LOYALTY ON THE LINE

Loyalty on the Line

Civil War Maryland in American Memory

DAVID K. GRAHAM

The University of Georgia Press
Athens

Paperback edition, 2023
© 2018 by the University of Georgia Press
Athens, Georgia 30602
www.ugapress.org
All rights reserved
Set in 10/13 ITC New Baskerville Std
by Graphic Composition, Inc.,
Bogart, Georgia

Most University of Georgia Press titles are
available from popular e-book vendors.

Printed digitally

Library of Congress Cataloging-in-Publication Data

Names: Graham, David K., 1988– author.
Title: Loyalty on the line : Civil War Maryland in
American memory / David K. Graham.
Description: Athens, Georgia : University of Georgia Press, [2018] |
Originally presented as the author's thesis (doctoral)—
Purdue University, 2015. | Includes bibliographical references and index.
Identifiers: LCCN 2018019197| ISBN 9780820353630 (hardback : alk. paper) |
ISBN 9780820353647 (ebook)
Subjects: LCSH: Maryland—History—Civil War, 1861–1865. |
Public opinion—Maryland—History. | Collective memory—Maryland. |
Memory—Social aspects—Maryland.
Classification: LCC E512 .G73 2018 | DDC 975.2/03—dc23
LC record available at https://lccn.loc.gov/2018019197

Paperback ISBN 978-0-8203-6488-9

For Kelsie

CONTENTS

ILLUSTRATIONS

ACKNOWLEDGMENTS

The thought of completing this book always seemed daunting to me. Fortunately, countless people have helped guide and assist me throughout this process. Their support has made writing a book much more enjoyable and rewarding.

The person who most directly influenced the scope and content of this project was my graduate advisor Caroline Janney. It was during the first few weeks of my first semester on campus at Purdue when Dr. Janney suggested that I continue to pursue my research on Maryland in Civil War memory. In addition to providing several jumping-off points, Dr. Janney challenged me to push my analysis, demonstrate the significance of my arguments, and refine my writing. Any positive contribution this book makes is primarily thanks to her guidance.

Several other faculty members of the history department at Purdue University offered their support. John Larson, Michael Morrison, Dawn Marsh, and Nancy Gabin also provided valuable assistance throughout the process of working on the manuscript and my time at Purdue. Dr. Larson challenged me to make national and broader connections. Dr. Morrison asked thoughtful questions about my project that generated different avenues of inquiry. Additionally, Dr. Barbara Gannon helped in my research on the Maryland GAR and provided information on the Charles Sumner Post.

Snow College has also helped in my development as an educator and supported my growth as a historian. At Snow, I have learned from my colleagues what it means to be a professor and how to put students first. The students at Snow College have pushed me to explore history from different perspectives and to appreciate the importance of cogent historical analysis. Thank you to Mike Brenchley and Nate Caplin for mentoring me as a teacher and for their friendship.

I owe a tremendous amount of thanks to the editorial staff at the University of Georgia Press for their assistance in developing this book. Bethany Snead and Thomas Roche provided thorough instructions and suggestions in the final preparations of the manuscript. A special thanks is owed to my editor Walter Biggins. Walter guided me through every stage and offered meaningful suggestions for how to strengthen the book.

I also benefited immeasurably from assistance provided by the staff at multiple archival institutions. The archivists at the Maryland State Archives not only fulfilled my research requests in a timely manner, but they also led me to other relevant materials within the collection. The staff at the Maryland Historical Society was also exceedingly gracious and helpful. Finally, a special thanks is owed to Scott Hartwig, who recently retired as the supervisory historian at Gettysburg National Military Park. Mr. Hartwig went above and beyond the call of duty with the help he provided in my research on the Second Maryland Confederate Infantry Monument.

I am most indebted to my family. Thank you to all of my family who expressed interest in my project and offered their support throughout my education. My parents have always supported me and were enthusiastic about this project. Thank you to my wife Kelsie for her unflinching support of me and my academic pursuits. She has not only been there for me throughout my educational journey, but she has also proved to be a brilliant college educator and an incredible parent. I am constantly in awe of her. Finally, thank you to my children Eli, Lincoln, and Olivia. Although you did not provide any research assistance or comments on chapter drafts, you reminded me every day of what is most important. I am forever grateful.

LOYALTY ON THE LINE

INTRODUCTION

Upon crossing the Potomac River and entering Maryland in early September 1862, the commanding general of the Army of Northern Virginia, Robert E. Lee, issued a proclamation to the citizens of Maryland. Through his proclamation, Lee expressed his hope that the people of the border state would welcome the liberating Confederate forces and join their sister states in their cause. In the second to last sentence of his proclamation he stated, "It is for you to decide your destiny, freely, and without constraint." While the proposition seemed straightforward to Lee, the people of Maryland struggled with deciding their destiny not only during the Civil War but also for more than a century after the conflict concluded in 1865. The people of Maryland clashed over their Civil War loyalty during the war and their subsequent Civil War identity and memory after the peace at Appomattox.[1]

During the American Civil War, Maryland did not join the Confederacy, but its citizens were divided. Although Maryland's government remained loyal to the Union during war, many regions and cities in the state harbored strong Confederate sympathies. A strong Unionist sentiment existed in northern and western Maryland while in eastern and southern Maryland there were many who advocated for secession and the Confederate cause. Additionally, Baltimore was a bastion for Confederate sympathizers and became a central setting for contention between those supporting the Union and those in favor of secession and the secessionist cause. Approximately twenty-five thousand soldiers from the state joined the Confederate army while more than forty-six thousand fought for the Union, nearly doubling the state's manpower contribution to the Confederacy. As a slaveholding state that did not secede, Maryland,

along with Missouri and Kentucky, occupied a unique position in terms
of its governmental policies on slavery. All of these factors came to a head
in the aftermath of the war during monument dedications, anniversary
celebrations, Grand Army of the Republic (GAR) and United Daughters
of the Confederacy (UDC) meetings, and mass cultural representations
of the Civil War. The divisions that characterized Civil War Maryland
continued into the postbellum period.

In 1922, critic, journalist, and Maryland native H. L. Mencken wrote
of the divisiveness of his home state. He argued that the boundary between North and South in the United States ran directly through his
home state, adding that a "Marylander from St. Mary's County or from
the lower reaches of the Eastern Shore is as much a stranger to a Marylander from along the Pennsylvania boundary, or even from Baltimore,
as he would be to a man from Maine or Wisconsin." Turning his attention
to Maryland's Civil War experience, Mencken claimed that during the
conflict "the State was even more sharply divided than Kentucky or Missouri, and that division still persists." The persistence of these divisions is
the defining feature of Maryland's place in Civil War memory.[2]

The Civil War fractures ran so deep within the border state's society
that it never adopted a clear postwar Union or Confederate identity.[3]
Maryland's postwar legacy and memory was divided between those emphasizing the state's Unionist efforts and those underscoring Maryland's
connections to the Confederacy and its defeated cause. Depictions of
Civil War Maryland both inside and outside the state hinged on interpretations of the state's loyalty. Maryland did not assume a clear, dominant
postbellum Civil War identity. Additionally, Unionists and Confederates
in Maryland were still waging the war through memory-making well after
the war, and this led to a postwar society in Maryland that was deeply
fractured. From 1861 to the Civil War centennial during the 1960s and
beyond, competing memories of Maryland and its loyalty clashed.

Although historians have examined Maryland's role in the war, none
have yet sufficiently looked at how the divisive nature of its wartime existence significantly affected both its internal postwar memory and its
broader national Civil War legacy.[4] This book views Civil War memory
through the lens of Maryland. To support this research aim, the book
draws on a variety of primary sources, including periodicals, dedicatory speeches, fraternal organization records and publications, personal
correspondence, court records, plays, novels, historical accounts of the
Civil War, and Civil War centennial commission records. It also includes
representations of Civil War Maryland from Unionist and Confederate

Marylanders as well as Unionists and Confederates from the entire nation. This methodological approach not only allows for an examination of Marylanders' struggle over their own Civil War identity but also sheds light on the border state's importance to broader conversations of Civil War memory in the century following the conflict. Additionally, a state-level study provides a different perspective in analysis on Civil War memory, which is often focused at the national or regional level. A state-level examination points to moments of congruence as well as moments of fracture with broader, more overarching national narratives.

Two debates existed concerning the Civil War memory of Maryland: one internal to the state and one external. Internally, the state was unquestionably divided over its Civil War identity. Externally, various groups and individuals attempted to superimpose an identity on Maryland. There was no sense of uniformity or consensus in these efforts. Those that tried to ascribe Confederate identities and memories to Maryland varied widely in their narratives. The same was true of Unionist attempts at cultivating a Civil War memory for Maryland from outside the state. These external pressures faced resistance, whether from Confederate or Union perspectives, time and time again from Marylanders. The value of an examination of postbellum Maryland points to how Marylanders received and processed these various collective national narratives at the ground level.

The contested Civil War memories of Maryland not only mirror a much larger national struggle and debate, they also reveal a clashing of memories that is more intense and vitriolic than the traditional national narrative has suggested. The close proximity of conflicted Civil War memories within the state contributed to a perpetual contestation. Marylanders waged their fight for the border state's postwar identity with unrivaled determination because they feared if they did not, their memory of the war and their state would fade from Maryland's and the nation's consciousness. Those outside the state also vigorously argued over the place of Maryland in Civil War memory in order to establish its place in the divisive legacy of the war. By using Maryland as a lens to Civil War memory, we can see how truly divisive the war remained and the centrality of its memory to the United States well into the twentieth century.[5]

The history of Maryland's Civil War legacy reveals the importance of border states to the national memory of the war. Americans, northern and southern, understood that Maryland's fractured society both during and after the war reflected the country's wounds for decades after the peace at Appomattox. They realized the importance of border states to the larger legacies of the Civil War. Those outside Maryland argued so ardently on behalf of the state's identity because, unlike more decidedly northern or southern states, it remained a battleground for contested memories of the war. Maryland's Civil War identity was constantly in flux, and, as a result, attempts to cultivate sectional legacies had increased significance. The ebbs and flows of Maryland's Civil War identity and memory were vital to those active in commemorating and remembering the Civil War. The Old Line State quickly emerged as the frontline for contested Civil War memories. This book uses Maryland as a case study to demonstrate the centrality of border state Civil War memory and identity to the postbellum United States.

The significance of Maryland to competing memories is evident throughout the century following the war. Veterans and politicians who gathered on the Antietam battlefield to commemorate their fallen com-rades and their actions on the bloodiest day in American history also reflected on the loyalty of the divided border state. Civil War Maryland featured prominently in mass culture throughout the late nineteenth and early twentieth centuries, and its internal divisions were highlighted. Union and Confederate veterans who recalled their experiences during the war in speeches and publications often framed their views on Civil War Maryland with the nation's memories of the war in mind. All of these constitute the various forms of memory-making that took place in the decades following the war. The importance of memory-making to postbellum American society is difficult to overstate. The meaning of the war to subsequent generations stemmed from how they, as a society, remembered the conflict. The different ways of commemorating the war greatly influenced that remembrance. The Civil War was the defining historical moment for those who experienced it and how the nation re-membered that moment was of the utmost importance because of the sacrifice it demanded.

Maryland's status in Civil War memory sheds light on another aspect of American society that this book explores: the centrality of loyalty in the postbellum period and its influence on and relationship with poli-tics, reconciliation, society, and culture. Historian William Blair outlines conceptions of loyalty and treason during the Civil War era in his book *With Malice toward Some*.[6] This book attempts to build on Blair's work by centering on what role Maryland's Civil War loyalty played not only during the war but also well into the twentieth century. The state's Civil War loyalty developed into an important political point that demanded the attention of state politicians. The governor of Maryland during most of the war, Augustus W. Bradford, was well aware of this fact. Bradford was a Unionist and actively sought to keep Maryland within the Union while simultaneously opposing the military occupation of his state. Although he was in favor of the Union, he understood the political ramifications of strict military occupation and the turmoil it would unleash among his already divided citizenry. Bradford's Unionism cost him his home as raiders under Maryland Confederate general Bradley T. Johnson burned it down during the war. Even after the war, Bradford understood how Civil War loyalty was important politically. In his remarks at the dedication of Antietam National Cemetery in 1867, he argued on behalf of his state's Unionist loyalty and Civil War identity in an attempt to justify his wartime policies as governor. Pennsylvania governor James A. Beaver discovered the political influence of Maryland's Civil War loyalty when Confederate veterans from the border state dedicated a monument on the Gettysburg battlefield and veterans from his own state expressed their frustrations. One hundred years removed from the war, the governor of Maryland was still attempting to navigate the Old Line State's Civil War loyalty and memory. Throughout the Civil War centennial, Governor J. Millard Tawes tried to oversee the state's Civil War commemorations by making sure both Confederate and Union contributions in the state received equal recognition. Many scholars have noted the fact that Civil War commemorations and remembrances were often highly politicized and used for political aims. The century following the Civil War in Maryland shows how this politicization took on a much different tone and complexity within a society that was so deeply fractured by the war.[7]

This book also analyzes the relationship between loyalty and reconciliation. Reconciliation for Civil War veterans meant no longer viewing wartime foes as enemies. It implied that veterans accepted their former opponents as fellow soldiers living together in postwar America. The contested memories of Civil War Maryland reveal that most who lived through the war did not simply resist reconciliation. They viewed reconciliation as disloyal to their wartime causes and believed that it undermined their continued loyalty and devotion to those causes in the postbellum period. Maintaining a Unionist or a Confederate identity meant refusing to forget the causes for which one fought and the enemies one faced. Maryland veterans who strived to maintain their loyalty made sure their former comrades knew that even though they resided in a divided border state, they remained intensely devoted to their causes and rejected reconciliation.

These notions of Civil War loyalty affected other aspects of society beyond politics. As the rest of the United States continually reflected on the Civil War, Maryland did as well. Veterans not only returned to rural battlefields to dedicate monuments and reunite with their comrades, but they also put forth a variety of publications that helped shape American culture. Maryland's place within these publications influenced the nature of the discussion and often represented a point of conflict. The Civil War also deeply affected American culture in the century following its conclusion. Playwrights and novelists used the Civil War to frame their narratives, and those who used Civil War Maryland discovered the complexity and controversy that came with commenting on the state's Civil War loyalty and identity.

Similarly, the influence of Maryland's Civil War loyalty on notions of equality in memory is clearly seen in this book. Marylanders constantly fought for an equal place in the larger legacies and remembrances of the war. They struggled against perceptions that dismissed their state's contributions because it was so divided throughout the war. Marylanders, both Confederate and Union, wanted to be remembered without qualification. From Marylanders resenting what they perceived as unequal treatment on the part of the Lincoln administration during the war to African Americans pushing back against a white, Confederate memory of the war in Maryland, equality in Civil War memory was central to citizens of the Old Line State. Some even went further by stating that because they came from a state that was so deeply divided during the Civil War, they were in fact even more loyal and devoted to their respective causes than their more northern or southern counterparts.

This book is organized both chronologically and thematically. The first chapter focuses on Maryland during the Civil War. It argues that divides formed during the war created a foundation from which the subsequent struggle over memory would build. The chapter highlights a few key events in Maryland's Civil War history that had lasting influences, including the Baltimore Riot of 1861, the federal government's actions in the state, and the Battle of Antietam. The trial of the conspirators of the Abraham Lincoln assassination is also detailed. The majority of the conspirators were from Maryland, and their status as residents of the conflicted border state was an important component of the trial.

The second chapter examines the history of commemoration at Antietam and the Second Maryland Confederate Infantry Monument at Gettysburg, the first Confederate monument dedicated on the battlefield. It looks at Maryland's place within these commemorations and how its loyalty was depicted. The efforts of Marylanders to inscribe their memories of the war on the battlefields of Antietam and Gettysburg underscore the degree to which the state's veterans rejected much of the reconciliationist sentiment of the era. Using commemorations of Antietam and Gettysburg as case studies sheds light on the relationship between perceptions of loyalty and reconciliation.

Chapter 3 explores attempts at southernizing and feminizing Maryland through Lost Cause histories and mass cultural representations of the Civil War border state. These two processes were inextricably connected and reinforced one another. Postbellum historians, playwrights, and novelists both inside and outside the state attempted to cultivate a Civil War identity for Maryland in which it was a passive actor during the war and in postwar depictions. Several early Confederate histories, the plays *The Heart of Maryland* and *Barbara Frietchie*, and the novel *For Maryland's Honor* serve as case studies for analyzing the feminization and southernization of Maryland in mass culture. Even in those moments where writers put forth a southern identity for the state, there was opposition.

Chapter 4 centers on the two-front war that Marylanders faced in maintaining their dual-identity as Civil War veterans and citizens of the Old Line State. Veterans from Maryland advocated on behalf of the causes of their particular side, but they also had to defend their contributions within their respective causes. This made maintaining a dual-identity as Civil War veterans from Maryland a struggle that was unique to them. Veterans from South Carolina and Pennsylvania did not have to justify or explain their state's position during the war. This, of course, did not stop Union and Confederate veterans from touting the contributions their states made in the conflict, but it did not require the continuous defending Marylanders did.

The fifth and final chapter looks at the relationship between race and Civil War memory in Maryland. The history of race relations and civil rights in Maryland, and in particular Baltimore, during the 1930s created an environment in which divisions of Civil War memory were no longer split merely along sectional lines. Remembrances of the war in Maryland became more intensely fractured across white and black memories. Furthermore, the final chapter demonstrates how the nature of Unionist memories was evolving in the twentieth century to include and hinge on the broader legacy of freedom inherent in narratives of the Civil War era. It follows the history of racial policies in Maryland from Jim Crow through the 1960s and demonstrates how the evolution of race law in the state influenced memories and commemorations of

the war. Successes in beating back the reach of Jim Crow were often met
not only with racialized responses but also with a Confederate, white
identity that harkened back to the Civil War. The Maryland Civil War
Centennial Commission attempted to quell the longstanding divisions
over the state's Civil War identity, but it was unable to fully achieve this
goal as controversies emerged throughout the commemorative period,
including race-driven disputes.

The paucity of scholarship on Maryland in Civil War memory itself is
a reflection of the state's conflicted postbellum identity. Maryland does
not fit clearly within a particular Civil War identity nor does it serve as a
beacon of reconciliation within the United States. Instead, its divisions
reveal the complex legacy of the Civil War. Describing Civil War Maryland
is a difficult challenge enough without trying to uncover its ambiguous
postwar legacy. This book is an attempt to shed light on a divided border
state's history by highlighting its perplexity.

CHAPTER 1

Maryland on Trial

The Old Line State in the Civil War and the Trial of the Lincoln Conspirators, 1861–1865

Baltimorean Virginia Craig's words to her husband U.S. Army captain Seldon Frank Craig just a few days after the assassination of Abraham Lincoln targeted her native state. She met her husband while he was stationed in Baltimore, and they married in April 1864. In her April 19, 1865, letter, she remarked that even in Baltimore a "shadow of grief appeared to hover about the countenances of all of our loyal citizens, and indeed over many who have always been considered the enemies of Mr. Lincoln." This expression of grief, however, was not enough for her to take pride in her home state.

Craig lamented her own connection to Maryland: "The South! How I detest the name, and everything with the horrid doctrine of Secession! How I wish that I had been born a 'Yankee' (though I once disliked them) or anything but a Marylander, for our state has produced some of the worst characters which this rebellion has brought to light." She insisted that from "the 19th of April '61 until the present time, the meanest most cruel and wicked acts of this accursed war (I blush to say it) have been done by Maryland villains." In her mind, Craig did not believe anything "could have exceeded in wickedness and blood-thirstiness, the acts of the lawless mob on the 19th of April 1861," with the exception of the "last desperate act of Maryland 'rebels,' the assassination of Abraham Lincoln." Craig claimed that even among those responsible for the horrid conditions of Confederate prisons, "none were so harsh or so cruel as those who claimed Maryland as their native state." She took comfort in the fact that Lincoln's remains would not travel through Baltimore because "there would be too many who would look at them with joy in their hearts." Craig's disdain for the citizens of her own state underscored the divisiveness of Civil War Maryland.[1]

The American Civil War fractured and disrupted Maryland society deeply. The divides that developed over the issue of secession continued to grow throughout the course of the war and, unlike the fighting that ceased in 1865, remained long after its conclusion. Maryland's schism over Union and Confederate identities and sympathies between 1861 and 1865 set the stage for debates and conflicts over postwar memory that persisted well into the twentieth century. Maryland during the Civil War era represented points of fracture for many of the states' citizens as well as those outside the state. From the Baltimore Riot of 1861 to the assassination of Abraham Lincoln, Maryland was a focal point of the Civil War, and its centrality contributed to its conflicted legacy. Many in the state resisted the changes the war wrought and longed for a sense of equality that they felt the war unfairly hijacked. The trials Maryland faced in the mid-nineteenth century were only the beginning but nevertheless created a foundation for divided Civil War memories.

Maryland on the Eve of the Civil War

Maryland was divided years before the outbreak of the Civil War. The eastern and southern regions of the state were vastly different from the northern and western counties. The varied nature of the economies throughout Maryland played a central role in their dichotomous relationship. The Eastern Shore developed its own unique culture apart from the mainland portion of Maryland. With the growing inability to produce tobacco on the Eastern Shore, the region witnessed a dramatic decrease in the number of slaves and a tremendous rise in the number of free blacks in the decades prior to 1860. The white population grew wary of the growing free black population and struggled to sustain its farms financially in a region of the state that lacked significant land transportation.[2]

The issue of transportation marked the most important difference between the two regions. Western Maryland's industries and economy experienced unprecedented growth in the first half of the nineteenth century with the construction of canals, railroads, and roads. The Chesapeake and Ohio Canal, the Baltimore and Ohio Railroad, and the National Road played vital roles in expanding the reach of western Maryland and providing opportunities for export. By 1850, western Maryland was home to nearly "70 percent of the state's total white population, nearly half of its free blacks, and less than 20 percent of its slaves."[3]

What set southern Maryland apart from other portions of the state was the persistence of the institution of slavery and the region's reliance on farming for the subsistence of its economy. Improved farming techniques and diversifying crop output aided the survival of white famers in southern Maryland. The white planter class in southern Maryland also enjoyed the benefits of new farming techniques and provided a steady demand for slave labor. The expansion of slavery into the southwest during the first half of the nineteenth century added value to slave labor and encouraged southern Maryland slave owners' participation in domestic slave trading.[4]

Northern and southern Maryland was also divided on the eve of the Civil War. Historian Charles W. Mitchell notes, "Maryland's economy in 1860 was a blend of Northern mercantilism and Southern agrarianism" and Baltimore "reflected this dichotomy." The commercial development occurring in the city certainly resembled the growth of industry in the North, but the population of Baltimore emanated a more traditionally southern culture.[5] Baltimore also possessed a complex black population in 1860. The free black population in the city numbered approximately 25,000 compared to 2,218 slaves. Competition for jobs with native and immigrant whites ultimately forced many free blacks in Baltimore to look elsewhere for work. Added to this complex racial society was the rise of the Know-Nothing Party in the 1850s. Founded and focused on nativist principles, the Know-Nothings thrived in Baltimore by preying on the fear of an ever-growing immigrant population.[6]

The growing sectionalism occurring throughout the United States in the years immediately preceding the outbreak of hostilities only furthered the divides in Maryland. Although the Know-Nothing Party emerged prominently in Baltimore during the 1850s, the issue of slavery subsumed it and other social concerns as the United States and Maryland grappled with heightened sectionalism. Historian Kevin Conley Ruffner notes that throughout the secession crisis "Marylanders could not decide whether they were northern or southern."[7] The presidential election of 1860 underscored the state's conflicted position amid the growing sectional crisis. Although the nationwide election was a four-candidate race, there were only two candidates who garnered significant votes in Maryland: John C. Breckinridge, the southern Democrat from Kentucky, and Tennessean John Bell, representing the Constitutional Union Party. Breckinridge appealed to voters who were invested in the institution of slavery and favored the expansion of slavery into new territories in the United States. Bell advocated on behalf of compromise and devotion to the Union. Although Bell garnered votes across the state, he failed to win Baltimore. Breckinridge's success in Baltimore, along with his popularity in southern and Eastern Shore counties, allowed him to claim the state's electoral votes. Maryland was the northernmost state to give electoral votes to the southern Democratic candidate. The much-maligned "Black Republican" candidate, Abraham Lincoln, received less than 3 percent of the vote in Maryland.[8]

The election of Abraham Lincoln sent ripples of discontent across the state. Constitutional Union supporters were disappointed with Bell's loss and fearful of the consequences of Lincoln's election. Southern Democrats expressed their support for the first states to secede and pledged to contribute volunteers to their cause. White Marylanders feared that the racial foundation of their state was shifting beneath their feet. Lucinda Rebecca Beall of Frederick County, Maryland, wrote to her brother James Francis Beall, a teacher and farmer from Frederick, in the winter of 1860 in this growing climate of paranoia. "There has been a great talk about a company of abolishionist being in the mountain," she warned. She confessed, "Some of the folks was afraid to sleep at night."[9]

Not all Marylanders were disappointed with the results of the 1860 election. An African American man sat down among white passengers on a train in Baltimore and when he was confronted he responded "that Lincoln was elected, and he would ride like 'any other man.'" The conductor removed the man from the train. The passenger believed that Lincoln's election meant his equality was finally realized. He would inevitably be disappointed by the persistent racial inequality that would characterize Maryland for the rest of the nineteenth century and beyond.[10]

As other states seceded from the Union following Lincoln's election, Maryland leaders wrestled with what course of action to take. Governor Thomas H. Hicks refused requests for a special session of the General Assembly, as it was an off-year for the legislative body, and in the first few months of 1861 individuals in counties across the state organized committees to discuss, debate, and promote actions on behalf of Maryland. In February 1861, James Beall received a letter from his uncle that expressed his fear that "Governor Hicks and Mister Davis will sell if not already don it Maryland to Black republicans." The tensions between opposing sides in Maryland and the growing resentment of the president-elect prompted Abraham Lincoln to sneak through Baltimore in the middle of the night on February 22, 1861, en route to Washington, D.C., for his inauguration. Internal divisions were present in Maryland well before the country fully fractured in two, and the political developments of early 1861 highlighted the points of separation. The debates over Maryland's position escalated into more visceral and physical expressions of conflict as the secession winter melted away and the reality of war became clear.[11]

The Baltimore Riot

One week after the first shots fired at Fort Sumter, the start of war for Marylanders and the rest of the United States echoed in the streets of Baltimore on April 19, 1861. Responding to Lincoln's call for troops on April 15, federal troops scattered about the country made their way to Washington, D.C., to prepare for war and receive their orders. News of U.S. troops' planned marching path through Baltimore reached the city's citizens, and many southern sympathizers expressed their resistance to this action. Lincoln was aware of rumblings of discontent and potential unrest prior to the troops' arrival in Baltimore. Secretary of War Simon Cameron wrote Governor Hicks on April 18 to implore him and the city of Baltimore to prepare for their arrival. He noted that Lincoln "thinks it his duty to make it known to you so that all loyal and patriotic citizens of your State may be warned in time and that you may be prepared to take immediate and effective measures against it." In the eyes of Cameron and Lincoln, the best possible outcome would be averting violence while simultaneously demonstrating the power and authority of the loyal sentiment in Maryland.[12]

They were ultimately disappointed with the events in Baltimore the following day. The Union soldiers from Massachusetts and Pennsylvania arrived in Baltimore on April 19 and prepared to transfer railroad lines while in the city. Their cars were hitched to horses for the transfer through Baltimore. A mob formed around the cars on their journey, and as the crowd grew in number they were eventually forced to stop as cobblestone pieces crashed into the cars' windows. The Sixth Massachusetts disembarked and was assaulted by the angry crowd hurling stones. Two shots were fired and the situation escalated with fist fighting. The Baltimoreans grabbed weapons from the soldiers and used them on the soldiers themselves. Once the riot died down, two Massachusetts soldiers were dead and dozens more wounded; twelve Baltimoreans lay dead on the streets.[13]

Reports of the activities in Baltimore recounted the frenzied state of the secessionist-leaning city. Colonel Edward F. Jones of the Sixth Massachusetts Militia authored his report of the events on April 22, 1861. He recalled the orders he personally gave his troops on the train to Baltimore on learning that they would likely face a resistant crowd. After distributing ammunition to his soldiers, Jones warned the troops of the opposition and challenge awaiting them: "You will undoubtedly be insulted, abused, and perhaps, assaulted to which you must pay no attention whatever, but march with your faces square to the front, and pay no attention to the mob, even if they throw stones, bricks, or other missiles." He qualified this order by stating that "if you are fired upon and any one of you is hit, your officers will order you to fire" and "select any man whom you may see aiming at you, and be sure you drop him." Upon arriving, Jones reported that his men "were furiously attacked by a shower of missiles" and as they quickened their marching pace the increase in speed "seemed to infuriate the mob, as it evidently impressed the mob with the idea that the soldiers dared not fire or had no ammunition." After pistol shots were fired into the crowd, the order to fire was given and "several of the mob fell" as the soldiers continued their trek through the streets of Baltimore. According to Jones, even the mayor armed himself with a musket, fired, and killed a man in his attempts to aid the Massachusetts men on their journey. Disgruntled over their fallen comrades and incensed by the continued assault, even aboard the departing train from the city, a soldier fired and killed a man who "threw a stone into the car."[14]

The Baltimore Police Commissioners delivered their report to the Maryland General Assembly on May 3. The commissioners asserted that neither they nor anyone else in the city's police department were made aware of the arriving federal troops until thirty minutes to an hour prior to their arrival. They also noted the controversial decision reached by the mayor, the governor, and the police to destroy bridges in order to prevent "further bodies of troops from the Eastern or Northern States" from passing through the city. The destruction of bridges further exacerbated Maryland's tenuous position in the eyes of the federal government and elevated the need for Lincoln to gain control of the important buffer-zone state around the Union capital.[15]

Baltimore mayor George William Brown and Governor Hicks both quickly wrote to Lincoln following the riot. Mayor Brown informed Lincoln that a delegation was en route to Washington "to explain fully the fearful condition of affairs" in Baltimore. He continued by asserting that

THE LEXINGTON OF 1861.

FIGURE 1.1. Rioting in Baltimore, April 19, 1861,
by Currier & Ives (courtesy of the Library of Congress).

the citizens of his city were "exasperated to the highest degree by the
passage of troops" and were "universally decided in the opinion that no
more should be ordered to come." He stated that the authorities did
their best to protect Baltimoreans and the soldiers but their efforts were
"in vain," despite the fact that their actions prevented "a fearful slaugh-
ter." As Brown concluded his letter, he took a more direct tone in his
message to the president: "it is not possible for more soldiers to pass
through Baltimore unless they fight their way at every step." After explicitly requesting that no more soldiers pass through Baltimore, he warned
that if they did come through "the responsibility for the blood shed will
not rest upon me." Hicks appended a brief letter to Brown's in which he
endorsed the statements and requests made by the mayor and noted that
he had been in Baltimore attempting to mitigate the situation.[16]

The following day Hicks penned a letter to Secretary of War Cameron
in which he outlined the challenges he was facing in the secessionist
stronghold city. He confessed that "the rebellious element had the control of things. They took possession of the armories, have the arms and
ammunition." Lincoln wrote Hicks the same day requesting his immediate presence along with the mayor of Baltimore in Washington to discuss

issues "relative to preserving the peace of Maryland." The Baltimore Riot
and the need to control "the rebellious element" in Maryland moved to
the forefront of the federal government's consciousness within the first
few weeks of the Civil War.[17]

The Baltimore Riot not only started speculation on Maryland's loyalty;
it was also often a point of contention for those who debated the state's
wartime position well into the twentieth century. The city, in particular, was on the lips of both Confederate and Union sympathizers. Those
who believed in the Confederate cause upheld Baltimore as a shining example of devotion in the face of intense opposition. Conversely, Unionists loathed Baltimore and its citizens for their rebellious spirit. The riot
added another dynamic to these debates and was used by both sides in
an attempt to prove Maryland's true Civil War identity.

Hicks faced other pressing issues on the ground in Maryland and ultimately decided to move the General Assembly west to Frederick and
discuss the course Maryland should take while Lincoln made plans for
occupying and securing Maryland under federal control. The decision
to move the legislature was due in part to federal occupation of Annapolis, and Hicks also later pointed to the large pro-Union population in
Frederick as the primary factor in his decision. The session was called
on April 22 in order to decide on a policy of secession or loyalty to the

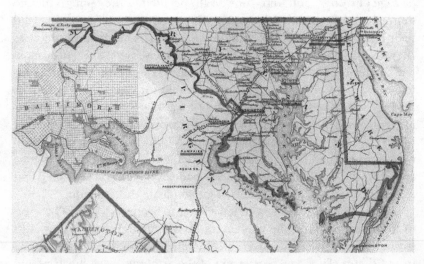

FIGURE 1.2. Pocket map of Maryland (1861)
by G. A. Aschbach (courtesy of the Library of Congress).

Union. On April 27, the Maryland Senate and House of Delegates resolved that the state would not secede and informed their constituents
that any fears of such an action were "without foundation." The legislative body understood they had "no constitutional authority to take such
an action." The General Assembly also approved a bill on behalf of the
City Council of Baltimore "for the defence of the city, against any damage
that may arise out of the present crisis."[18]

While Hicks and the General Assembly were making their plans for
Maryland's Civil War path, Lincoln and the federal government had their
own policies. Maryland was too crucial a state for Lincoln to trust the
state government and its word of loyalty. It was the northernmost border
state and its proximity to Washington, D.C., made it a critical region to
both Union and Confederate strategy. If Maryland was lost, Washington,
D.C., would be within the borders of the Confederacy. The riot in Baltimore in mid-April forced Lincoln to take significant steps in securing
the state under Union control. By early May, Maryland was under federal
occupation and would experience its own unique wartime home front
that would be the topic of debate and conflict for decades after the final
shots of war ended.

Benjamin Butler and Union forces seized control of Maryland within
the first several weeks of May 1861. In a series of well-orchestrated ma-
neuvers, Butler gained control of the Baltimore and Ohio Railroad between Frederick and Baltimore, thus securing the railroad and preventing a potential invasion point into the Union capital. He then moved to
Baltimore and with the aid of Union troops positioned on Federal Hill, a
strategic vantage point above the city, occupied the turbulent town. Butler's decision to occupy Baltimore and use military force if the rebellious
element inside the city acted again was not approved by Lincoln. Both
Lincoln and General Winfield Scott were angered by Butler's actions,
and he was removed from his command and sent to Virginia. The soldiers, however, stayed in Baltimore to prevent further unrest. Although
disappointed with Butler's insubordination, Lincoln understood the importance of maintaining control of Maryland so much so that he would
invoke an unprecedented amount of federal power. He suspended the
writ of habeas corpus and arrested numerous Marylanders of questionable loyalty, including newspaper editors, judges, and politicians among
other influential state citizens. Kevin Ruffner characterizes the ensuing
period in Maryland Civil War history as "four years of constant military
activity and occupation" that residents of the state were forced to endure

"whether they liked it or not." Mitchell qualifies, however, that only Baltimore and Annapolis featured permanent military installations for the entire duration of the war.[19]

For many Marylanders, the federal occupation of the state and the subsequent arrests and detainments represented an infringement on their liberty and unequal treatment on the part of Lincoln and his policies. The dissatisfaction and discontent of those opposed to such policies created friction with those who wanted to rein in the rebels and control the state's loyalty. The fight over Maryland's loyalty that began in the streets of Baltimore in the spring of 1861 set in motion the continued struggle over the state and its legacy well into the twentieth century. The state was dividing, and while Lincoln's aggressive policies toward the border state helped it from falling to the South, they also widened the cracks developing in Maryland's society.

Maryland under Arrest

The arrest and imprisonment of Robert Winans was one of the first incidents to create backlash and divisions in Maryland. Winans was a member of the Maryland House of Delegates from Baltimore. The Maryland General Assembly issued a resolution putting forth its opinion on the fact that Winans "was arbitrarily and illegally arrested on a public highway in the presence of the governor of this State by an armed force under the orders of the Federal Government" on his way home on May 14, 1861. The legislature noted other instances of "despotic and oppressive" actions of the "same usurped authority." After citing the illegality and unconstitutionality of the federal government's policies of arrest and imprisonment of Marylanders, the members issued on behalf of its citizens "their earnest and unqualified protest against the oppressive and tyrannical assertion and exercise of military jurisdiction within the limits of Maryland over the persons and property of her citizens by the Government of the United States, and do solemnly declare the same to be subversive of the most sacred guarantees of the Constitution and in flagrant violation of the fundamental and most cherished principles of American free government." To the Maryland General Assembly, the actions of the federal government's unconstitutional policies were destroying their guaranteed rights of equality.[20]

The issue of equality was even more paramount to Marylanders than most other individuals because of their tenuous status within the Union.

They longed for equal treatment under the law and governmental policies. This desire for equality remained with residents of the state when they attempted to stake a claim for their own contributions to opposing Civil War causes. Marylanders worked doubly hard to do so, knowing they had to overcome the ambiguous legacy of their home state.

The case of John Merryman's arrest was another early occupation effort that proved controversial and would eventually make its way to the U.S. Supreme Court and represent a landmark ruling in American history. Merryman, acting on the orders given by Governor Hicks, helped with the controversial destruction of bridges north of Baltimore to prevent further through-marches on the part of U.S. troops. He was arrested by federal soldiers on the charge of treason and imprisoned in Fort McHenry. Merryman was able to petition Chief Justice Roger B. Taney of the U.S. Supreme Court for a writ of habeas corpus and, after hearing the case, Taney concluded that Merryman was unlawfully detained and must be released. Merryman's case and Taney's ruling upheld the writ of habeas corpus during times of war and the inability of the president to suspend it, deferring the power to Congress. Merryman viewed his arrest as a violation of a constitutional right granted to all Americans and, as a Marylander, he protested for an equal claim to that right. The Winans and Merryman cases proved to the Maryland population that the distinctiveness of their wartime situation made equal treatment nearly impossible whether they were in favor of Lincoln's approach or not.[21]

Lincoln, however, did not accept Taney's decision and expressed his position in his message to Congress on July 4, 1861. Historian Brian McGinty traces the evolution of the suspension of habeas corpus from a military measure to a constitutional debate. Lincoln weighed the importance of violating the law versus maintaining the Union by stating, "I should consider my official oath broken if I should allow the government to be overthrown, when I might think the disregarding the single law would tend to preserve it." He was quick to assert, "In my opinion I violated no law." Lincoln argued that in terms of who had the authority to suspend the writ of habeas corpus, the Constitution was "silent," and that under such extenuating circumstances as civil war, it was within the president's power to suspend the provision.[22]

Throughout the first year of the war, Lincoln continued to arrest individuals who posed perceived political and social threats in Maryland. The state legislature expressed continued frustration as the summer turned to fall and the imprisonment of Maryland politicians continued at an alarming pace. The month of September was particularly active in terms of political arrests, and the federal government maintained frequent communication and correspondence with its officers in the field in charge of occupying various sections of Maryland. On September 11, 1861, General George B. McClellan forwarded a letter to Secretary of War Cameron written by General John A. Dix. Dix was the commanding officer charged with the task of preventing Maryland secession and arresting pro-South members of the Maryland legislature. In his preface to Dix's letter, McClellan informed Cameron that it seemed "necessary to arrest at once the parties named" and they should be taken to Fort Monroe in Virginia "in order to get them away from Baltimore as quietly as possible, and would suggest that they ultimately be sent North." Cameron responded to Dix by providing the names of six people for him to arrest and keep in "close custody." He also wrote to Major General Nathaniel P. Banks, commanding troops near Darnestown, Maryland, on September 11, urging him that "the passage of any act of secession by the Legislature of Maryland must be prevented" and if Banks deemed it necessary "all or any part of the members must be arrested."[23]

The federal government also received valuable information from Unionist private citizens in Maryland, including the editor of the *Examiner,* Frederick Schley. Schley reported to Secretary of State William Seward what he knew regarding the makeup of the legislature and who could be trusted and who possessed more questionable loyalties. He informed Seward of an upcoming meeting of the Maryland legislature and cautioned, "Many loyal citizens believe that at the coming session some effort will be made on the part of the 'Tory' majority to convulse the State and force it into an attitude of hostility to the Government." By his count of the twenty-two senators, "eight are loyal and reliable, leaving fourteen in whom I have not faith and I speak the sentiment of many."[24]

Schley wanted to make a claim of support on behalf of the loyal citizens of Maryland, an approach that many Union-supporting Marylanders would continue to employ when making postbellum claims on behalf of the state's wartime contribution to the North. Helping the Union by reporting on the pro-Confederate Marylanders was a way of highlighting the Unionist sentiment in the border state. Schley utilized this tactic with the hope that the loyal Marylanders were far more valuable than the state's Confederate sympathizers and, at least partially, redeemed the state.

Dix informed Cameron of the ten arrests he made as of September 13, 1861. The prisoners were mostly either Baltimorean members of the Maryland House of Delegates or editors of southern-sympathetic newspapers and viewpoints. Over the course of the following week, Union officers continued to arrest Marylanders with questionable loyalties. A camp aide informed General Banks on September 15 that they had "seized seven members of the house of a very bitter character, and four officers, clerks, &c., who are intensely bitter and are said to have been very forward and to have kept some of the weaker men up to the work." He would also send four men to Dix who were "very bad men." Banks was proud to report that "all the members of the Maryland Legislature assembled at Frederick City on the 17th instant known or suspected to be disloyal in their relations to the Government have been arrested." Dix notified Seward of the arrest of E. G. Kilbourn, the president of the House of Delegates and "a dangerous secessionist." Dix also included the names of two individuals whom he believed should be released on taking an oath of loyalty to the Union. The oath that political prisoners in Maryland were forced to swear to required them to "bear allegiance to the United States of America" and "support, protect, and defend" its government and the Constitution.[25]

Many Marylanders were quick to express their gratitude for and support of the federal government's policies on disloyal members of the border state's society. W. G. Snethen, an abolitionist, thanked Seward and the federal government "in the name of every truly loyal man in Baltimore" for the arrest of "the traitors." He viewed the arrest of disloyal Marylanders as a "great and a good Work," and he believed that the rebellion was dealt "a staggering blow" by the decisive action taken by the federal government. A doctor from Baltimore, Arthur Rich, espoused a similar sentiment. He felt that apprehending secessionist Maryland congressmen "soothed down the temper of the disunionists prodigiously." Rich also thought more nationally about the potential benefit of arresting those opposed to the Union. He hoped that the U.S. government was "strong enough to arrest such characters as Breckinridge, Magoffin and Burnett, of Kentucky." He was cognizant of the importance of other border states to the Union cause as well as the power of disloyal sentiments within those states. Even Governor Hicks offered his approval, noting "the good fruit already produced by the arrests." The Union, Hicks contended, could "no longer mince matters with these desperate people."[26]

Not everyone in Maryland was pleased with the course of actions implemented by Lincoln and the Union forces occupying the state. Much like the Maryland legislators who protested the unconstitutional arrests, citizens also voiced their frustration. Those Marylanders irritated with the federal government, however, expressed their opinions in their own unique fashion. By September, General Dix had earned a reputation among those sympathetic to the Confederate cause as an agent of tyranny so much so that a satirical piece was published in Baltimore under the heading "General Dix's Proclamation." Written from the perspective of Dix, the proclamation referred to the federal government as "His Majesty's government" and called for the removal of the rebel color red from babies' stockings, brick houses, watermelons, mint candy, barber's poles, flowers, and persons with red hair. Red and white cows would be forced "to change their spots or take the oath of allegiance," sunrises and sunsets "which exhibit such combinations" were forbidden, and the drinking of "red and white wines alternately" was also not permitted under the terms of Dix's decree. The only exception to the banning of red was red noses due to the fact that they were "greatly in vogue among Federal officers." The proclamation concluded, "Done at the Baltimore Bastile, this 4th day of September, the 1st year of Abraham's glorious and peaceful reign."[27]

Even into the spring of 1862, Baltimoreans continued to protest the political arm of the Union in their lives. The *Savannah Republican* featured a story titled "The Spirit of the Ladies of Baltimore." The narrative in the newspaper recounted the outward forms of protest and southern pride on behalf of a group of women living in Baltimore, namely, their clothing. Despite the insults and treatment they faced as a result, the group of women "appeared daily in the streets, in secession colors, to wit, 'red, white and red.'"[28]

The transition from 1861 to 1862 did not bring about immediate changes to the political and military force applied to Maryland and its citizens. Union forces detained F. Key Howard and W. W. Glenn, editors of the *Baltimore Exchange*, in September 1861 due to their and their paper's Confederate leanings. Howard was eventually released in February 1862, while the date of Glenn's release is unknown. *The South*'s Thomas W. Hall Jr., a secessionist-sympathetic Baltimorean, was also arrested in September 1861 and eventually released the following February.[29]

The arrest of Judge Richard Bennett Carmichael also pointed to the persistent hostilities and distrust between some Marylanders and the U.S. government. Carmichael served as circuit court judge for four Eastern Shore counties and requested the indictment of the men who arrested three Marylanders in November 1861 charged with "interfering with the election process after they heckled Unionists at a rally." Due to Carmichael's challenge to the federal government's arrests, Seward called for his arrest, and on May 27, 1862, Union soldiers entered his courtroom and assaulted him with a pistol before physically dragging him from his bench. Repressing pro-Confederates in Maryland was still central to Lincoln and the federal government in mid-1862. After spending the summer and fall in several Union prisons, Carmichael was released on December 4, 1862. He was therefore deemed to be "incompatible with public safety" or rejected an oath of loyalty per the terms of Lincoln's Executive Order No. 1 relating to political prisoners. The executive order, issued on February 14, 1862, sanctioned the release of "all political prisoners or state prisoners now held in military custody" with the qualification of "their subscribing to a parole engaging them to render no aid or comfort to the enemies in hostility to the United States."[30]

The War Comes Home

As the political turmoil that federal occupation and imprisonment created in Maryland waned in 1862, the devastation of war hit the border state's soil in unprecedented fashion. The split in wartime loyalties throughout the state was reflected in the military contributions Marylanders made to both the Union and the Confederate forces. More than forty-six thousand Maryland men joined the Union army, while twenty-five thousand mustered into service on behalf of the Confederacy. By way of comparison to other border states, Kentucky contributed between ninety thousand and one hundred thousand men to the Union and twenty-five thousand to forty thousand to the Confederacy with comparable numbers for Missouri. Maryland accounted for twenty infantry regiments, four artillery regiments, and six artillery batteries within the Union army as well as many smaller units. Confederate Marylanders formed a single infantry regiment as well as one infantry battalion, four artillery batteries, and two cavalry battalions. Additionally, many Maryland men headed south and joined other state regiments. Historian Daniel E. Sutherland notes that the rebellious Marylanders who remained in the state "caused alarm among Maryland Unionists." They feared "the elements" of the Baltimore Riot were still present inside the state. The split between Maryland soldiers and civilians perpetuated the dichotomous relationship that continued well into the twentieth century between the state's Civil War veterans.[31]

Even within their own ranks, Maryland soldiers faced divisions and internal strife. Charles H. Russell, a Presbyterian minister from Williamsport, Maryland, raised a cavalry company and received a commission as a captain with the Union First Cavalry Regiment Virginia in the summer of 1861. By January 1862, his company transferred into the First Maryland Cavalry Regiment. On more than one occasion, Russell wrote to Ward Lamon, a personal friend of Abraham Lincoln, imploring him to use his standing with the president to reassign his company to its original regiment. His greatest frustration was with the commanding officer of the regiment, Colonel Andrew G. Miller. In a letter to Lamon in April 1862, he characterized Colonel Miller as "a miserable drunkard" and recalled an occasion in which he "was so drunk he could hardly sit in the saddle." Russell concluded that his men were "very very much dissatisfied here." Charles Thornton Moore, a soldier in the U.S. Second Maryland Infantry Regiment, recounted the problems caused by alcohol within his regiment in a letter to his mother in August 1863. Moore said that when two men who were tasked with finding and bringing back a missing drunken soldier, the inebriated soldier resisted and one of the men "upped with his gun and shot him dead." As soldiers from the Old Line State realized throughout the conflict, the effects of war were not limited to their own ranks.[32]

As expectations and predictions that the war would be brief dissipated, the success and confidence of the Confederacy swelled during the first year of the Civil War. The Army of Northern Virginia, under the leadership of General Robert E. Lee and his two most trusted subordinate commanders, generals Thomas "Stonewall" Jackson and James Longstreet, rattled off numerous victories in Virginia in 1862, aiding in the protection and security of the Confederate capital in Richmond; to most observers they "appeared poised to capture Washington." The success of Jackson in the Shenandoah Valley and Lee in the Seven Day's Battles and the Battle of Second Bull Run helped fuel Lee's decision to move north and his confidence that such a move would prove successful.[33]

The Confederate troops lacked sufficient rations and ammunition needed to engage a siege on the city of Washington after the success at Second Bull Run, and the number of troops at Lee's disposal also seemed inadequate. Washington was heavily fortified with a large number of federal troops and artillery situated to defend the Union capital. Lee decided that the best course of action was to invade north of the capital by marching into Maryland with the hope of eventually pushing into central Pennsylvania and drawing federal forces away from Washington as well as Baltimore. Lee and the Army of Northern Virginia crossed the Potomac River and began marching toward Frederick, Maryland, in the early days of September 1862.[34]

Once in Frederick, Lee issued a "Proclamation to the People of Maryland" on September 8 in order to explain his purpose for entering the state and his hopes for its citizens. He expressed empathy early, noting that the Confederacy had "long watched with the deepest sympathy the wrongs and outrages that have been inflicted upon the citizens of a Commonwealth, allied to the States of the South by the strongest, social, political, and commercial ties." He then appealed to Marylanders' constitutional rights and their hopes for equality. Maryland, he asserted, was "deprived of every right, and reduced to the condition of a conquered Province," and its citizens were arrested with no formal charges "in violation" of the Constitution's "most valuable provisions." Lee recalled the many variants of federal occupation in Maryland and made clear that the states of the Confederacy believed "that the People of Maryland possessed a spirit too lofty to submit to such a government" and that they "long wished to aid you in throwing off this foreign yoke." The ultimate goal of this process was, of course, a restoration of "independence and sovereignty" for the state and ability of its citizens to "once more enjoy their ancient freedom of thought and speech." Lee's army and "the power of its arms" would achieve the "throwing off." The issue of equality and inequality was important to those who challenged federal occupation in Baltimore, and Lee used that point of frustration as a key component of his proclamation.[35]

Lee was ultimately disappointed by the lack of response his proclamation to Maryland generated. The state's citizens did not come rushing to the Army of Northern Virginia with gratitude and relief. Western Maryland, the region of the state Lee invaded, was not particularly sympathetic to the Confederate cause and not surprisingly spurned the Confederate general's invitation. Additionally, the condition of Lee's army was also a factor contributing to the unenthusiastic response to the invasion north. The Confederate forces struggled with stragglers, had tattered uniforms, and many were barefoot. The status of the army did not inspire confidence in Maryland's citizens. The apathy with which Marylanders viewed Lee's invitation would be noted for years after the Civil War in debates over Maryland's wartime loyalties. The refusal became a point of pride among Maryland Unionists after the war and a strike against the Old Line State from those questioning the state's contribution to the South.[36]

Not everyone in western Maryland resented the presence of Confederate troops. James Francis Beall from Frederick expressed his disdain for the actions of Union forces on their way to Sharpsburg. In his September 16, 1862, diary entry he lamented, "When I arrived home this evening

I found that the Yankees had killed my hog, stolen all our peaches, some sweet potatoes, tomatoes, beets, carrots, cantelopes & keyan pepper." He concluded that the Union soldiers were "the most wicked & meanest set of men in the civilised world." Beall was politically sympathetic to the Confederacy and had both a brother and a brother-in-law who fought in the Confederate army. His experiences with the Union army only reaffirmed his personal sentiments on the war and the opposing sides. William Harrison Beach of the First New York Cavalry remembered things differently. He recalled in his memoir that the "Federal army had not before seen such a reception" as it was given in Maryland in 1862. He remembered "women and young girls waving the Union flag" from "every doorway and at every window." The divergent narratives of Beall and Beach speak to the ambiguity of Maryland's Civil War loyalty.[37]

After several small skirmishes and battles in Maryland during the first two weeks of September, the forces of General Robert E. Lee and General George B. McClellan met in Sharpsburg on September 17, 1862. The Battle of Antietam, fought on September 17, 1862, was the bloodiest day in American military history. More than seventy thousand federal troops participated in the conflict, and of those soldiers, approximately thirteen thousand were killed, wounded, or missing in action; the casualty number of the thirty-five thousand Confederate troops that fought in the battle was similar to that of the Union army. The result of the battle was a technical draw but a tactical and strategic victory for the Union forces as they thwarted General Lee's first invasion into northern territory and his Maryland campaign of 1862.[38]

Newspapers, including the *Herald of Freedom and Torch Light*, a local newspaper printed out of Hagerstown, Maryland, were quick to relay the events of the day to the public. The *Herald*, in reference to the aftermath of the battle, noted that "heap upon heap lay piled the dead and wounded" and "in one field where their advance was checked lay 1,217 rebel dead, while on the hill beyond a number of nearly as great of our own men were left to the mercy of the enemy." The author of the article praised the Union army for its performance during the battle and stated that "consummate valor marked the actions of every division in the field." The article also cited the early questioning of McClellan's decision making during and immediately after the Battle of Antietam. The author noted that "there are those who blame McClellan for granting the armistice, yet his course was a wise one." The questioning of McClellan and his seemingly evident pacification and hesitancy would not dissipate in the few days after the final shots at Antietam. McClellan's leadership became a point of controversy for many years to come and posed perhaps the greatest difficulty for Lincoln.[39]

The Hagerstown article concluded with the statement that "the rebels have been driven out of the State, and we believe that the footsteps of not a single one of them now pollutes the soil of Maryland." The loyal citizens of Maryland were aware of the fragility of their state's tenuous position. Its dubious early history in the war was already a mark against its Union character. Expunging those of questionable loyalty as well as the rebel army itself was paramount to loyal Marylanders who were worried about not only the safety of their state but also the safety of its legacy. The problem of rebel pollution would vex Unionist Marylanders for years to come.[40]

Two weeks after the Battle of Antietam's conclusion, Lincoln became the first official tourist to the battlefield. He spent four days touring the field and speaking with General McClellan as well as visiting the wounded of both the Union army and the Confederate army.[41] Before Lincoln, however, there were other important visitors to the Antietam battlefield. On September 19, 1862, Mathew Brady's staff photographers Alexander Gardner and James F. Gibson photographed the aftermath of the battle. Their photographs once again placed Maryland in the national consciousness, even if merely as a backdrop for the destruction and violence of the Civil War that plagued the American landscape. There is no evidence as to where Gardner and Gibson stayed on the night of September 18, but it is clear that Gardner began taking photographs on September 19, most likely in the early morning. Dunker Church, the small unassuming white church located "in the heart of the battlefield," was the first site Gardner photographed. The first series of pictures taken by Gardner centered on several dead Confederate soldiers lying in an open field in front of the church with a cluster of trees in the background. Gardner and Gibson had to confront the issue of time and race against soldiers hastily burying the dead on the battlefield. Taking photographs on a remote battlefield was a time-consuming process. Gibson probably helped prepare the plates while Gardner operated and set up the camera. After photographing around Dunker Church and near a fence line along Hagerstown Pike, Gardner and Gibson made their way to the Sunken Road, later to be remembered as "Bloody Lane." At the Sunken Road, Gardner and Gibson exposed the final three plates in the late afternoon of September 19.[42]

The Baltimore Riot the previous year garnered national attention and represented the turbulent society that made up Maryland's populace.

The Battle of Antietam and the photographs of its aftermath, however, showed those outside the state in a more visceral and graphic manner the trauma Marylanders faced during the war. The first photographs of the dead at Antietam marked the beginning of remembering, capturing, and commemorating the landscape of wartime Maryland as well as grappling with its conflicted nature.

Photographs of Civil War dead were primarily of fallen Confederates, as Union soldiers often buried their fallen comrades when they held the field. Manipulation of Civil War photographs and scenes was prevalent among post-battle images. Photographers employed manipulation as a way to "appeal to a sentimental, even romantic, sense in public attitude." Gardner and his assistants moved one Confederate soldier at Gettysburg more than forty yards to a barricade in order to make it appear as if the soldier was a sharpshooter. Gardner then placed a rifle carefully over the soldier's body; the use of props to add to the emotional imagery was a common tactic employed in photographic manipulation. Although Gardner later used manipulation in his subsequent photographs of Civil War dead, there is no evidence of manipulation in his photographs taken at Antietam, most likely because he did not yet realize the potential market value of sensationalized images.[43]

Gardner and Gibson brought the photographs to Brady in Washington, and by the middle of October the images were on display in Brady's gallery on Broadway, under the title "The Dead of Antietam." Crowds flocked into the second-floor reception room to gaze at a spectacle never before seen in the United States. As historian Bob Zeller notes, "The photographs of the dead of Antietam were the first American images of the carnage of war."[44]

One visitor to the gallery, a *New York Times* reporter, put forth his interpretation of the display in an article titled "BRADY'S PHOTOGRAPHS; Pictures of the Dead at Antietam" published on October 20, 1862. The reporter began his article by acknowledging the distance between the home front and the front lines. Historian Earl Hess refers to this distance as the "gulf of experience" that existed between soldiers and home front civilians.[45] The reporter noted that the citizens living on the home front "recognize the battle-field as a reality, but it stands as a remote one" and they "see the list [of fallen soldiers] in the morning paper at breakfast, but dismiss its recollection with the coffee" much like when a funeral takes place next door; "it attracts your attention, but does not enlist your sympathy." The author speculated on how different the perception or reality of war would be if the dead "fresh from the field, laid along the

FIGURE 1.3. Confederate dead in front of Dunker Church
(courtesy of the Library of Congress).

FIGURE 1.4. Confederate dead by a fence on the Hagerstown road
(courtesy of the Library of Congress).

pavement" of Broadway or if the corpse of a fallen soldier was "carried out over your own threshold."

According to the *New York Times* reporter, Mathew Brady's gallery of the fallen of Antietam served to "bring home . . . the terrible reality and earnestness of war." Even though he did not literally bring the bodies home and lay them in "dooryards" or "along the streets," he did "something very like it." The reporter anticipated a feeling of "repulsiveness" but was surprised that he also experienced a "terrible fascination" that drew him near the pictures and made him "loath to leave them." He observed "hushed, reverent groups standing around these weird copies of carnage, bending down to look in the pale faces of the dead, chained by the strange spell that dwells in the dead men's eyes."

Although the reporter recognized that the photographs possessed "a terrible distinctness" and the "very features of the slain" could be distinguished with "aid of the magnifying glass," he made one interesting point as to what the detailed photographs could not capture. The one aspect that eluded the skill of the photographer was the "background of widows and orphans, torn from the bosom of their natural protectors." The suffering of those who survived was not present in the photographs of the slain. The reporter concluded that "all of this desolation imagination must paint—broken hearts cannot be photographed."[46]

When Lincoln visited the battlefield in early October, Gardner returned to Antietam to take more photographs, this time of several prominent Union generals along with the president. Brady made his first visit to the site shortly thereafter in late October and took his own pictures of Union soldiers not far from the site of the original battle.[47] The more significant decision made by Lincoln following the battle came one week prior to his visit to the battlefield.

The Battle of Antietam provided Lincoln the opportunity to issue the preliminary version of the Emancipation Proclamation. The fact that Antietam led to the Emancipation Proclamation forever tied Maryland with emancipation. In commemorations and remembrances of the battle, Marylanders often connected the policies of emancipation with Antietam. Decades later, those advocating on behalf of their civil rights in the Old Line State reminded its citizens as well as the nation that, in many respects, Maryland was the birthplace of emancipation but still lagged behind socially in matters of race and equality. The significance of issuing the Emancipation Proclamation following a battle that took place in a loyal, slaveholding state was, however, felt almost immediately.

When officially enacted on January 1, 1863, the Emancipation Proclamation not only granted freedom to slaves in the states in rebellion against the U.S. government but also started the recruitment of African Americans into the United States Colored Troops (USCT) regiments. Maryland African Americans made up several USCT regiments. An estimated one-third of Maryland's military-aged enslaved black male population fought in the U.S. Army, with approximately nine thousand African American Marylanders serving in six regiments of the USCT as well as several serving in the U.S. Navy. By the fall of 1863, the U.S. government was recruiting slaves of loyal masters from several border states, including Maryland, under the terms of General Order 329. The order "promised freedom to the recruits and compensation to loyal owners." It also fostered and encouraged the flight of Maryland slaves from their masters' bondage and, in many cases, subsequently led to their enlistment in the Union army. General Order 329 pushed Maryland further to the brink by bringing another factor into the divisions over loyalty within the state. The federal government was undermining slaveholders sympathetic to the Confederacy in Maryland, and this exacerbated their frustrations with Lincoln's policies.[48]

Similarly, reactions to Lincoln's proclamation in Maryland were unsurprisingly mixed. One Frederick newspaper lauded a policy of emancipation because it "would afford relief to thousands of slave holders and if accompanied with Federal compensation for the public and private inconvenience attendant upon a change of system . . . would promote the welfare and prosperity of the State." Another, a Maryland man, pinned the blame for the secession of the southern states and the outbreak of war on emancipation. "Had it not been for them [the abolitionists]," he stated, "the bad men of the south could not possibly have succeeded in their state rights and state sovereignty doctrine." He referred to abolitionists as "that horrid faction" and confessed that his "disgust" for them "only increases as the awful fruits of their leanings are being manifested." Many in Maryland also expressed their hopes and fears that a similar proclamation would apply to their own state. The realities of war complicated life in the state, but the tangible and economic impact of policies of emancipation made unquestionably clear that the war was altering traditional ways of life and that Maryland society was being pulled in different directions. This polarization continued beyond 1865 and would not stop.[49]

Marylanders were once again exposed to the conflicting armies in the aftermath of the Gettysburg campaign in the summer of 1863. Frederick Shriver of Union Mills, Maryland, noted that the presence of the Army of the Potomac was not a burden for the citizens of Maryland because the army "left the most favorable impression on the citizens imaginable" and the only trouble they had was from some of the stragglers who stayed after the army had left, some of which "were extremely saucy" and, in Shriver's estimation, "every saucy one was an *Irishman.*" Shriver's positive experiences with the Union army certainly differed from the experience of Francis Beall less than one year prior. Although many Maryland citizens possessed loyalties to a particular side prior to contact with Civil War armies, some Marylanders' experiences on the home front with Union or Confederate soldiers shaped their wartime sympathies.[50]

Shortly after Marylanders and the rest of the country grappled with the changes to slavery and the evolution of war through 1863 into 1864, the reality and violence of battle once again arrived on the doorstep of the conflicted border state. Confederate military forces returned to Maryland; this time Lee sent Jubal Early and his corps to support approximately six thousand Confederates already in the Shenandoah Valley. After successfully controlling the valley, Early moved into Maryland. Virginia Craig characterized the mood of the loyal citizens in Baltimore in a letter to her husband. She claimed that "in the present panic which pervades the city, if a hundred rebel cavalrymen were to ride into the city, the cowards here would be so frightened they would surrender the city to them." The goal of the strategy to once again move into Maryland was that it would divert some of Union general Ulysses Grant's men from the siege of Petersburg and a successful attack could be launched on the scantly defended Union capital. Grant responded to the movement of Early and his men by sending 5,000 federal soldiers and General Lew Wallace to confront them. Early and his force of approximately 14,000 met Wallace and 5,800 Union soldiers in the early morning on July 9, 1864, outside Frederick, Maryland. Although Wallace and his men were eventually defeated, they managed to hold off the Confederate forces for ten hours and stalled Early's march to Washington by a full day. The delay allowed Grant the opportunity to reinforce Washington's defenses and led to a successful defense of the capital when Early attacked Fort Stevens on July 11. Although it was not the same magnitude of the Battle of Antietam nearly two years earlier, the Battle of Monocacy was a crucial Maryland battle that earned the nickname "The Battle that Saved Washington."[51]

With the Union and its capital preserved on the field near Frederick, Maryland, just three months later the state's devoted Unionists made a move to push Maryland further to the north politically. Maryland's Constitution of 1864 was drafted in April 1864 and narrowly ratified the following fall. In addition to disenfranchising the white population that was disloyal and engaged in actions in support of the Confederate cause, Article 24 of the Declaration of Rights coupled with the Constitution outlawed slavery in the state. It read: "That hereafter, in this State, there shall be neither slavery nor involuntary servitude, except in punishment of crime, whereof the party shall have been duly convicted: and all persons held to service or labor as slaves are hereby declared free."[52]

Despite the shifts in Maryland's legislation, the Union army and the Lincoln administration still did not fully trust the state in late 1863 and even into 1864. On October 31, 1863, Maryland governor Augustus Bradford, who assumed the office in January 1862, wrote to Lincoln expressing his concern over General Order No. 53, which called for the presence of troops at polling places in Maryland to ensure peace. Bradford, although sympathetic to the Union, took issue with this order and what he saw as an infringement on the political process in his state. Lincoln's reply to Bradford showed that he did not have the same level of confidence in Maryland as its governor did. Lincoln wrote, "Your suggestion that nearly all the candidates are loyal, I do not think quite meets the case. In this struggle for the nation's life, I can not so confidently rely on those whose elections may have depended upon disloyal votes." He also pointed out the hypocrisy of Bradford's complaint, noting that the governor was elected with the presence of military force at the polls. Lincoln's rebuttal to Bradford serves as an unambiguous indication that the disloyal acts of Maryland were still fresh in the mind of the Union and its administration.[53]

The skepticism about the state's loyalty was not restricted to the political landscape. Maryland units were not permitted to fulfill some duties required by the Union military. For instance, an Ohio regiment replaced the Fifth Maryland Infantry Regiment as guards for Fort Delaware because Secretary of War Edwin Stanton received a recommendation that the Maryland regiment had "too many sympathizers in it to be intrusted with the charge of prisoners of war." Union soldiers and leaders alike remembered Maryland's problematic and quarrelsome factions from the earliest days of the war and would not forget even long after the war concluded.[54]

Maryland Unionists once again outwardly proved their loyalty in late 1864 by casting their ballots in the presidential election of 1864. Virginia Craig of Baltimore ordered her Union officer husband to "tell the boys they must not vote for Mc" because "his election would please the Rebels too much." Lincoln defeated General George McClellan soundly in the election and, in the state of Maryland, he managed to earn 54 percent of the vote. Winning the majority of the vote in Maryland represented a marked shift from Lincoln's performance in the state four years prior. The shift is reflected in the effectiveness of federal occupation in the state, the growing successes of the Union military, and the fact that many Marylanders who would have voted for the Democratic candidate were no longer residing in the state in the fall of 1864.[55]

By the time of Lincoln's second inaugural address on March 4, 1865, the writing was on the wall for the South and the Confederate cause. Maryland, though divided in sentiment, had not fallen to the Confederacy. Lincoln, through aggressive policies and initiatives, managed to hold on to the conflicted border state for the entirety of the war. The state was a key battleground for the armies of both sides, in part, for its geographic position as well as for the advantage its citizens could bring to either side. Maryland would once again take center stage in the national consciousness just one month later. The war had ended, but Maryland's divisions endured, and the first postbellum debate over the state took place in the months immediately following the peace at Appomattox.

Maryland on Trial

During the early secession crisis that reached a fever pitch in Baltimore, John Hay, Lincoln's personal secretary, recalled that the president believed "if quiet was kept in Baltimore a little longer Maryland might be considered the first of the redeemed."[56] The redemption of Maryland was not fully realized, and the events of the spring and summer of 1865 brought that reality into sharper focus. Four years removed from Lincoln's early hopes for Maryland, a bullet fired from a Marylander's gun took his life.

On April 14, 1865, John Wilkes Booth entered Ford's Theater in Washington, D.C., at approximately 10:00 p.m. The play in progress that evening was *Our American Cousin*, and the distinguished guest of the evening was Abraham Lincoln. The president viewed the play from a private box in the balcony with his wife and another couple, Major Henry Rathbone and Clara Harris. Booth made his way easily through the theater, aided by his notoriety as an actor. He reached Lincoln's box and shot the president in the back of the head. After struggling with Rathbone and amid screams from Harris and Mary Todd Lincoln, Booth jumped down onto the stage, shouted "sic semper tyrannis," and darted out into street.[57]

While Booth was committing his crime in Ford's Theater, Lewis Thornton Powell arrived at the home of Secretary of State William Seward. Powell posed as a prescription deliverer for the injured Seward. William Bell, a black servant of the Sewards, welcomed Powell into the residence. Powell first faced resistance from William Seward's son Frederick William Seward. He hesitated momentarily but then regained his nerve and attempted to fire on the secretary's son. The gun misfired; however, Powell continued his assault by beating Frederick Seward with his pistol. He made his way into the secretary's bedroom and managed to wound him several times before Seward's aide and another son, Augustus H. Seward, were able to drive the assailant out of the home, but not before receiving wounds of their own from Powell's blade.[58]

The simultaneity of the events of April 14 made clear to those entrusted with seeking justice, especially Joseph Holt, that the crimes were facilitated through a network of conspirators. Holt was the judge advocate general of the U.S. Army at the time of the assassination. Several of the conspirators were charged with aiding Booth in his flight from the scene into southern Maryland. Immediately after committing his crime in Ford's Theater, Booth made his way to the Naval Yard bridge in Washington, D.C., and crossed it unopposed into Maryland. Once in the borders of his home state, he met up with David Herold, who helped escort him across the Maryland countryside. Herold and Booth were eventually cornered by federal troops in the barn of farmer Richard Garrett in Port Royal, Virginia. Soldiers set the barn ablaze and Boston Corbett, a soldier acting without orders, gunned down Booth in the barn on April 26, 1865, twelve days after the assassination.[59]

Even before Booth's death on April 26, a list of those who aided him in his crime was growing, and authorities began to question and arrest those suspected of involvement in the conspiracy to assassinate the president. The conspirators played a variety of roles in Booth's plot, including simultaneously attacking other political figures, helping with supplies needed both leading up to and after the assassination, providing a meeting place for the conspirators to meet and discuss their plot, and offering houses of respite on his flight through Maryland. Those eventually charged as conspirators were Samuel Arnold, George Atzerodt, David Herold, Samuel Mudd, Michael O'Laughlen, Lewis Powell, Edman Spangler, and Mary Surratt.[60]

Maryland's loyalty and divisiveness during the Civil War featured prominently in the trial of the Lincoln conspirators for the simple reason that the majority of the conspirators had strong ties to the Old Line State. John Wilkes Booth was born in Harford County, Maryland, and lived in the state. Samuel Mudd was raised near Bryantown, Maryland. George Atzerodt ran a small carriage-making and painting business in Port Tobacco, Maryland. David Herold was born to native Marylanders Adam and Mary Porter Herold. Michael O'Laughlen and Edmund Spangler were from Baltimore. Mary Surratt owned and operated a boardinghouse in Surrattsville, Maryland.[61] Due to the status of Maryland as a border state, the conspirators' home state came under more scrutiny, and at times Maryland was put on trial along with the defendants.

The trial of the Lincoln conspirators and the position of Maryland within the testimonies and dialogue of the trial represented a larger conversation and debate over the state that Americans would grapple with for decades following the conclusion of the Civil War. In the first few decades of the postbellum period, northerners, southerners, and Marylanders themselves tried to place Maryland within the larger narrative of the war and delineate its role for the Union and the Confederacy. Throughout the course of the trial, former Unionists attempted to demonstrate the Confederate underpinnings of Maryland, and the defendants and their attorneys tried to prove their loyalty to the Union and, in turn, the loyalty of their home state.

The trial began on May 9, 1865, and the Military Commission included Judge Advocate General Joseph Holt, his two assistant judge advocates Colonel Henry Burnett and John A. Bingham, and nine military commissioners. After nearly two months of testimony, the commission came to a decision on June 30, 1865. Due to President Andrew Johnson's illness, the decision was not made public until July 5. All those charged were found guilty to varying degrees. Samuel Arnold, Samuel Mudd, and Michael O'Laughlen received life sentences; Edman Spangler received a six-year sentence; and Lewis Powell, David Herold, George Atzerodt, and Mary Surratt were condemned to hang. The execution of Powell, Herold, Atzerodt, and Surratt took place on July 7, just two days after sentencing.[62]

The details of the conspirators' involvement in the assassination plot and their connection to John Wilkes Booth were the central components of the trial both to the Military Commission and to the general public following the ebbs and flows of the trial in newspapers across the country. Maryland, however, also figured prominently in the proceedings and was a vital piece of the conspiracy puzzle to both the judge advocates and the defense. Civil War Maryland was more than just a backdrop for arguments over the conspirators' loyalty and guilt; it was a political and legal tool used deliberately and pointedly throughout the trial.

The loyalty of Maryland and the conspirators was a primary target of the prosecution. Pointing to the disloyal elements within the state and connecting the defendants to them not only underscored their treasonous behavior but also provided a tangible link to the conspirators' culpability in the assassination of Lincoln. The prosecuting officers referred numerous times to the questionable loyalty of Maryland during the Civil War. The commission also attempted to prove that the conspirators placed their loyalty to their home state of Maryland over their loyalty to the Union.

Early in the trial, the commission directly linked Maryland and John Wilkes Booth. The prosecution called Henry Van Steinacker, a former Confederate engineer-officer, who recounted his experience in meeting Booth and two other men while taking a sick engineer to his home in Virginia in 1863. He stated that he "got better acquainted after having ridden a while with them" and he "found them out to belong to Maryland."[63] Steinacker's comment was a subtle one but still pointed to not only the Confederate sympathies of Maryland but also the Maryland roots of the most notorious individual in American society at the time. The country had not forgotten the secessionist tumult in Baltimore at the beginning of the war and the extreme measures the Union government implemented in order to hold on to Maryland.

The prosecution also noted on several occasions the questionable military record of Maryland on behalf of the Union. General Thomas Maley Harris of the Military Commission objected to the presence of Reverdy Johnson, Mary Surratt's defense attorney from Maryland, as legal counsel based on his actions during the war, namely, a controversy surrounding a loyalty oath in Maryland in 1864. Harris cited Johnson's opposition to the law that required Maryland citizens to take a loyalty oath before voting. Johnson believed the law making voting conditional on taking the oath was unconstitutional but not the oath itself. He laid out this position to the court and was ultimately approved as legal counsel. During the course of his objection and the back-and-forth exchange with Johnson, Harris cited the mixed record of Maryland during the war by giving credit to the state for its role in the "great contest" but also noting that in Maryland "a portion of the people stand in a very different attitude, and have made for themselves a terrible record."[64]

The commission also attempted to discredit the witnesses called by the defense by questioning their loyalty to the Union during the war and their role within the secessionist element in Maryland during the war. Assistant Judge Advocate Major Henry Lawrence Burnett grilled J. Z. Jenkins, a witness called on behalf of Mary Surratt, with a litany of questions concerning his loyalty: "Where did you stand when it was discussed that the State of Maryland was about to secede, and join the Southern Confederacy? Did you ever take any part in any way against the Government during this struggle? Have you been entirely on the side of the Government? During the entire war? Have you never by act or word given aid or sympathy to the Rebellion? You never fed any of their soldiers? Nor induced any soldiers to go to their army? Nor aided or assisted them in any way?"[65] Burnett also questioned the affiliations and loyalties of defense witness Joseph T. Nott. Nott responded by asserting he never acted against "the Union party in Maryland" nor did he take "sides with secession elements there."[66] The prosecution probed into defense witness Jeremiah Dyer's participation in military organizations in Maryland that placed devotion to the state over devotion to the Union. He confessed that he was a member of an organization in 1861 that was committed "to stand by the State of Maryland in the event of its taking ground against the Government of the United States." Dyer defended his position, however, stating that by the time Richmond was taken his "sympathies were on the side of the Government." He believed "the United States were pursuing the right course, except in emancipating the slaves," adding that he "thought that was wrong."[67] By centering on the Civil War loyalty of not only the conspirators but also the defense witnesses, the prosecution could weaken the testimony brought forth by the defense and generate skepticism concerning its validity.

The prosecuting officers not only questioned Jenkins's loyalty but they also called their own witnesses who challenged Jenkins's testimony and his devotion to the Union. One witness recalled, "For the last three years he has been one of the most disloyal men in the county." Another remarked, "He pretended to be a loyal man in 1861, as a great many in Prince George's, St. Mary's, and those lower counties did," but his "reputation and conduct since 1861 has been disloyal. I call him a rebel. His sympathy with the rebels has been open and outspoken." John L. Thompson, a witness for the prosecution, stated that Jenkins "is regarded as a disloyal man in that community; his disloyalty is open and outspoken."[68]

The role and loyalty of Maryland during the war figured most prominently in the prosecution's case against Samuel Mudd. Both the prosecution and the defense devoted time to an alleged statement made by

Mudd where he asserted that "every Union man in the State of Maryland would be killed in six or seven weeks." Both sides also debated the credibility of supposed claims made by Mudd that "Maryland had been false to her duty in not going with other States in rebellion against the Government." Mudd supposedly issued these statements in early March 1865 to John H. Downing and Daniel J. Thomas.[69] The judge advocates tried to link Mudd with secessionist elements in Maryland and prove his disdain for those in Maryland who did not support the Confederacy.

The defense attorney for Samuel Mudd, Thomas Ewing Jr., and defense witnesses used the Civil War legacy of Maryland in a different fashion. When cross-examined regarding the Civil War loyalty of Mudd, defense witness Julia Ann Bloyce placed Mudd in context with southern Maryland to prove his loyalty. She recalled that in terms of his opposition to the U.S. government, "he was very temperate in this regard . . . very much more so than many of the citizens of benighted Charles County, in Southern Maryland."[70] Characterizing southern Maryland as a radicalized Confederate region allowed the defense to justify Mudd's Confederate sympathies and paint him as a moderate compared to his neighbors. While it would be difficult for Mudd's defense to argue he possessed unbridled devotion to the Union, the context of Maryland during the Civil War provided a tangible counterpoint.

The attorneys defending the conspirators also pointed to the Unionist efforts of their clients and witnesses amid the secessionist movement in Maryland. J. Z. Jenkins stated that he had spent $3,000 during the war in his district in order to "hold it in the Union." When the prosecution questioned Jenkins's loyalty, Mary Surratt's defense attorney Frederick Aiken called in several witnesses to attest to his loyalty to the Union. One in particular, William P. Wood, made note of Jenkins's efforts in keeping Maryland a Union state. According to Wood, Jenkins went as far as to travel to "obtain voters who had left the State of Maryland, but who had not lost their residence, to return to Maryland to vote the Union ticket."[71] Maryland's ambiguous Civil War legacy benefited those representing the accused, to a certain extent, because it accentuated the defendants' acts of loyalty and Unionism and made those acts seem more committed in light of the circumstances in Maryland. Maryland's mixed record during the war was a double-edged sword that could be used both for and against the conspirators' behalf.

The conflicted nature of Maryland's Civil War status and its connection to the assassination of Abraham Lincoln as the home state of those who conspired to kill him was not a discussion point limited to the courtroom. Much like the debate in the courtroom, American society writ large disagreed over the Civil War Maryland and its loyalties. *Harper's Weekly* recorded the debate over Reverdy Johnson's loyalty and his legitimacy as a defense attorney for Mary Surratt. The magazine noted that during Johnson's self-defense speech he "digressed from the subject to eulogize the people of Maryland, and said they were the equals morally and patriotically of the General's fellow-citizens of West Virginia." *Harper's Weekly* ultimately sided with Johnson regarding this incident and stated emphatically that the "court was not competent to measure the moral character of the counsel."[72]

Not everyone defended Maryland's loyalty so ardently in the wake of the conspirators' trial. New York Civil War correspondent George Alfred Townsend posited that Booth's flight through Maryland was significant and underscored Maryland's disloyal history. Townsend asserted that "the western shore of Maryland is a noxious and pestilential place for patriotism." He also detailed the motivations of one of the officers involved in the pursuit who was once "driven" out of lower Maryland "for his loyalty." Townsend added that the citizens of lower Maryland "had reserved their hospitality for assassins."[73]

The accounts from *Harper's Weekly* and Townsend's reports reveal that there was no consensus in the immediate postwar period on Maryland's Civil War loyalty emanating from the North. In the wake of the Civil War, many northerners would not forgive Maryland for its Confederate sympathizers, most notoriously Booth and his fellow conspirators. Many in the North, however, acknowledged and appreciated Maryland's contribution to the Union cause and understood its significance to the ultimate success of the Union army. The divide in the North over Maryland's Civil War position persists throughout the history of the state in Civil War memory. The centrality of Maryland to the history of the Civil War ensured the Old Line State's prevalence in postbellum remembrance, perhaps most notably in battlefield commemorations.

CHAPTER 2

"An Ungenerous Sneer"

Commemorations at Antietam and Gettysburg

On November 16, 1886, three days before the dedication of the Second Maryland Confederate Infantry Monument in Gettysburg, a group of Confederate veterans met in Baltimore to discuss their Confederate identity and why they should be proud of it. The main feature of the evening was a speech by General Bradley T. Johnson in which he defended Confederates "from the charge of being 'Rebels' and 'traitors'" and argued that they were "well worthy of preservation" in the historical record. Johnson was not only vital in commanding Confederate Marylanders during the war; he also was central to the development of Confederate memorialization from his efforts in promoting the veterans' organization the Society of the Army of Northern Virginia and through his postbellum promotion of Confederate Marylanders. A major theme of Johnson's speech was being a Confederate Marylander after the war. Early in his speech, Johnson noted two possible fates for Confederate soldiers returning home after the war. One was that of outcasts, in which they "would rapidly degenerate into the outlaws of the community, and would be thrust aside as unworthy of respect." The other potential outcome was that they would return home as "respected citizens" and be able to leave to their "children the priceless heritage of honored fame and name." Johnson believed this polarity to be particularly tumultuous for Marylanders who did not possess "State organizations to justify them." He then outlined several legal cases that exemplified the struggle over which postwar identity society would force on Confederate veterans. The result of these struggles, according to Johnson, firmly established former Confederate soldiers "as equal citizens, with equal rights to respect and recognition." Johnson was speaking at a time in which debates over reconciliation were on the lips of veterans from both sides.[1]

The history of commemoration at Antietam and the first Confederate monument at Gettysburg highlights the incompleteness of reconciliation. It demonstrates that appeals for reconciliation and displays of
persistent bitterness occurred side by side in the late nineteenth century
and that in their struggle to establish their own postwar identities and
legacies, many veterans as well as civilians resisted reconciliatory efforts.
Studying the commemoration histories of Antietam and Gettysburg and
Maryland's place within them, however, reveals something else: the connection between perceptions of loyalty and reconciliation. Discussions
over loyalty were not restricted to Maryland's status during the war. To
many soldiers, loyalty did not end at Appomattox. Many Union veterans
interpreted offers and evocations of reconciliation, this chapter argues,
as not only misguided but also disloyal and anti-Union. Accepting reconciliationist sentiment meant not only forgetting and forgiving the wrongs
of the Confederacy but also the dissolution of the Union soldier's loyalty
to the nation he fought so ardently to preserve.[2]

Maryland veterans from both sides resisted reconciliation not only because they feared the dissolution of their respective loyalties but because
they were fighting for an equal claim to their Civil War legacies. Those
Marylanders who remained loyal to the Union wanted to make clear to
other Union veterans their equal devotion to the cause they fought for.
They had to argue more passionately on behalf of their own efforts because of the divided state from which their troops mustered into service.
Union citizens from the Old Line State not only highlighted their personal contributions but also argued that the true loyalty of their state,
despite the internal strife, always resided with the North. Confederate
Marylanders, such as Johnson, wanted to be on equal ground as their former in-state foes. They feared the Union veterans from their state as well
as others might overshadow their own contributions. Within Maryland as
well as beyond the state's borders, the issues of reconciliation and loyalty
were tied directly together, and early battlefield commemorations shed
light on this connection.

Antietam National Cemetery

As is the case with most Civil War battlefields, including most notably
Gettysburg, Antietam's formal commemoration and preservation history
began with the call for a national cemetery on the battlefield. Maryland
state senator Lewis P. Firey introduced a proposition to the Maryland

legislature for a state and national cemetery honoring the fallen soldiers of the Battle of Antietam in early 1864, before the war's conclusion. By 1864, other national cemeteries were already established. General George H. Thomas established the cemetery at Chattanooga in the winter of 1863 through a general order, and the national cemetery at Gettysburg was transferred from the Pennsylvania state government to the federal government in November of the same year. In his resolution for a cemetery on the Antietam battlefield, Firey requested "a portion of the battlefield of Antietam" in order to more properly bury "the bodies of our heroes who fell in that great struggle and are now bleaching in the upturned furrows."[3]

Shortly after the appointment of the committee for the proposed cemetery, the committee members visited the battlefield and "selected that most eligible and beautiful site where the National Cemetery is now located." They also received a "positive offer of sale" from the property owner on that same trip. On March 10, 1864, the General Assembly of the state of Maryland unanimously passed an act that approved $5,000 for the purchase of lands for the cemetery and its enclosure. The act also gave the governor permission to hire an agent in charge of supervising the construction of the cemetery's enclosure as well as the exhuming of the bodies. Additionally, the act provided "that those who fell in the army of General Lee should be buried in a separate portion of the Cemetery from that designed for those who fell under General McClellan."[4]

The burial of Confederate dead at the Antietam cemetery developed into a point of controversy during the period before and after the cemetery's official dedication on September 17, 1867. The issues and controversy surrounding the establishment and dedication of Antietam National Cemetery are indicative of the larger complexities and disparities in the remembrance and commemoration of the Battle of Antietam, namely, the issues of loyalty and reconciliation. In many ways, the dedication of the cemetery serves as a foundation for the persistent anti-Confederate sentiment that frequents the history of Antietam remembrance and commemoration.

Although the act passed by the Maryland legislature called for the incorporation of Confederate dead in the cemetery, the Maryland trustees of the Antietam National Cemetery Association decided to exclude Confederate burials from the board's initial plans. This decision was more than likely a result of the strong anti-Confederate sentiment that still pervaded the society in the Sharpsburg area. The Unionist political leanings of western Maryland still lingered after the war. Several months after the cemetery's dedication, an article printed in the Hagerstown *Herald and Torch Light* revealed the community's anti-Confederate attitude. It cited "one of the Maryland Commissioners from the vicinity of Antietam" who stated that if there was any attempt to commemorate the Confederate soldiers who "devastated their homes and spread ruin through the surrounding country," the local citizens "would seize them and burn them to ashes."[5]

The board of trustees continued to table and ignore motions and resolutions put forth to enact plans for the reburial of fallen Confederate soldiers within the enclosure of the Antietam National Cemetery. A final proposal put forth in December 1869 calling for the purchase of lands for a separate Confederate cemetery failed, marking the conclusion of the struggle to incorporate Confederate dead in the cemetery. No soldiers of the Confederate army were ever buried at Antietam National Cemetery. The Maryland legislature approved the creation of a separate burial ground for fallen Confederate soldiers several miles from the Antietam cemetery in 1870.[6]

Before the dedication of the cemetery in 1867, the board members faced the issue of what to do with Lee's Rock. The rock was a simple stone located within the boundary of the cemetery grounds but created a dilemma for the trustees. According to legend, Lee stood on the rock to watch the progress of his army during the Battle of Antietam. The board wavered on the issue of whether or not to retain Lee's Rock. They feared that if it remained it might become a sacred site to former Confederates and, therefore, an indirect offering of reconciliation. Some board members were certainly concerned that such a physical symbol would contradict the intention of honoring loyal Union veterans. The majority opinion depended greatly on which members were at the meetings, specifically whether or not there was a Republican majority in attendance.

Popular opinion of what to do with Lee's Rock and its appropriateness within the enclosure of Antietam National Cemetery was also varied. An article featured in the *Lancaster Intelligencer* referred to Lee's Rock as a "memorable spot" and upheld its historical significance. The *New York Times* also analyzed the debate surrounding the rock. "Although the rock has been pressed by traitors' footsteps," the author conceded, "few will be pilgrims to this spot, now made sacred by the nation's soldiers, who will not stand upon it and recall the scene which Gen. Lee gazed upon that bright September morning."[7]

Conversely, a visitor to the cemetery reported in the *Boonsboro Odd Fellow* of the visitors removing chunks of the rock and keeping them as their own personal souvenirs. He concluded his discussion on the topic by clearly showing his disdain for the stone with the words, "Lee's Rock!—Bah!!!" The controversy surrounding whether or not to retain Lee's Rock eventually dissipated as public interest waned and the board of trustees ordered the removal of the rock. The issue of Lee's Rock serves as a foreshadowing of the tensions that came to fruition during the official dedication of Antietam National Cemetery on September 17, 1867, the fifth anniversary of the Battle of Antietam.[8]

The formal dedication of Antietam National Cemetery was attended by, among other notables, President Andrew Johnson, his cabinet members, and seven governors. A crowd of ten thousand to fifteen thousand gathered to witness the ceremonies at Antietam. The ceremony included several speeches and addresses, the reading of a poem written for the occasion, and the laying of the cornerstone of the Private Soldier Monument by the Free Masons. The dedication of the cemetery represented the immediate postwar debates over Maryland's loyalty.[9]

Maryland's unique position both geographically and in the Civil War led to the state being a major topic of discussion during and immediately after the dedication of Antietam National Cemetery. At the dedication, former Maryland governor Augustus Williamson Bradford made an impassioned plea for his state's loyalty during the Civil War. Bradford was well aware that in the immediate postwar memory of many in the North, Maryland was not counted among the Union's most loyal. As a former governor of Maryland, Bradford felt it necessary to dedicate a substantial portion of his speech to addressing and challenging the common criticism and perception about Maryland's loyalty to the Union cause. Bradford's speech was an opportunity to ensure his state had an equal place in Union Civil War memory alongside more northern and unquestionably loyal states. Perceptions of Maryland's loyalty dictated its Civil War legacy. Maryland Unionists needed to affirm their state's devotion to the Union in order to solidify their wartime contributions for future generations. At stake for Bradford and his fellow loyal Marylanders was the enshrinement of their devotion in the pages of history and the respect and recognition of their compeers. Bradford began by laying out the popular opinion of many northerners who were "taught to believe that the loyalty of Maryland had at best but an apocryphal existence" and that the "patriotic and spontaneous impulse" of the state was "limited to a few" and "induced chiefly by the presence of the National force."[10]

Bradford continued by noting all of the opportunities Maryland had to submit to Confederate appeals to the citizens of Maryland, attempting to sway their political loyalties in the direction of the Confederacy and secession. According to Bradford, Marylanders, in response to Confederate appeals, "rushed into their houses and slammed the doors." He further stated that the rebels "were regarded not as friends, but enemies." He concluded his discussion on Maryland's loyalty by once again laying out the common perception of many Unionists and then challenging it. Despite all the tests of loyalty Maryland had passed, "there are still those who still make it the subject of an ungenerous sneer," he lamented. Bradford took solace in the fact "that it never comes from that gallant host that accompanied her sons to the field"; rather, it comes "from those whose well calculated distance from the scene of conflict placed them as far out of the reach of information as of danger." Those who truly knew Maryland's loyalty were equally devoted to the Union; those who questioned Maryland's status were individuals not fully committed to the Union cause.[11]

Despite Bradford's defense of Maryland, there were still those who questioned Maryland's loyalty and role in the preservation of the Union during the Civil War. The day after the dedication of the cemetery, the Philadelphia *Daily Evening Bulletin* made its own "ungenerous sneer" in reference to Maryland's loyalty to the Union. The newspaper praised Bradford for his "eloquent, interesting and elaborate account of the battle of Antietam." The *Daily Evening Bulletin*, however, believed that the speech was "marred by an abortive attempt to set up a claim for Maryland loyalty during the rebellion." The article continued with its own analysis, acknowledging the intense devotion of the "loyal men in Maryland" but arguing that "the whole world knows how that State lay as a stumbling block and an embarrassment in the way of the North, and its official standard of loyalty to-day is only measured by such dubious characters as Swann and his Johnsonized body-guards." The author of the article not only questioned Maryland's loyalty during the war but also characterized the state as a problem for the goal of Union victory and went even further, claiming that the state's leadership and political affiliations did not improve after the war by classifying the current governor as "dubious." The tactic of acknowledging the devotion of particular Marylanders while dismissing the state as a whole was common among veterans reflecting on the Old Line State, as chapter 4 shows.[12]

The governor of Maryland at the time of the dedication was Democrat Thomas Swann. He opened the ceremony with a short address welcoming those in attendance, namely, the prominent guests participating in the proceedings. Although his speech was brief, the central theme running throughout it was an appeal for reconciliation between former Unionists and Confederates. This is not surprising given his support for Andrew Johnson's Reconstruction policies. Much like Johnson, Swann faced intense opposition from Radical Republicans in his home state for advocating on behalf of reconciliation in Maryland. The governor concluded his address hoping "for a speedy restoration of harmony and brotherly love throughout this broad land," and he left the stage with the words "May this Union be perpetual."[13]

President Andrew Johnson expressed similar thoughts in his speech at the dedication. He stated that he did not want to comment on the meaning and inspiration prompted by the prayers, addresses, and hymns. Instead, he implored the citizens of the United States to "live together in friendship and peace" and "to restore harmony to our distracted and divided country." Although the cemetery interred only Union dead, the president made sure to note that when he looked upon the battlefield he thought of "the brave men on both sides" who lost their lives during the conflict.[14]

Johnson's reconciliationist overtures must not have come as a surprise to those present at the cemetery on September 17, 1867. Prior to 1867, the Democrat president from Tennessee demonstrated his views of Reconstruction through the policies he enacted, most notably his proclamations of May 29, 1865. The first proclamation granted amnesty as well as pardoned former Confederates who claimed their loyalty to the Union and the cause of emancipation. Former Confederates possessing taxable property worth more than $20,000 had to apply for individual presidential pardons. There was a disagreement about Johnson's intentions in including the $20,000 clause. Some argued that he included the clause to prevent ex-Confederate elite from having a significant voice in the Reconstruction process and instead pushed for "yeomen to shape Reconstruction." Others believed Johnson incorporated the clause to force the southern "aristocracy" to agree to his terms and policies for Reconstruction. Despite his rationale, his proclamations of 1865 demonstrate his far-reaching policies of amnesty and reconciliation, which extended far beyond anything ever envisioned by Lincoln.[15]

The *History of Antietam National Cemetery* recorded that many of Johnson's comments received applause from the crowd; however, several newspapers noted a much different account of the crowd's reaction to him and other proponents of reconciliation. The *Daily Evening Bulletin* noted, "The impatience of the great concourse of the spectators at the manifest indignity offered to the loyal North could not be restrained."

The crowd began calling out for Governor Geary and he eventually came to the stage to "quite the generous tumult of the loyal audience which even Governor Swann had not been able to keep away." The article interpreted the reconciliationist tone that ran through many of the speeches as anti-Union and anti-North. The "loyal" crowd longed for a speaker who would reject traitorous reconciliation and trumpet their own achievements. Obviously, the *Daily Evening Bulletin* would praise Governor Geary, born in Pennsylvania and at the time the state's active governor. The *Boonsboro Odd Fellow*, published out of Maryland, corroborated the story published by the *Daily Evening Bulletin* and reported that Geary was "loudly called for." Geary then cited his absence in the program and posited that if the ceremony was in Pennsylvania, "the programme would have been that whoever the people desired to hear should have spoken." His omission from the program was assuaged by his knowledge that he was "in the hearts of the loyal people." Through this statement Geary implied the disloyalty of those running the ceremony in Maryland as well as those promoting reconciliation for it was only the "loyal people" who wanted to hear him speak and having the respect of the loyal citizens was of the utmost importance.[16]

The newspapers also challenged the reconciliationist speeches delivered at the ceremony. Many Republican and Unionist newspapers were quick in their criticism of the proceedings. The Waynesboro, Pennsylvania, *Village Record* opened its account of the dedication by stating that "the idea of turning a solemn ceremony into a political ovation is repulsive to every patriot, but it was doubly so to-day when all the incidents connected therewith are considered." The article expressed a strong disdain for President Johnson, citing the dedication ceremony at Antietam as "another opportunity to observe what an object of disgust he [Johnson] is, and will probably never forget his visit to Antietam." It contained strong anti-Confederate sentiment, stating, "Liquor stands lined the roadside up to the gates of the cemetery, and the graves of the Union soldiers who died on this field for their country were trampled upon by the returned rebels as they gallanted their ladies through the cemetery."[17]

Similarly, a *New York Times* article questioned the substance of Governor Bradford's speech. It critiqued the "unnecessary fullness in the historical recital of the action and antecedents" within the speech and argued that the "true spirit in which such ceremonies are to be regarded will forever remain embalmed in the almost inspired language used by Mr. Lincoln in his remarks on the Gettysburg dedication." This statement reveals the author's disappointment in the proceedings at Antietam and the unfulfilled hope that the dedication of the Antietam National Cemetery would have taken a style similar to that of the National Cemetery at Gettysburg. Although President Lincoln's address at Gettysburg received initial criticism, as the years passed and the war concluded the nostalgia and legend of the speech began to swell. The proceedings at the Antietam cemetery, however, did not contain a Gettysburg Address. Although the addresses, poems, and hymns delivered at the ceremony contained approbation for the soldiers who lost their lives on the battlefield, the divisiveness of postwar America and, in particular, Maryland overshadowed the honoring of the fallen. Additionally, the fact that Antietam was not a clear Union victory facilitated an even more contested memory of the battle. Lincoln's address focused on the Union cause and therefore came to embody loyalty to the Union even after the war. Perhaps it would have been impossible, maybe even for Lincoln, to deliver a Gettysburg Address in 1867 on such a contested spot as Antietam and in such a contested state as Maryland.[18]

The *Daily Evening Bulletin* also disparaged the proceedings at Antietam. The newspaper noted that Virginia-born Governor Swann's "incivility to his official peers from the Northern States" was the only part of his role in the ceremonies that required noting. The paper reserved its fiercest written attacks for its critique of President Andrew Johnson's address. "It is thoroughly Johnsonian," the author chided. The article counted "about two hundred and eighty words, and its 'I's' and 'my's' number fifteen, or one allusion to himself in each eighteen words uttered." The article compared Johnson's speech to Lincoln's Gettysburg Address, noting that its "characteristic egotism is in painful contrast with the noble simplicity of the speech of his great predecessor, at Gettysburg, in which Mr. Lincoln never once alluded to himself, but devoted his brief words to the nation and to the nation's dead." Johnson was characterized as a self-absorbed individual by noting the number of times he referred to himself, but what is more telling is that the president was once again compared to his predecessor Lincoln and his speech at the dedication of cemetery at Gettysburg. Through this portion of the article, we can see the combination of dissatisfaction with Johnson and his administration and the disappointment and letdown of the dedication of Antietam National Cemetery. Many newspapers that commented on the ceremony at Antietam compared the Antietam dedication to that of Gettysburg and felt that Antietam, with its several reconciliationist speakers, including President Johnson, did not measure up to the dedication of the national cemetery in Gettysburg and the words spoken by the preserver of the

Union, Abraham Lincoln. Dr. J. E. Snodgrass, a trustee on the Antietam board from New York, was also highly critical of the proceedings at Antietam in an article in the *New York Tribune* that was reprinted in the *Boonsboro Odd Fellow*. In the article, Snodgrass stated that "taken as a whole, a more stupidly farcical affair than that at Antietam could scarcely be imagined."[19]

The *Daily Evening Bulletin* also implied that anti-Union sentiment was underlying Johnson's endorsement of reconciliation. The reviewer remarked, "Mr. Johnson knows no distinction between 'the brave men who fell on both sides,' but, with a broad Irish bull, he desires to 'imitate their example as they lay sleeping in their tombs, and live together in friendship and peace.'" The most outlandish component of his speech was that he did not distinguish between Union and Confederate men. Living "together in friendship and peace" could only be characterized as disloyal and anti-Union if there was not an acceptance of the righteousness of the Union cause and the treasonous nature of the Confederate cause.[20]

The anti-reconciliation sentiment was not unique to the reaction of the audience in attendance or in the newspapers, and it did not stop at mere resistance to reconciliation. Many of the speakers participating in the dedication of the Antietam cemetery expressed strong anti-Confederate attitudes and a refusal to forgive those who rebelled against the United States. The speeches of the former Maryland governor Augustus Bradford and Pennsylvania governor John W. Geary are particularly indicative of the anti-Confederate sentiment that seeped into the ceremony. By resisting reconciliation and scolding former Confederates, Bradford and Geary were able to publicly reaffirm their loyalty to the Union cause. Anti-reconciliation, in the eyes of many Union veterans, was equal to pro-Union sentiment and rhetoric. This outlook fostered intense resistance to reconciliationist overtures throughout the first fifty years following the war.

Bradford dedicated a portion of his lengthy speech to challenging the numbers of soldiers engaged in the Battle of Antietam suggested by Confederate historians and newspapers immediately following the battle. He noted that Confederate newspapers "might at times have attempted to deceive us by an inflated account of their military power." His use of the word "us" is significant in that he still viewed the North and South as separated, not as one nation. He utilized inclusive language to exclude former Confederates. What is more telling is Bradford's criticism of the estimates put forth by Confederate historians and newspapers even five years after the battle. He argued that Confederate sources initially inflated the numbers to exaggerate the Confederacy's military power but then claimed to fight the Union to a stalemate with significantly fewer troops. It is also interesting that he felt it necessary to argue about the relative equality of the forces at Antietam, implying that it was the Union army's will and tact that led to its victory in the Battle of Antietam. Bradford obviously believed that establishing the relative strength of McClellan's and Lee's armies was an important topic "to consider" at the official dedication of the cemetery.[21]

Governor Geary of Pennsylvania, the governor requested and cheered by the crowd in attendance, was much more obvious in his anti-Confederate and anti-reconciliationist speech. Geary opened his speech with a passive criticism of the dedication ceremony at Antietam, stating that when a monument is dedicated at Gettysburg "we will tender you the hospitalities of the State, and permit every man to speak." This was an obvious backhanded condemnation of the proceedings at Antietam. He continued by stating that the program at Gettysburg would contain "no gag." His comment, however, was not only a slight at the Antietam dedication; it was also a criticism of the state. Geary wanted to make clear that the "hospitalities" of his home state of Pennsylvania would exceed that of Maryland, a state with divided loyalties and questionable character.[22]

Although Geary noted the importance of the Battle of Antietam in preventing the exposure of "both Washington and Baltimore" to the Confederate army, the main focus of his speech was praising the Union army and isolating and at times even condemning the Confederate military. Geary was especially harsh in his discussion of General Lee. He stated that the battle helped dispel "the arrogant assumptions of superior valor, so vauntingly advertised by Lee and his followers." In many ways, Geary reflected and expressed an opinion of Lee that many citizens of Pennsylvania shared. Lee's invasion of Pennsylvania in 1863 brought the war to its most northern point and into the backyards of Pennsylvanians and northern citizens for one of the first times. The war became much more personal for northern citizens after the Battle of Gettysburg.[23]

Geary continued with his address by honoring, by name, the units from Pennsylvania that participated in the Battle of Antietam and stated that all of the soldiers "who perished while contending for the Union, are just as dear and will be hallowed as sacredly by the people of Pennsylvania as the memories of their own beloved sons who here lie buried." His most blatant exclusion of the Confederates who fell at Antietam was near the conclusion of his speech. "The blood of the North, of the East, and of the West flowed in the same sacred stream, and broke from the same

ranks to crimson the waters of Antietam," he said. The following morning, "the Union dead from every section were mingled upon the field of
strife." Geary was careful to note every cardinal direction and geographic
region except the South, almost denying any suffering or loss felt by the
South during and after the Battle of Antietam, much like the cemetery
itself. The loyal North should be remembered, not the disloyal South.[24]

The history of establishing and dedicating the cemetery at Antietam
revealed Maryland's place within the growing debates over loyalty and
reconciliation. Those defending Maryland's Civil War identity as well as
those challenging its claim to Union victory argued over the state's loyalty
in a climate in which veterans were struggling with reconciliation. Union
veterans returned to the border state to commemorate and remember
their fallen comrades, and, for many veterans, returning to Maryland
provided the opportunity to demonstrate their continued devotion to
the cause by recalling the wrongs of the Confederacy.

The Private Soldier Monument

One day before the dedication of the cemetery, the board of trustees
of the cemetery passed a resolution for a monument on the cemetery
grounds. The board also entered into a contract with James C. Batterson of Hartford, Connecticut, designer of the monument. The contract
covered the time span of approximately two years to allow for the completion of the monument. The design of the monument was a soldier
leaning on his rifle standing in a "place rest" position.[25]

Historian Thomas J. Brown notes that the design of "a uniformed
standing soldier holding the barrel of a rifle that rests upright on the
ground in front of him" was the dominant form that many Civil War
monuments took during this time frame. The "watchful sentinel" served
as a representation of the common Civil War soldier and was the preferred choice of monument design by sculptors and designers. There
were more than two hundred "single-figure soldier statues" erected
around the country by the late 1880s. Although the design of the monument at Antietam was not the most original, it was and remains to this
day unparalleled in terms of its size. The monument is made of granite
and weighs 250 tons. The height of the structure is 44 feet, 7 inches, with
the soldier alone reaching 21½ feet in height and weighing more than
30 tons. The entire structure consists of twenty-seven pieces, and the
soldier is made of two pieces connected at his waist.[26]

FIGURE 2.1. Private Soldier Monument, Antietam National Cemetery (photographed by Jack E. Boucher, courtesy of the Library of Congress).

The Antietam cemetery board of trustees was able to make the first four payments on schedule between 1871 and 1873; however, it was unable to make the final payment of $10,000 and the U.S. government took control of the cemetery in 1877. The trustees of Antietam National Cemetery voted to transfer control and ownership of the cemetery to the United States and the War Department on June 6–7, 1877. The secretary of war, G. W. McCrary, assumed control of and responsibility for the national cemetery on June 22, 1877. The U.S. government eventually paid the remaining balance, with interest, on the monument.[27]

After several delays, the War Department finally officially dedicated the monument on September 17, 1880, the eighteenth anniversary of the Battle of Antietam. The dedication took place during a three-day campfire event held in Hagerstown on September 15–17, 1880. The event represented one of the first major reunions of Union veterans to take place on the battlefield at Antietam. During the afternoon of September 16, Hagerstown hosted a parade including two thousand uniformed men from numerous posts of the Maryland portion of the Grand Army of the Republic (GAR). The official unveiling and dedication of the Private Soldier Monument took place on September 17 with more than fifteen thousand spectators in attendance. The ceremony's notable attendees included dignitaries and officers from the GAR, Maryland Republican congressman Milton G. Urner, and the main speaker of the occasion, Republican congressman Marriot Brosius from Lancaster, Pennsylvania.[28]

Brosius advocated reconciliation but, like others before him, made sure to qualify his call for reconciliation and note who was to blame for the devastation of the Civil War. He noted that the "war became a high and responsible duty" when it became necessary "to crush bad principles, destroy tyrants, and rescue society from evils incomparably greater than itself." He continued with a detailing of the "abuses" that precipitated the Civil War as well as with an account of the Battle of Antietam "described in vivid and stirring language." Brosius made mention of the North's "magnanimity" to the "conquered South" in his speech and "condemned" those that practiced "blind adherence to party or faction," arguing that if party loyalty promoted behavior and actions against the public good it represented the highest form of "disloyalty to the Government." The *New York Times* noted Brosius's conditionality in his call for reconciliation: "He believed, however, that there should be no obliteration of the distinction between loyalty and treason by equality of rights and ceremonies in their commemoration; no immunity to crime, by venerating the memory of its perpetrators." The only path to reconciliation was "the recognition of the rightfulness of the war for the Union and entire acquiescence in its results." Brosius's idea of reconciliation amounted to a complete submission on the part of the former Confederacy to the loyal Union, an admittance of its wrongs, and even through this form of reconciliation, "crime" should not be forgotten and the "distinction between loyalty and treason" should remain in commemoration.[29]

The creation and dedication of the Private Soldier Monument at Antietam National Cemetery is notable for several reasons. The dedication ceremony and the address delivered by Brosius serve as examples of continued resistance to reconciliation. The most significant contribution of the Private Soldier Monument, however, was that it marked the beginning of prolific monumentalization of the battlefield at Antietam. The

Private Soldier Monument was the first of many monuments that would dot the battlefield and serve as permanent forms of commemoration and remembrance of those who served, fought, and fell in the Battle of Antietam. Antietam continued to provide a platform for discussions over reconciliation, sectionalism, loyalty, and Maryland's postwar status in subsequent monument dedications. The Private Soldier Monument set in motion a commemoration tradition that would have an enduring impact on Maryland's Civil War memory.[30]

Historian Timothy B. Smith refers to the period of the 1890s as "the golden age of battlefield preservation" in his book of the same name. He notes several factors that allowed preservation to take place, including "veterans returning to the fields to document what had happened, the opportunity to preserve almost pristine fields that had not yet experienced the development that would later come in the second industrial revolution, and massive government support from Congress and state legislatures dominated by veterans." These same factors also contributed to the drastic increase in the monumentalization of Civil War battlefields that took place during the late nineteenth and early twentieth centuries. Thomas Brown characterizes the late nineteenth century as the "peak" period for the establishment of Civil War monuments up until 1920. After 1920 and the "technological innovations" of the time, "monuments tended to be obstacles for rapidly proliferating automobiles."[31]

The growth of sprawling cities and large corporations during the rapidly changing environment of the Progressive era fostered an impulse to hold on to what remained of the earlier periods of the nineteenth century. Yosemite National Park was established in 1890, and two years later the Sierra Club was created with the mission of preserving the American wilderness. Veterans and civilians alike saw the benefit in protecting bucolic landscapes that contained memories of America's defining conflict. It was during this "golden age" that a group of Maryland Confederate veterans attempted to dedicate a monument on the Gettysburg battlefield.

The Second Maryland Confederate
Infantry Monument at Gettysburg

Standing before a crowd of two thousand veterans and civilians on November 19, 1886, Captain George Thomas was aware of the magnitude of the moment. Recalling the "bitterness and heartburning" of recent American history, Thomas reminded his audience of the incredibility "that the men of the South could be here to perpetuate by monumental record the memory of their own achievements." The story of sacrifice and heroism was no longer "half told" and "the survivors of the Confederate commands" were now free "to complete the record." Thomas concluded his forty-five-minute speech by stating that this now completed monumental and historical record of battlefield heroics belonged "to no section, and to no time" but was, rather, a "joint heritage of the North and of the South." Thomas's speech was the dedicatory address for the Second Maryland Confederate Infantry Monument, the first Confederate monument established on the Gettysburg battlefield.[32]

Not everyone, however, endorsed Thomas's vision for the Gettysburg battlefield and its historical record. Up until this point, Gettysburg was exclusively a Union military park with the purpose of honoring loyal soldiers. Three years after the dedication of the Confederate monument, various GAR posts across Pennsylvania began to adopt resolutions voicing their frustration and dissatisfaction with the notion of former rebel soldiers establishing permanent forms of commemoration on a northern battlefield. In Pittsburgh, Post 88 passed a resolution that contended that "if such monuments were permitted to be built it would make treason honorable." The post also argued that Confederate monuments at Gettysburg represented a form of "sacrilege," an "intrusion by traitors upon sacred soil." The resolution requested that Pennsylvania governor James A. Beaver "prevent the erection of any more rebel monuments on the battlefield at Gettysburg" and the removal of the Second Maryland monument.[33]

Utilizing the Second Maryland Confederate Infantry Monument as a case study provides a unique lens through which to view the nascent stages of reconciliation during the late nineteenth century. Much like the dichotomy and exchange between reconciliationists and those resistant to reconciliation, many Union veterans expressed a willingness to reunite and reconcile in postwar rhetoric, but the reality of dedicating a Confederate monument for perpetuity at Gettysburg struck many former Union soldiers in a jarring fashion. Additionally, while the Gettysburg Battlefield Memorial Association (GBMA), made up predominantly of GAR members, approved the monument, there existed a simultaneous resistance from other GAR members. Loyalty to the Union was most important, and permanent forms of reconciliation would stand out as treasonous symbols of anti-Unionism.[34]

On August 11, 1885, the board of directors of the GBMA discussed the contents of a particularly interesting letter. The vice president read the letter to the individuals gathered that requested the permission of the GBMA "to erect a memorial to the Second Maryland Confederate regiment." The board of directors, on the motion of John B. Bachelder, superintendent of tablets and legends, agreed to allow the group of Confederate veterans to establish "a monument on their position on this field, subject to the rules of the Association in regard to historical accuracy and inscription." Prior to the Second Maryland Confederate veterans' letter, Bachelder had contacted the regiment to gauge their interest in placing a monument on the Gettysburg battlefield.[35]

Historian Carol Reardon provides a possible reason for inviting Confederate veterans to return to the Gettysburg battlefield and officially commemorate their role. She notes that Bachelder was the "unofficial government historian" of the Battle of Gettysburg and that his early drawing of the battle was based "on eighty-four days of interviews with wounded soldiers of both armies." Given his long-standing commitment to a complete history of the battle, including both sides of the conflict, it is not surprising that he would offer Confederate veterans the opportunity to mark their positions on the field and commemorate their service with a monument. Bachelder and the GBMA might also have considered the tourism benefits a Confederate monument would bring. Some former Confederate veterans remained hesitant and resistant to the idea of returning to a field of such a devastating defeat, but by the 1880s, as Reardon states, Bachelder was attempting to "change their minds."[36]

The GBMA approved the initial concept of placing a monument to honor the Second Maryland Confederate Regiment rather painlessly, but the issue of where to locate the monument proved more troublesome. During the same meeting, the directors also decided to write the group of veterans, suggesting "that a committee of the organization visit the field before locating the site of the monument." More than eight months after the initial meeting over the monument, the board met once again; this time, a committee of the Second Maryland Confederate Regiment veterans joined the GBMA board of directors. The committee of veterans "submitted a design of their proposed regimental monument, and requested the association to assign the proper location for it." Before the conclusion of the meeting, the GBMA debated the options for a location and agreed that three board members would accompany a group of the Second Maryland veterans to the battlefield to "select a correct historical site for said monument." At the May 7, 1886, meeting of the GBMA, the board read a report from Major Bell on the visit to the battlefield by the committee in charge of finding a proper location for the monument.

Bell's report, dated May 2, stated that the veterans' preferred position was "within the line of Union works on Culp's Hill near the monument of the 20th Connecticut Regiment, and at the point where the regiment entered and occupied our line on the night of July 2d, 1863." The veterans also hoped "to erect a marker on their extreme advanced position," which would be near the Twenty-ninth Pennsylvania Monument.[37]

The board of directors was not blind to the controversy that such a location would undoubtedly prompt and therefore proceeded with caution. Bachelder had established the guidelines for placing monuments, and according to his battle line regulations, monuments were to designate the locations from which units began their attacks. The members present noted that "the erection of an ex-Confederate monument within the Union line raises an important precedent, which should be wisely settled." Placing such a monument within Union lines would probably generate strong responses from Union veterans and could lead to a negative controversy for both the association and the battlefield. Those in attendance "were unwilling to assume the responsibility of deciding" on the issue of location without the input of some of the GBMA's senior members. Therefore, action on the subject was deferred. The final decision of the board, after hearing from General Barnum and John M. Vanderslice, was to inform the Confederate veterans that the monument must be "outside of the Union breastworks, and the inscriptions on said monument to be subject to approval by this Association." The issue of precedent would come up again amid the cries of sacrilege and treason. The phrases "our line" and "ex-Confederate" reveal an interesting mindset on the part of the GBMA board of directors that would also prove potent among other Union veterans and their response to the monument: they still retained their identity as Union soldiers, as well as their loyalty to their cause, but assumed that their former enemies had shed their own as Confederates.[38]

In his November 16, 1886, address, Bradley T. Johnson reflected on the predominant identity of Maryland both during and after the war. He contended, "Even here in Maryland, where the Confederate soldier has not always been recognized as he should be, not ten can be found who have proved recreant to their comrades and their faith." Johnson clearly believed that Confederate soldiers were not only underrepresented in Maryland but also not honored to the same degree as Union veterans. In spite of these facts, they maintained pride in their Confederate heritage. Placing these remarks in context with his statements just a few sentences later makes his speech all the more significant. As part of his answer to

the question of why public exhibitions and demonstrations were still necessary, he claimed that they "have been intended to keep, and they have
succeeded in keeping, alive that heartfelt sympathy which Maryland felt
so deeply for us." In some respects, Johnson's statements on Confederate
soldiers being undervalued but simultaneously receiving "heartfelt sympathy" from the people of Maryland were conflicted. The pervasiveness
of the Lost Cause sentiment in the Civil War memory of not only Maryland but also the United States facilitated the assumption on the part of
Confederate veterans that their history in the conflict deserved equal
recognition and respect. While Confederates from all southern states
wanted to enshrine their legacies and preserve their pride, Confederate Marylanders struggled for equality in memory, for they came from
a state that did not secede. They had to overcome perceptions of their
state's half-hearted devotion to the Confederacy from other Confederate
veterans.[39]

Maryland veterans, both Union and Confederate, were forced to fight
a two-pronged war over their Civil War memories. They struggled to justify their wartime efforts to their own ranks while simultaneously combating the commemorative efforts of their in-state foes. This was a process
that was unique to border states, in particular to Maryland. The multi-
tude of major events and battles that occurred during the Civil War in the
Old Line State created more moments that Marylanders felt obligated to
defend in the postwar period.

Johnson's closing remarks were perhaps the most noteworthy and
demonstrated the role Maryland's status as a border state played in the
process of establishing the monument. He remarked that during the
dedication ceremony at Gettysburg he possessed no desire "to revive
the issues or rekindle the passions of the civil war" and that any who did
"has a bad heart and is a bad citizen in Maryland." Johnson expected
"equal recognition and respect" from Union veterans that he insisted
he granted them over the years. As he wound down his address, Johnson
made an appeal for pride in a shared heritage between both Union and
Confederate veterans. He stated, "I claim a share in the reputation won
by Kenly, Phelps, Horn, and every Maryland soldier on every stricken
field, and I will everywhere and at all times guard their honor as my own."
Johnson implored veterans from both sides to let "every laurel won by
either side be the common right of all Marylanders" and future generations to "take equal pride and do equal honor to the memory of their ancestors who fought under McClellan and Grant, Hancock and Buford, or
who followed Jackson and Ashby, and charged under Lee and Stuart." To

Johnson, the combined Union and Confederate contributions of Maryland are what made it special in the larger narrative of the Civil War.[40]

Johnson was surely aware of the potential for blowback from placing a Confederate monument on a Pennsylvania battlefield, and the final words of his speech at the preliminary meeting demonstrate his awareness of the sensitivity of the process. By alluding to the heritage and heroics of Union Marylanders, Johnson tried to preempt the potential criticism by emphasizing similarities and continuities between the two sides rather than underscoring their differences. Historian David Potter argues that citizens and soldiers of the North and South possessed both sectional and national loyalties. These loyalties were not mutually exclusive. Johnson's plea embodies this point. The unique position of Maryland during the war gave Johnson the supporting ammunition through which to stifle the outcry that the monument would probably produce. Maryland, according to Johnson, should take pride in its dualistic Civil War heritage and not chastise or devalue one particular side. He would, however, be disappointed not necessarily by the immediate reaction to the monument but by the delayed response several years later initiated by members of the Grand Army of the Republic.[41]

The monument's design was unassuming and modest in size. Subsequent observers of the monument would note its benign appearance. In her 1911 book on southern monuments, Bettie Alder Calhoun Emerson found the monument's appearance particularly poignant: "Its severe outlines and absence of the usual ornamentation that marks memorial structures as a rule, is in keeping with the plain, whole-souled heroes whose valor it commemorates." According to Emerson, the monument simply and quietly stated "here came the sons of Maryland, fighting for a cause they believed to be just—a cause they believed meant the life of their State and the liberties of its people." Other Confederate monuments that dotted the southern landscape were much taller, were more elaborate, and often featured a soldier at the top of the monument.[42]

One can speculate that the plainness of the monument and the fact that it is the first Confederate monument at Gettysburg are not simply coincidental. Any mention of a "ruthless foe" was certainly out of the question given the reaction that such an engraving would create. The simplicity of the monument serves a similar purpose. The GBMA probably would not have approved a Confederate monument design that included extravagant ornamentation and, even if it had, the boldness of the monument would disturb some northern citizens. The humility of the monument's design served as another method through which to soften the controversy surrounding its dedication at Gettysburg.

Approximately two thousand people, civilians and veterans, attended the dedication of the Second Maryland Confederate Infantry Monument on the Gettysburg battlefield on Friday, November 19, 1886. Veterans strolled around the battlefield reminiscing and exchanging old war stories. Both veterans and civilians in attendance gathered in disparate groups all over the field for "luncheon parties" before the start of the dedication ceremony. The official ceremony began with a prayer delivered by Rev. Dr. Randolph H. McKim. McKim prayed "that the liberty for which the South had fought and the Union for which the North had contended might never be broken asunder." After McKim's prayer, Captain George Thomas delivered the dedicatory address, the day's main event.[43]

FIGURE 2.2. The Second Maryland Confederate Monument, Gettysburg Battlefield (George Grantham Bain Collection, courtesy of the Library of Congress).

In addition to Thomas's lines on the narrative no longer being "half told" and his references to the "joint heritage of the North and of the South," his speech also exemplified two of the most important themes of the day's festivities. The first reflected the unassuming and nonpolitical appearance of the monument. Throughout the speech, Thomas demonstrated keen cautiousness and carefulness not to offend the Union veterans and northern supporters in the audience. He noted that there "was no paltering upon either side with the magnitude of the interests at stake," and even after the first two years of the war "the fire of battle still fiercely glowed in every heart" in both opposing armies. By appealing to the nobility of both the Union and the Confederacy, Thomas helped delicately ease the idea of a Confederate monument on northern soil into the minds of those in attendance, including the more ardent anti-reconciliationists.[44]

The second theme focused more specifically on Maryland during and after the Civil War. Thomas concluded that it was "not altogether inappropriate" that the Second Maryland be the first regiment to establish a Confederate monument at Gettysburg. He recalled that the men of the regiment "with the courage of their convictions, left their homes in Maryland to cast their fortunes with the South." This was a subtle, yet clever, statement to appeal to a northern crowd. By characterizing Maryland as a non-southern state, and thus a northern state, Thomas justified why a monument to a Maryland regiment on the Gettysburg battlefield was "not altogether inappropriate." Thomas made a similar statement a few moments later. He claimed, "The representatives in the Confederate service of this phase of Maryland sentiment were scattered far and wide." Thomas once again alluded to the fact that finding Confederate sentiment and sympathies in the state of Maryland was a difficult task because the predominant attitude was one of loyalty to the Union. Thomas was aware of the significance of the first Confederate monument at Gettysburg, and by disguising some of its groundbreaking qualities, he hoped to make the process as smooth as possible.[45]

After Thomas's speech, John M. Krauth of the GBMA accepted the monument. Throughout the proceedings the "Fifth regiment band" performed various familiar numbers, including two dirges. The *Baltimore Sun* also reported that "it was noticeable that during the whole day no National or Southern airs were played."[46] The careful selection of musical scores played during the dedication represents another conscientious effort to avoid polarizing the audience or isolating the Pennsylvanians or Union veterans in attendance. Not all veterans, however, were pleased with the new addition to the Gettysburg landscape.

David A. Buehler tried to warn Bachelder of the consequences of the monument and the precedent it would establish. Buehler was the postmaster of Gettysburg, a lawyer, a politician, and the editor of a Republican newspaper. Less than a month after the dedication of the monument, he wrote to Bachelder expressing his concerns. Buehler stated in regard to the Confederate monument that the "historical delineation of the field is one thing, the erection of monuments in honor of what was done here is quite another thing." He argued that the latter was the "basis of our Association, recognized in the charter, and we dare not ignore it" but only "as far as concerns the Union forces." To Buehler, the GBMA served as an organization that was designed to honor and commemorate the Union, its army, and its veterans and not its enemy. He concluded his letter by positing that if the GBMA did not adhere to its principal goal of commemorating Union soldiers it would "do violence to the basis of the Association & will get into trouble." Trouble would arise from sanctifying disloyalty to the Union. Buehler's foreshadowing came to pass not only for the members of the GBMA but also for Union and Confederate veterans as a whole.[47]

For nearly three years, the Second Maryland Confederate Infantry Monument sat in relative peace and silence. In the fall of 1889, however, the fears of many of those involved with the completion and dedication of the monument were realized. Pennsylvania governor James A. Beaver and the GAR Abe Patterson Post of Pittsburgh put forth a formal protest and resolution in regard to the three-year-old monument. The multiyear delay in a response to the monument might seem arbitrary at first, but a closer look at the structure of the GBMA provides some clues to better understanding the resolutions against Confederate monumentalization on the Gettysburg battlefield.

The April 10, 1885, amendments to GBMA charter represented a significant factor in the strong Union veteran and northern opposition to the monument. Section 3 of the amendment read, "The Governor of the Commonwealth of Pennsylvania shall be, *ex officio*, President of the Association." The governor of Pennsylvania as well as the president of the GBMA at the time of the establishment of the Second Maryland monument was Robert E. Pattison. Pattison was a Democrat from Maryland and the only Democrat elected between the conclusion of the Civil War and 1935. Born in 1850, Pattison did not fight in the Civil War, but his ties to the state of Maryland more than likely influenced his role in the oversight of the Second Maryland monument building process during his tenure as president of the GBMA. James A. Beaver replaced Pattison as governor of Pennsylvania in 1887. Beaver was a Republican and served with the Second Pennsylvania Volunteers as a second lieutenant and, by 1864, rose to the rank of brigadier general. Although most of the newspapers only referenced Beaver's endorsement of the Abe Patterson Post resolution, his role as president of the GBMA during the most stringent protests and outcry over the monument was a significant factor in 1889 being the critical year. Whether Beaver helped initiate the resolution or the veterans saw the opportunity to appeal to a former comrade and ally, the transition from Pattison to Beaver helped facilitate an environment in which strong resistance to Confederate commemoration could occur.[48]

Another factor in the delayed Union response was the Blue-Gray reunion on the twenty-fifth anniversary of the Battle of Gettysburg held on the battlefield. Those in attendance included numerous Pennsylvania veterans and Governor Beaver. Many of the Union veterans probably did not realize that a Confederate monument was on the Gettysburg battlefield until they attended the reunion ceremony in 1888. Seeing the monument for the first time while reminiscing with fellow veterans was jarring for many of the former soldiers. The reunion ceremonies the year before the twenty-fifth anniversary also undoubtedly played a role in the ignited animosity over the monument. In 1887, Confederate veterans of Pickett's Charge gathered on the battlefield and stated their desire for a monument to honor Pickett's division. Many Union veterans expressed their dismay over the possibility of a Confederate monument on "their field." The GBMA ultimately denied the request, and the veterans placed the monument in Hollywood Cemetery in Richmond, Virginia. The bitterness over Confederate monumentalization lingered, however, and it came to a head in 1889.[49]

The Abe Patterson Post did not hide its disdain in the rhetoric of its resolution. The opening line of the resolution read, "The survivors of the Second Maryland rebel regiment have erected on the battlefield of Gettysburg, within four feet of the monument erected by a loyal Maryland regiment, a monument commemorating the disloyal deeds of said rebel regiment." By allowing a monument to disloyalty to stand in close proximity to one that represented loyalty, the GBMA was welcoming anti-Unionism onto their battlefield. The members of the GAR post also expressed their concern over the precedent the monument would establish, contending that "there is every indication that other rebel organizations and regiments will, if permitted, follow the example, and thus make treason honorable." It was in this vein that the post challenged the Second Maryland monument. In addition to its references to "sacrilege" and "treason," the resolution not only called for the prevention of further Confederate monuments, it also demanded that the Second Maryland Confederate Infantry Monument be removed from the battlefield.[50]

Newspapers across the country reported on the Abe Patterson Post resolution against Confederate monumentalization on the Gettysburg battlefield. Once the newspapers picked up on the story of the resolution, they moved quickly to inquire about Governor Beaver's position on the monument and the Abe Patterson Post. Beaver commented that he "read the resolutions and they show the right spirit" but that in terms of the Second Maryland monument he confessed, "I don't know just what it is" (an interesting comment" considering he was president of the GBMA). After someone explained the position of the monument on the battlefield to him, Beaver said that if the monument fell outside the land owned by GBMA, which it did not, then there was no issue but if it was inside the lines of the GBMA that was a completely different issue. He unequivocally stated, "I am and was always opposed to any rebel organization erecting its monuments within the grounds of the association." To Beaver and many rank-and-file Union veterans, it did not matter that the monument was to a Maryland regiment, only that it was Confederate.[51]

The Abe Patterson Post and Governor Beaver were not alone in their assessment of the Second Maryland Confederate Infantry Monument. The GAR John C. Dickey Post of Greenville, Pennsylvania, characterized the Second Maryland monument as "commemorating the disloyal deeds of said Rebel regiment." The post passed their own resolution against Confederate monuments on the battlefield and asked that it be attached to that of the Abe Patterson Post. The *New York Times* was also cognizant of the ubiquity of negative responses to Confederate monumentalization and explicitly acknowledged its awareness in its coverage of a congressional appropriation "to mark the Confederate lines at Gettysburg." The editorial noted that the appropriation "will arouse the ire of the Grand Army post in Pittsburg[h], which lately denounced the monument set up to a Maryland organization in Lee's army at that battle." The author of the article argued that the real issue, however, "is the size of the proposed appropriation, which is to exceed $300,000."[52]

Despite the intensity of the protests to the Second Maryland Confederate Infantry Monument, not every northerner objected to the monument. The South Carolina *Anderson Intelligencer* included a discussion of the sectionalism in its December 19, 1889, issue, and within that dialogue Bill Arp quoted a letter he received from a James Yanney on the Confederate Maryland monument. Yanney wrote in regard to the monument, "I was on the field last September and saw the monument and I dident hear any unkind remarks made about it by the boys in blue" and was relieved "the time had come when the graves of the blue and the gray could be marked together where they fought and fell for the cause they thought was right." He was disappointed with the negative response to the monument and said, "It looks like death will only close the bitter contention" despite his status as "a Republican and a northern man" and his belief that "we were all of one country and ought to love one another." Yanney was unaware of the criticism of the monument until Arp raised the issue and did not believe that the monument warranted any sort of disparagement. To Yanney, the Second Maryland monument represented a fitting expression of reconciliation almost twenty-five years after the conclusion of the Civil War. His, however, appeared to be the minority opinion among Union veterans, and the South, including Confederate veterans, felt it necessary to respond to the majority opinion of those in the North.[53]

It did not take long for Confederate veterans and white southerners to learn of the protests to the monument and offer their rebuttal to the northern response. The nature of the rebuttal and tone of the Confederate reaction was varied, ranging from apologetic to unmitigated rage. The *Winchester Times*, a Virginia newspaper, published a scathing article, originally appearing in the Shepherdstown, West Virginia, *Register*, under the heading "They Are Good Haters," representative of a response from the angrier end of the spectrum. The article began by pointing out the falsity, pretentiousness, and, at the very least, infrequency of Blue-Gray reunions, noting that there were rare occasions "when the veterans of either side shake hands across the bloody chasm and conduct themselves as brethren once at variance but now happily reunited." The editorialist went on to conclude that these instances were much more rare than the "exhibitions of bitter hatred manifested by northern soldiers against those of the South." According to the *Winchester Times*, the action of the Maryland veterans dedicating their monument was "worse than shaking a red flag at a mad bull" and the Abe Patterson Post "immediately flew to arms." The editorial proceeded to quote a few of the post's resolutions regarding the monument and subsequent attempts at Confederate memorialization and critiqued the fraternity, arguing that the "Abe Patterson Post never stopped to consider . . . there was no objectionable inscription which could arouse their anger." The post "simply took advantage of an opportunity to display their hatred of the soldiers who fought so bravely against them 25 years ago."[54]

The tone of the piece shifted from a critique of the Abe Patterson Post's resolution to more personal and severe insults to the members of the organization. The third paragraph began, "The opinion of Abe Patterson Post, fortunately, doesn't have a great deal of weight, and certainly cannot affect those at whom it is aimed." Speculating on the makeup of its membership, the author of the editorial suggested that the "Abe Patterson Post is probably composed chiefly of bummers. Manliness is at a discount among its members." After pondering how Governor Beaver of Pennsylvania could possibly endorse such rhetoric, the article concluded emphatically, "As to Abe Patterson Post, G.A.R.—whoof!!!"[55]

Others quickly chimed in with equally strong responses and reactions to the words of the Abe Patterson Post and Governor Beaver. In a speech before a group of South Carolina Civil War veterans, Senator Matthew Butler of South Carolina "severely criticized the action of Abe Patterson Post, G.A.R., for protesting against" the Maryland Confederate monument at Gettysburg. The impetus for Butler's speech likely came from a letter penned by General Bradley T. Johnson. He detailed the history of the monument as well as the Abe Patterson Post controversy and concluded, "I thank God you and I and our comrades have lived in the heroic age of the republic—we marched with Lee and stood with Stonewall and rode with Stuart." Johnson went on to claim that the North fought against the South solely for profit and monetary gains and encouraged Butler to "let them write their own history; we have made ours." In response to the letter and the Abe Patterson Post Butler replied, "I would much rather be the dead lions whom this shaft was intended to commemorate than the live animals practicing their heels against the Second Maryland monument." Butler's statement embodied the triumphant tone of the Lost Cause by celebrating loss and emphasizing the honor of the losing side over the tyranny of the victorious Union army and its veterans. In another short article, Johnson stated that "there was certainly nothing objectionable in the monument, and Confederates had no apologies to make." He also commented that the monument "was the result of a pressing invitation" from Bachelder and his fellow Confederate veterans "can not understand how the Pittsburghers could have been led to such action." The *Alexandria Gazette* sarcastically replied to the Abe Patterson Post resolution, "Oh! how they love us."[56]

The *Columbus Enquirer*, published out of Georgia, noted a letter exchange between Major Goldsborough, an officer in the regiment, and the secretary of the GBMA, John M. Krauth. Goldsborough wrote Krauth "asking if the association's views had changed since the erection of the monument, and if they desired its removal." Krauth replied, "stating that the question of removal . . . from the field has not been entertained or considered by the association." The article ended authoritatively: "Abe Patterson Post may now crawl into their hole and keep quiet."[57]

Not all Confederate veterans reacted in as strong a fashion. Captain W. T. Thelin, a veteran of the Second Maryland Confederate regiment, expressed a more measured reaction to the Abe Patterson Post. He conceded, "If they want us to take the monument away . . . we will do it." The same editorial acknowledged additional ex-Confederates who "said they were rather nonplussed by the action of Patterson Post, but no action would be taken in the matter." Although Thelin and James Yanney represent the minority opinion of veterans from both sides, their views indicate that even in a climate of persistent hostility and bitterness there were individuals willing to reconcile. To these individuals, staking a claim for their loyalty and their legacies was not worth impeding reconciliation.[58]

Not two years after the Abe Patterson Post controversy, Union veterans from Maryland gathered on the Gettysburg battlefield to dedicate their own monuments. In a preliminary meeting to discuss the prospect of establishing the monuments, Captain Frank Nolen asserted "that the only troops who there [Gettysburg] carried the standard of Maryland, by authority of the State, were fighting to protect the honor of the old flag and to perpetuate the union of the United States." Colonel Vernon emphasized the "part the loyal sons of the old Maryland line" played in the battle and the fact that "Maryland had sent more soldiers into the Union army than a number of States wherein there was no division of sentiment." During his speech at the meeting, Dr. George Graham also referenced "the loyal sons of Maryland" as well as Maryland's "erring brethren." An inscription on one of the Maryland monuments read, "Maryland's Tribute to Her Loyal Sons." Milton G. Urner recalled that "when the War began there was a division of sentiment among the people of our State"; therefore, when "the Maryland soldier enlisted at his country's call he placed country above section, above family ties, above *everything*, and manifested a patriotism equaled by few and excelled by none."[59]

There are two significant points to take away from the Union Maryland monument dedications at Gettysburg. First, the Union veterans at both the preliminary meeting and the monument dedication ceremonies made a conscientious effort to not only emphasize the Union loyalty of Maryland during the Civil War but also to establish the state as a truly Union state. Second, not a single one of the countless number of dedicatory addresses mentioned the Confederate monument or the controversy that surrounded it. Although the history of the Union Maryland monuments at Gettysburg does not indicate the same level of bitterness as the Second Maryland monument, it does, nevertheless, corroborate the incompleteness of reconciliation and coming to terms with Maryland's divisive past.

Regimental and State Monuments at Antietam

While controversy swirled over the monument in Gettysburg, the commemoration of Antietam continued at a rapid pace. The first monuments on the Antietam battlefield were regimental and brigade monuments dedicated during the late nineteenth century. States would often dedicate several monuments to various regiments at once. Pennsylvania and Connecticut monuments were among the first.

Several speakers at these early monument dedications reflected on the significance of the war to the people of Maryland. At the dedication of the Philadelphia Brigade Monument on September 17, 1896, Archbishop P. J. Ryan opened his address, titled "A Reunited People," with a discussion of the Old Line State. He stated, "No part of the country felt more deeply that separation than the Border States, like Missouri, Kentucky, and Maryland." He continued by recalling his time at a parish in St. Louis tending to "both the Union and Confederate sick and wounded that filled the hospitals in that city." Ryan believed that because those citizens of the border states experienced the divisiveness of the war more than anywhere else, they rejoiced "more on an occasion of the reunion of the people." David Cunningham, president of the Ohio Antietam Battlefield Commission, expressed a similar sentiment in his speech at the dedication of Ohio regimental monuments and the McKinley monument on October 13, 1903. He began by thanking the citizens of Maryland who gathered near Dunker Church, acknowledging their unique and difficult position of residing in a border state during the war, for they "were exposed to all the vicissitudes and annoyances of active warfare, and therefore have less reason to remember with pleasure those trying days." He also noted the divisiveness of the state and the fact that "one-half of the community recognized the stars and bars as their national emblem, and the other half still holding to the stars and stripes" but now that the country was once again united the people of the United States "have but one national emblem, recognized and acknowledged everywhere, and that emblem is old glory." The place of Maryland in Civil War memory and the debates that surrounded it proved that any "rejoicing," as Ryan suggested, would be short-lived. "Those trying days" would remain in the popular consciousness for Marylanders for a long time.[60]

In addition to regimental and brigade monuments, states began placing monuments to represent the entirety of their contribution and their sacrifice at Antietam. The most notable state monument as well as the first was the Maryland State Monument, dedicated in 1900. The Maryland State Monument is particularly worth noting in that it is the only monument on the field of Antietam devoted to soldiers of both the Union and the Confederate armies. Scholar of the Antietam battlefield Susan Trail points to the reconciliation effect of the Spanish-American War as central to the success and development of establishing a Maryland monument to both Union and Confederate soldiers.[61]

The Spanish-American War, fought in 1898, was the first major American war after the Civil War and provided the first opportunity for former Confederate and Union soldiers to once again join each other on the battlefield, this time on the same side. As later remembrance ceremonies indicate, however, the Spanish-American War did not completely reconcile the divisive memories of the war. As historian Caroline Janney documents, the Spanish-American War did not simply enhance reconciliationist sentiment in the United States. It also provided Confederate veterans the opportunity to bolster the Lost Cause by placing the war of 1898 in the broader context of American history, citing all the instances that southerners fought for liberty and self-government. In the eyes of former Confederate veterans, the Spanish-American War proved they were right in 1861.[62]

The Maryland state legislature committed $12,500 to all of its monuments for the Antietam battlefield and selected a spot near the Dunker Church in the heart of battlefield to place its primary state monument. On the soil of a border state with contending loyalties during the war, the Maryland State Monument was to serve as a beacon of reconciliation and reunion at Antietam. The eight-sided monument bears a gazebo-type framework with each side devoted to a Maryland unit that participated in the battle, six Union and two Confederate. The Maryland state government hoped that the equal sides of the monument would represent the now parity that existed between the once divided sections of the country and the state.[63]

FIGURE 2.3. Maryland State Monument, Antietam National
Battlefield (courtesy of the Library of Congress).

The dedication of the Maryland State Monument took place on Memorial Day, May 30, 1900, despite initial plans for dedicating the monument on the anniversary of the battle the previous year. The ceremony was well attended with between fifteen thousand and twenty-five thousand people in the audience. Many notable individuals and dignitaries attended the event, including the current president William McKinley, Maryland governor John W. Smith, and several prominent veterans and officers of the Civil War. In his speech, the acting secretary of war, Elihu Root, retold the heroics of McKinley as a young sergeant at Antietam and expressed his belief in the monument's mutual commemoration. McKinley reportedly transported under fire food and coffee to his regiment and served them himself. President McKinley also stated his satisfaction with the process of reconciliation that was taking place as a result of the Maryland monument's dedication. He shared his gladness in seeing men from both the former Union and Confederate armies gathering "not with arms in their hands or malice in their souls, but with affection and respect for each other in their hearts." McKinley also pointed to the Spanish-American War as a reconciling force in the United States, noting that "the followers of the Confederate Generals, with the followers of the Federal Generals fought side by side in Cuba, in Porto Rico, and in the Philippines, and together in those far off islands are standing to-day fighting and dying for the flag they love."[64]

Notably absent from the formal proceedings of the monument dedication ceremony was the Maryland GAR. In their report of the 1901 state encampment proceedings, the department commander, John R. King, noted that the organization had originally accepted an invitation "at the last Encampment from the Antietam Battlefield Commission to participate May 30, (Decoration Day)" in the dedication of "the monument erected by the State to the memory of the Soldiers, Union and Confederate, of Maryland, who were engaged in that battle." "I felt that the 30th of May was a day set apart sacred to the memory of our *own* dead, and that to divide our duty to them would be a perversion of the spirit of the occasion," King stated. He also referenced "conditions" that he "could not subscribe" to that were imposed by the commission. The real issue to King, however, was the "perversion" of spending any amount of time on Memorial Day honoring Confederate veterans alongside Union veterans. The shared citizenship to Maryland was not enough to engage in a moment of reconciliation when Memorial Day was intended to honor the country's loyal sons. In other words, honoring Confederate veterans on Memorial Day would represent disloyalty to the Union.[65]

Even beyond the absence of the Maryland GAR, the reconciliationist tone of the monument and its dedication could not escape the ever-common politicization of Civil War commemoration as demonstrated in the *Chicago Chronicle* article reprinted in the *Marion Sentinel.* In 1900, the *Chicago Chronicle* was a Democratic newspaper and clearly demonstrated its political loyalties and its lack of reservations in bringing politics into commemoration ceremonies when it openly criticized McKinley and his speech at the monument dedication. The article noted that the echoes of McKinley's speech "are those of reproof and censure," and the newspaper criticized McKinley for not mentioning McClellan, "who gained the union victory over Lee at Antietam." In reference to McClellan's efforts during the Maryland Campaign the author of the article recorded: "President McKinley ignored this memorable chapter in the history of the war. He not only neglected to mention McClellan as the hero of Antietam, he neglected to mention Abraham Lincoln, who derived from McClellan's victory inspiration for the emancipation proclamation, the most notable act of his life."[66]

Other state monuments soon followed and quickly showed that the hope for reconciliation embodied in the form of the Maryland State Monument would not be realized. The dedication of the New Jersey State Monument in 1903 is particularly worth noting because of the presence and speech of President Theodore Roosevelt. Although Roosevelt briefly alluded to the soldiers of the Confederacy, he dedicated the great majority of his speech to recalling "the patriotism, the courage, the unflinching resolution and steadfast endurance" of those "who wore the blue . . . in the great years from '61 to '65," once again proving that even though reconciliation was a common theme among the speakers of the Maryland monument dedication ceremony, the monument devoted to soldiers of both sides did not represent the beginning of movement toward reconciling Civil War memory in the North. Roosevelt devoted the rest of his speech to what contemporary citizens and government officials should take away and remember from those who fought to preserve the Union.[67]

Reaction to Roosevelt's speech in Democratic newspapers was not surprising; however, the speakers', namely Roosevelt's, omission of mentioning General George B. McClellan garnered a particularly strong response. The *New York Times* reported that "the name of Gen. McClellan, the Union victor at Antietam, was never once mentioned by any of the speakers, although the names of other Union Generals were mentioned by both the President and Gov. Murphy," and that such an incident "probably has never been duplicated in the dedication of any similar monument." The negative reaction compounded because McClellan was not only the commanding Union general at Antietam but also a Democrat and former governor of New Jersey.[68]

The national reaction to Roosevelt's omission of mentioning McClellan not only demonstrates the contention among various groups and factions in remembering the Battle of Antietam; it also shows the politicization of commemoration during the contentious period of Gilded Age politics. Elections during the late nineteenth century were hotly contested and resulted in narrow margins of victory. Voter turnout was also high near the turn of the century. As a consequence, Civil War commemorations and responses to them were characterized by politicized overtones. Establishing a monument was not only an opportunity to honor Civil War soldiers, it was also a chance to appeal to voters while also offering political adversaries potential ammunition.

Three years after the dedication of the New Jersey State Monument, Pennsylvania Union veterans once again returned to Antietam to honor their reserve regiments—the Third, Fourth, Seventh, and Eighth. Major G. L. Eberhart of the Eighth Reserve Regiment and his address put any hope for Antietam as a site of reconciliation to rest. In reference to the Battle of Antietam, Eberhart characterized it as an "act of treason" and "one of the bloodiest crimes against civilized society that blackens the history of mankind." He likened the Civil War to a struggle between good and evil, between God and Satan, and the conflict would not come to a close until God commanded "the stormy waves of treason and discord to cease." Eberhart rarely referred to the Confederacy or Confederate army by name; instead, he preferred "bloody treason" or "bloody treason's forces." He also preferred "the Slaveholders Rebellion" over the "Civil War." Perhaps the most significant point to take from Eberhart's speech is that for many, the war, its participants, and its memory were not completely reconciled.[69]

The commemorative efforts at Antietam and the Second Maryland monument at Gettysburg inform our understanding of reconciliation and loyalty during the late nineteenth century. When one critically evaluates the tenor of the reaction and exchange regarding the monument, it becomes clear that the more famous Blue-Gray reunions possessed some level of superficiality. Some, such as John Bachelder, genuinely desired reconciliation on some level. By inviting the Maryland Confederate veterans to place a monument on the Gettysburg battlefield, Bachelder expressed a willingness to reconcile. The GBMA's approval of the monument also demonstrates a form of rapprochement. These appeals were not warmly accepted by all and the reaction they received points to the impracticality of full reconciliation and the persistence of wartime loyalty two decades removed from the Civil War. Struggles for equal claims and Maryland's conflicted Civil War history amplified the discord of veterans returning to consecrate their valor and devotion.

CHAPTER 3

The Heart of Maryland

The Feminization and Southernization of Maryland
in Lost Cause History and Mass Culture

"Barbara Frietchie's work is o'er, / And the Rebel rides on his raids no more." The work that John Greenleaf Whittier referenced in his poem was Barbara Frietchie's proud display of the U.S. flag as Confederate forces marched past. The legend of Frietchie, an elderly Unionist woman living in Frederick, Maryland, during the war, swirled throughout the postbellum period. Marylanders debated vigorously the legend and loyalty of Frietchie and the appropriateness of commemorating her throughout the postwar period. She embodied the memory of Civil War Maryland writ large as a point of contention and the earnestness with which individuals strived to establish her identity and loyalty. Additionally, as this chapter demonstrates, the fact that a woman represented Civil War Maryland was not surprising given the history of the state in mass cultural mediums in the first sixty years following the conclusion of the war.[1]

While veterans inside and outside Maryland battled over the state's identity on rural battlefields, Confederate veterans as well as southern and northern writers, biographers, and playwrights attempted to cultivate their own image of Civil War Maryland. These writers did not deny the divisiveness of wartime Maryland, but they still worked to carve out a space for Maryland in the broader legacy and heritage of the Confederacy. Many were motivated in their desire to bolster the ideology of the Lost Cause and saw Maryland as a crucial point in this growing ideology.

In the process of southernizing Maryland, southern writers also contributed to the feminization of the border state. In their view, the state was relatively helpless during the war under the tyranny of aggressive and oppressive northern policies. The subjugation narrative of Civil War Maryland facilitated a popular image of the state as a feminine character that needed to be rescued by her southern protectors. Even if salvation from northern tyranny during the war was not realized, it was still possible in the postwar period through early southern histories of the war as well as plays and novels at the turn of the century. Redeeming Confederate Maryland through mass culture became a popular phenomenon throughout the second half of the nineteenth century and beyond. Not all were complicit in the southernization of Maryland, and many publicly challenged the process. Despite efforts to establish a clear Confederate identity for Maryland, the state remained divided in both internal and American memory. The malleability of Civil War Maryland is clearly seen in the writings of Lost Causers. No consensus of the state emerges from their works; rather, narratives of Civil War Maryland vary markedly. The divisiveness of the border state provided a powerful weapon for authors to craft the stories they wanted to tell. Maryland could support the legacy of the Confederacy in different ways, and the writings of former Confederates demonstrate this vividly.

Those producing early Lost Cause literature and mass cultural depictions of Maryland worked to create a southern Maryland as well as a feminine Maryland. Lost Cause authors did so through historical accounts from the perspective of those who fought for the Confederacy, while novelists and playwrights did so through fictitious narratives set in Civil War Maryland. The southernization and feminization of the state occurred simultaneously, and the processes were inextricably connected. These writers characterized Maryland as southern rather than Confederate because Maryland was sympathetic with its sister states but did not stand up with them as Confederate because of its subjugated history. While many defined "the South" as the states south of the Mason-Dixon line, Maryland's position bordering this line and its complex regional history rendered this a more complicated matter. "Southern" implied affinity for the South and its states, but the label and identity of "Confederate" was reserved for those who made substantial contributions to the Confederacy's wartime cause. In this respect, southernization and feminization went hand in hand. Maryland, although southern in sentiment and sympathetic to the Confederacy, needed saving from northern tyranny. Through this familiar narrative, writers, playwrights, and novelists often seamlessly blended the southernization and feminization of Maryland into one narrative.[2]

Northerners and southerners, who southernized Maryland, claimed and asserted Maryland's identity and therefore attempted to control the state's identity. To a certain extent, this reality further contributed to the feminization of the state. The border state served as a passive actor in many of the postwar narratives, and the writers behind them subjugated Maryland in their own way by manipulating the state to fit their own interpretations. Therefore, in the subjugation narrative of Civil War Maryland, the state was characterized as a female victim, while in the tangible action of asserting a particular identity for Maryland, the state fulfilled the role of the pliant female.

Maryland in Early Lost Cause Histories

The Lost Cause developed immediately following the war and originated from the writings of figures such as former Confederate general Jubal Early and Edward A. Pollard. It was not just through the written word that the Confederacy was memorialized and the Lost Cause promoted. Ladies' Memorial Associations set to work immediately following the war and organized cemeteries for Confederate soldiers that resided in unmarked graves. There was no standard formula put forth by authors of the Lost Cause but rather a loose set of tenets that justified the Confederacy and attempted to spin the failure of the Confederacy and its armies into something more glorious. Historian Caroline Janney identifies six recurring tenets within the ideology of the Lost Cause. The tenets include denying slavery as the cause of the Civil War, depicting African Americans as loyal slaves, and the unquestioned adoration of Robert E. Lee. The proponents of the early Lost Cause also argued that the Confederate military possessed the more chivalrous and intelligent leaders and the only reason the Confederate armies lost was because of the Union's overwhelming resources and manpower.[3]

Although historians have covered the Lost Cause extensively, depictions of Maryland by early Lost Cause authors remain unexplored.[4] Analysis of Maryland in early Lost Cause history reveals efforts to southernize the state despite its wartime divisions and the resulting feminization of Maryland in postwar memory. Maryland lent itself particularly well to the narrative of the Lost Cause. A noble, proud, and patriotic state that only fell short because of federal oppression fell in line with the ideology that postwar Confederates were putting forth in their manuscripts.

Many early Lost Causers praised Maryland for its contribution to the Confederacy and its military force. One of the founders of Lost Cause ideology in literature, Edward A. Pollard, lauded Maryland's Confederate and southern sympathies. Pollard served as editor of the *Richmond*

Examiner during the war, and although he was critical of Jefferson Davis, his postwar work, *The Lost Cause: A New Southern History of the War of the Confederates*, popularized the phrase "Lost Cause."[5] Despite the fact that he characterized Maryland governor Thomas Hicks's policy of neutrality as a sign of weakness and an "absurd piece of demagogueism," Pollard acknowledged Maryland's contribution to the Confederacy. He traced Maryland's history back to the 1780s and argued that Maryland had always been a southern state by citing a member of the South Carolina Constitutional Convention who defined southern as being "Maryland and the States southward of her." He continued by associating the Baltimore Riot of 1861 with Confederate patriotism and sadly recalled that "the first blood of Southerners was shed on the soil of Maryland." In one of the fundamental texts of the Lost Cause, the author honored the early sacrifice of Marylanders to the Confederate cause and therefore marked the beginning of the southernization of Maryland.[6]

Not all writers publishing immediately after the war agreed with Pollard's positive characterization of the Old Line State. Confederate army chaplain and Stonewall Jackson's chief of staff Robert Lewis Dabney began working on a biography of Jackson shortly after his death at the request of his widow, and it was published in 1866. In his *Life and Campaigns of Lieut.-Gen. Thomas J. Jackson*, Dabney frequently deviated from his central topic to provide context and through this process Maryland faced his judgment. He was often critical of the border states for their indecisiveness and their neutrality. "How grandly does the action of Virginia contrast with that of Maryland and Kentucky, which professing attachment to the right, subsided into a pitiful 'neutrality,' that was, in fact, slavish co-operation with their enemies," he wrote. The Virginia native was not as sympathetic to arguments of Maryland oppression. He dismissively noted that Marylanders justified their neutrality with "the plea that the military highway to the tyrants' capital lay through her heart." Although referring to Maryland in feminine terms, Dabney, rather than express sympathy for the border state's position, dismissed the state's neutrality as weakness.[7]

In particular, Dabney took issue with Maryland's timidity. He claimed that the Confederacy was patient with Maryland and hoped that it would eventually join its southern brethren. In his account of Lee's proclamation to Maryland, he regretfully remembered that "the people of that region were too timid and undecided to concur in such a plan." Additionally, he believed the importance of "decisive results" in the early stages of the war was of the utmost importance because they would help "determine the wavering judgments of Maryland, Kentucky, and Missouri."[8]

Dabney's analysis of Jackson's impact on the Maryland population was slightly different from his previous descriptions of the state. Wanting to highlight the influence of his subject, Dabney wrote with pride of Jackson's experiences with the divided citizens of Maryland. "The arrival of the Confederates in Maryland awakened in a part of the population a faint glow of enthusiasm," he wrote. Dabney argued that because of Jackson's strict regimented policies concerning troop conduct and "straggling," the citizens of Maryland were "almost unconscious of the inconvenience of hostile occupation." While still not applauding Maryland's loyalty, he was able to demonstrate the magnanimity with which Jackson dealt with a population that was divided in its sentiments.[9]

Several years after Dabney published his work, another biography of Stonewall Jackson emerged. George Francis Robert Henderson, a British officer and military scholar, penned a two-volume work that offered a different interpretation of Civil War Maryland. In the first volume of *Stonewall Jackson and the American Civil War*, Henderson gave the border state more credit than Dabney offered in his biography of the famed Confederate general. "The loyalty of Maryland to the Union was more than doubtful," he wrote. Henderson argued that "her sympathies were strongly southern" and that it was primarily because of the state's geographic location north of the Potomac River that it did not join the Confederacy. He also characterized Baltimore as the "very hot-bed of secession sentiment" and noted the "anxiety" the federal government exhibited in its dealings with Maryland.[10]

More than twenty years later, Henderson's second volume was published. In this volume, Henderson was not as committed to Maryland's southern affiliations. Perhaps other postwar writers who were more dismissive of Maryland than Henderson was in his first volume influenced his second volume. In his account of Jackson's occupation of Frederick, a topic that many postwar writers would remember, he recalled the apathetic response exhibited by the residents of Frederick. The "troops were not received with the enthusiasm they had anticipated," he wrote. He also distinguished between the reception provided by female and male Marylanders. Henderson fondly remembered that the women of Frederick, "emulating their Virginia sisters, gave a warm welcome to the heroes of so many victories" but stated that the men "show little disposition to join the ranks" whether it be because they were "terrorised by the stern rule of the Federal Government, or mistrusting the power of the Confederates to secure them from further punishment." By emphasizing the positive reception of Maryland women, Henderson added to the characterization of the state as feminine. While many contributed to the feminization of Maryland through portraying the state as a damsel in distress, he added another dynamic by highlighting Maryland's female population and its Civil War contributions. Remembering Maryland women as the most positive element within the state contributed to both the feminization and the southernization of the state as Confederate women and the sacrifices they made were held up in the ideology of the Lost Cause.[11]

Three years after the conclusion of the war, Frank H. Alfriend published his biography of an important Confederate leader, Jefferson Davis. Alfriend served as editor of the *Southern Literary Messenger*. Much like other postwar southern biographers, he also documented the federal government's aggressive polices toward Maryland and stated that Marylanders themselves understood the policy toward their state "as one of subjugation." The narrative of a subjugated Maryland supported the feminization of the state in the early postbellum period because it underscored its helplessness in the larger struggle of the Civil War. Alfriend's characterization, however, did not end with the state's subjugation but continued by noting the impact federal policies had on Maryland's population. He argued that the federal government's policies "greatly strengthened the already preponderant Southern sympathies" of Maryland.[12]

In his biography of the Confederate president, Alfriend reprinted Davis's February 1862 inaugural address. During the course of his remarks, Davis expressed his hope for the future of the Old Line State. Davis stated with pride the fact that the Confederacy had "grown from six to thirteen States." In his next breath he asserted, "and Maryland, already united to us by hallowed memories and material interests will, I believe, when able to speak with unstifled voice, connect her destiny with the South." Here in 1862, Jefferson Davis was expressing the subjugation narrative of Maryland well before countless writers and commentators of the Civil War would several decades later. Maryland and "her" voice were not strong enough to assert the true wishes of the state's inhabitants. Davis hoped that the coming year would free helpless Maryland from the tyrannical constraints of the federal government. The South must rescue Maryland in order for the proper marriage between the state and the region to be realized.[13]

Alfriend noted the response Maryland offered when the South did finally come to save the state from northern tyranny. Unlike other postwar writers who simply stated that Marylanders did not come running to the Confederate ranks when Lee entered the state in the fall of 1862, Alfriend did not pin the blame squarely on the state's residents. Instead, he suggested that the failure to deliver a crushing blow to Union forces at Antietam and Lee's retreat back across the Potomac River ultimately undermined any efforts to free Maryland from Union control. "As a consequence [of Lee's inability to win a decisive victory], the people of Maryland, of whom a large majority were thoroughly patriotic and warm in their Southern sympathies, were not encouraged to make effective demonstration which would inevitably have followed a defeat of McClellan," he wrote. By shifting the responsibility of Maryland's loyalty away from Marylanders, Alfriend not only justified the state's Civil War legacy but also protected the state from its critics and detractors who argued that it did not deserve to be placed alongside the truly southern states.[14]

Marylanders themselves also contributed to the immediate postwar discussions of their home state's loyalty. Baltimorean John Beauchamp Jones was an editor, journalist, and novelist in the years leading up to the Civil War. It was, however, his wartime diary *A Rebel War Clerk's Diary*, published in February 1866, which held the most significance for postbellum debates over the history of the war and Maryland's place within it. Jones served as a clerk in the Confederate War Department and provided postwar Americans with an unprecedented look into the Confederacy's government throughout the course of the war.[15]

Although Jones does not devote much attention to his home state in his diary, two particular points stand out in his wartime writings that touch on Maryland's Civil War loyalty. Just three days before the firing on Fort Sumter, he described his meeting with the founder and publisher of the *Baltimore Sun*, Arunah Shepherdson Abell. He characterized Abell as "an old acquaintance." Jones was aware of the fact that Abell was a native northerner, so he expected the publisher to be Unionist. He was surprised to learn that not only was Abell "an ardent secessionist" but he was also so invested in the Confederate cause that "he denounced both Maryland and Virginia for their hesitancy in following the example of the Cotton States." The remarks of Abell and Jones's decision to include them in his diary reveal an important strategy that Confederate Marylanders would employ through the postwar period. By condemning the actions and loyalty of their own state, they sought to underscore how intensely loyal they truly were to the Confederate cause. In other words, being a secessionist in Maryland was more heroic than being a secessionist in South Carolina. This approach ran counter to attempts at southernizing Maryland or maintaining a dual-identity (the topic of the following chapter), but it bolstered Marylanders' own personal identity as Confederates.[16]

The second point documented the early doubts surrounding Maryland within the higher ranks of the Confederate leadership. On April 20, 1861, Jones penned his entry and in it he offered his feeling on the Baltimore Riot that occurred the previous day. Although a secessionist, he was more than disappointed in the actions of the mob in the streets of Baltimore. "It was a brickbat 'Plug Ugly' fight—the result of animal, and not intellectual or patriotic instincts," he wrote. He feared the negative consequences of the riot and concluded that the "absence of dignity in this assault will be productive of evil rather than good" and "Maryland is probably lost." He even regretted the actions of the citizens of his hometown: "Baltimore has better men for the strife than bar-room champions." Again, Jones distanced himself from his native state, but in this entry he added the notion that his hometown was better than its secessionist mob.[17]

Jones's criticism of the Baltimore Riot in his diary was an anomaly among wartime and postwar Confederates. Many portrayed the riot as an expression of Confederate identity and resistance and then focused on the incivility of the federal government's policies toward the state. Jones's account, however, ran counter to this growing preponderant narrative and also challenged the feminization of Maryland. The barbarous nature of the mob represented Maryland as an uncontrollable brute, not a delicate damsel needing rescue. Over the next several decades, authors, playwrights, and novelists would work to counter this interpretation of the Old Line State.

Former president of the Confederacy Jefferson Davis presented a picture similar to that of Pollard in his analysis of Maryland during the conflict through his history of the Confederacy, *The Rise and Fall of the Confederate Government*. Davis as well as Robert E. Lee expected Marylanders to join the Confederate war effort after Lee entered the state in 1862. The citizens of the Old Line State ultimately disappointed both Confederate leaders when they did not rush to join or support the Army of Northern Virginia. In their respective histories of the Confederacy, Pollard and Davis both lamented the lack of response generated by Lee's proclamation to Maryland and his presence in the state. Comparable to Pollard's analysis of the Baltimore Riot, Davis underscored the heroism of those who resisted the Union forces in the state. He insisted, "The manly effort of the unorganized, unarmed citizens of Baltimore to resist the progress of armies for the invasion of her Southern sisters, was worthy of the fair fame of Maryland."[18]

The Southern Historical Society offered another outlet from which Lost Causers expressed their viewpoints on Civil War Maryland. The society formed in 1869 and collected a variety of materials including both sources from the war as well as postwar articles and recollections describing the southern experience in the Civil War. The society eventually published the collection in several edited volumes under the title *Southern Historical Society Papers.*[19] The *Papers* represent a variety of viewpoints from southerners on the war, including Maryland's role as a divided border state.

Many contributors to the *Papers* joined Pollard and Davis in their adoration for Maryland's Confederate war effort. Lamar Hollyday, a Confederate veteran from Maryland, authored an article in the third volume of the *Southern Historical Society Papers* in which he defended Maryland's contribution to the Confederacy. He acknowledged that early contributors to the *Papers*, including Confederate general Jubal A. Early, undervalued Maryland's role and countered that such "statements, coming from such high authority, are calculated to do great injustice to as gallant soldiers of the Confederate army as either shouldered a musket, straddled a horse or rode on a caisson." In this instance, Hollyday attempted to defend Maryland in the face of neglect and disrespect. More than a decade after the fighting had ceased, Confederates, inside and outside the state, felt compelled to protect Maryland.[20]

Another, more prominent Maryland Confederate veteran, Bradley T. Johnson, also outlined the state's southern roots in the pages of the *Southern Historical Society Papers*. During the war, Johnson served as commander of the First Maryland Infantry in the Confederate army. After the war, he became an advocate on behalf of Maryland Confederate veterans and was active in memorializing their efforts, including the Second Maryland Confederate Infantry Monument at Gettysburg. In his memoir of his regiment, Johnson remembered that the situation Marylanders faced at the outset of the war "was peculiar." He insisted the citizens of the state were "intensely Southern" but that their unique situation "on the frontier of the immense Northern empire" prevented them from following their brethren southern states fully and quickly in the secessionist movement.[21] Former Richmond, Virginia, mayor A. M. Keiley echoed Hollyday and Johnson in their adoration for Maryland Confederates in his Memorial Day address featured in the *Southern Historical Society Papers*. Keiley was particularly inspired by the fortitude of Maryland Confederates who left their divided home state to support the southern cause. He stated emphatically during his address, "Maryland's immortal children, in a banishment whose tenderest alternative was a dungeon, how these gallant souls kept their faith bright as their bayonets, and marched gaily to death as high carnival!"[22]

Several articles featured in the *Papers* did not possess such a laudatory tone, including some scathing admonishments directed at Maryland and its lack of commitment to the Confederacy. Private Carlton McCarthy of the Richmond Howitzers penned an article describing the "Camp Fires of the Boys in Gray" and in his listing of the songs they would sing he referenced "Maryland, My Maryland." He recalled that they sang "Maryland, My Maryland" until "about the third year of the war, when we began to think Maryland had 'breathed and burned' long enough and ought to 'come.'" McCarthy made sure to check his criticism of the state by adding that "what part of her did come was *first class*."[23] In an 1875 address before the Southern Historical Society, then governor of North Carolina Z. B. Vance wanted to distinguish the commitment of the "wholly committed" southern states and the border states, namely, Maryland, Kentucky, and Missouri, which "were only partially engaged, the great majority of their people remaining with the Union." These former Confederates accepted Maryland's connection to the South but they rejected identifications of the state as Confederate.[24]

These comments, however, were mild compared to those that held Maryland at least partially culpable for the ultimate defeat of the Confederacy. Finding scapegoats for the Confederate demise was a common practice among Lost Cause writers, including Jubal Early. The Lost Causers frequently targeted General James Longstreet, who bore the brunt of the blame for the Confederate failure at Gettysburg, while absolving Robert E. Lee of responsibility. Individuals were not the only targets; states were as well. Confederate general D. H. Hill pinned the blame for the fall of the Confederacy on the lack of commitment from the border states. In his address before the Mecklenburg (N.C.) Historical Society, he stated, "Had the South been united, our independence could easily have been established, but unfortunately, the South furnished, probably, as many native troops to the Federal army, as did the vast and populous North." The statement is an improbable exaggeration that Hill infused with the Lost Cause theme of an overwhelming northern population and military. Although he acknowledged that every southern state contributed to "Yankee service," Missouri, Kentucky, and Maryland were the only states he named specifically and the only states for which he listed the number of Union soldiers. Again, the southernization of Maryland was accepted but it did not necessitate a favorable review of Maryland's Civil War devotion and contributions.[25]

Not all early Lost Cause writers expressed such simple positive or negative sentiments regarding Maryland. Numerous authors attempted to justify why the state did not secede by pointing to the subjugation of the state at the hands of northern tyranny and oppression. Pollard linked Lincoln's "occupation" of Maryland and Missouri as a decisive factor in keeping them from seceding. He referenced policies of "coercion and subjugation of the South" and "systems of despotism in Maryland and Missouri."[26] He felt passionately enough about the topic of Maryland's loyalty to offer an extensive list of factors that impeded Maryland's Confederate status. After noting the many challenges the border state faced, Pollard concluded that it was no wonder "that Maryland became the easy prey of a Government that scrupled at no means of success and spared no opportunity for the perversion of the principles of men." In Pollard's narrative, the barbarous men of the North affronted the dignity, righteousness, and purity of Maryland during the mid-nineteenth century.[27]

Davis also mentioned the subjugation of "the State government of Maryland." He described the story of Maryland in the Civil War as "sad to the last degree, only relieved by the gallant men who left their homes to fight the battle of State rights when Maryland no longer furnished them a field on which they could maintain the rights their fathers left them."[28] To Davis, although Maryland suffered at the hands of northern aggression, only those who left the border state to fight with the Confederate army deserved the admiration of the South. Therefore, he dissented from those who tried to completely southernize the state and establish its unimpeded southern identity.

A few columns and speeches featured in the *Southern Historical Society Papers* supported the northern subjugation thesis of Maryland. The *Papers* reprinted the address of the Confederate Congress to the citizens of the Confederate States of America from December 1863. The resolution asserted that the Maryland judiciary was "made subservient to executive absolutism" and "the whole land groaneth under the oppressions of merciless tyranny."[29] Although the address made by the Confederate Congress was during the course of the war, the decision of the Southern Historical Society to reprint the resolution in its first volume speaks to the importance of explaining border state Civil War roles and identities in early Lost Cause literature. It also furthered the feminization of the state by pointing to Maryland's subservience to Union policies.

In the second volume of the *Papers*, the Southern Historical Society published a letter that General Jubal Early penned originally for the London *Standard* on the relative strength of the Confederate and Union armies. Documenting the overwhelming military odds the Confederacy faced in the Civil War would develop into a favorite pastime among promoters of the Lost Cause. By citing the insurmountable disadvantage the South faced, the ability of the Confederacy to last as long as it did and fight as admirably as it did was viewed as even more impressive. Early's analysis of Maryland is significant for two reasons. First, he supported the subjugation thesis on the state's loyalty. Second, he feminized Maryland in his analysis. Early wrote, "The strong hand of military power was put upon Maryland in the very outset, by which her voice was suppressed before there was an opportunity of giving expression to it."[30] Depictions of Maryland as feminine complemented and merged with the subjugation theory and implied submissiveness and fragility on the part of the state.

Characterizing Maryland as feminine took on even more significance in mass cultural depictions of the state, including plays and novels. The debates over Maryland's Civil War identity persisted and spread beyond the pages of historical manuscripts. The southernization and feminization of Maryland that early Lost Cause writers employed evolved into a cultural phenomenon that would reach another generation of Americans through a different medium.

Maryland in Mass Culture

Maryland exclaims, "The bell shall not ring! [*Maryland leaps and clings with both hands to the tongue of the bell. The bell moves higher and higher; she is dragged backwards and forwards by the swing. Shouting, etc., kept up until the curtain falls*]."[31] The late nineteenth-century play *The Heart of Maryland* received popular acclaim, in part, for the climactic conclusion of the third act in which the protagonist Maryland Calvert leaps onto the clapper of a large bell signaling an alarm in an attempt to deaden the sound and allow her imprisoned lover to escape. In addition to a story of young romance, *The Heart of Maryland* is a tale of Civil War Maryland, the divisions within families living in the Old Line State, and the southernization and feminization of the state in popular memory.

Maryland's role in the Civil War served as a prominent backdrop for a variety of artistic and literary cultural depictions of the war. Several playwrights and novelists set their narratives in the border state, and theirs were not arbitrary selections. A few examples serve to demonstrate the pervasiveness of Maryland's Civil War loyalties in popular memory, not only in Maryland but far more broadly: two immensely successful late nineteenth-century plays, *The Heart of Maryland* and *Barbara Frietchie*, and an early twentieth-century novel, *For Maryland's Honor: A Story of the War of Southern Independence*. Examining the different works, each separated from the next by several decades, contributes to a more complete answer to the question of how mass culture represented and, at times, manipulated the history of Maryland's Civil War loyalty.

Northerners, southerners, and Marylanders themselves used mass culture as a means to create a southern, white identity for the state. While not shying away from its wartime divisiveness, playwrights and novelists presented a romanticized image of a southern and Confederate Maryland. Writing in the age of Jim Crow, authors of mass culture largely created a racial and Confederate heritage for Maryland like those who used Kentucky as a backdrop.[32] Writers also contributed to the feminization of Maryland by personifying the state through a lead female character. As in the case of Barbara Frietchie, the implications of this literary decision could often prove controversial. A generation removed from the war, mass culture provided a medium through which writers could glorify Maryland and the Confederacy, in a captivating fashion, to those that did not experience the war directly.

The Heart of Maryland (1895)

David Belasco penned *The Heart of Maryland* with the intent that the production would serve as a melodramatic highlight for his protégée Mrs. Leslie Carter, who played the star role of Maryland Calvert. Mrs. Carter's path to the role of Maryland was not a smooth one. Caroline Louise Carter was married to Leslie Carter, a prominent and wealthy lawyer from Chicago. In 1887, Caroline Carter filed for divorce and accused her husband of physical abuse. In 1889, the trial was resolved and Leslie Carter was acquitted of the charges while Caroline was convicted of "intimacy with various men" via a "cross bill" filed by her husband. The trial was a high-profile case and widely reported in major newspapers. Caroline Carter retained her married name, Mrs. Leslie Carter, and used it as her stage name as a subtle form of revenge directed at her ex-husband. The role of Maryland Calvert would help launch Carter's career as an actress following several years of personal turmoil. After several failed attempts to have the play produced, *The Heart of Maryland* finally debuted at the Grand Opera House in Washington, D.C., on October 9, 1895. At the end of the month, the production moved to Herald Square Theatre on Broadway and opened the first of what would be more than two hundred performances. After its initial run in New York, *The Heart of Maryland* toured the country for the next several years and even played the Adelphi Theatre in London.[33]

Belasco, who spent considerable time in Maryland to enhance his play's sense of realism, centered it on the romantic relationship between young Union officer Alan Kendrick and Confederate sympathizer Maryland Calvert. Not only is their own relationship conflicted, but their familial bonds are also strained because Alan's father Hugh is a Confederate general and Maryland's brother Lloyd is a Union spy. Kendrick is captured while attempting to sneak through Confederate lines to see Maryland and is held prisoner under the authority of Colonel Thorpe, a former officer seeking to exact revenge because Kendrick had him court-martialed many years before. Maryland tries to dissuade Thorpe from executing Kendrick; Thorpe then advances on Maryland, who resists by stabbing Thorpe and presenting Kendrick with an opportunity to escape. Thorpe gives the order to ring the church bell and signal the attempted escape, but, in the play's most iconic scene, Maryland leaps onto the bell's clapper to muffle the bell and allow Kendrick to flee. He later returns with his troops and receives a letter indicating that Thorpe is in fact a Confederate spy, which leads to Thorpe's imprisonment and the reunion of Kendrick and Maryland.[34]

Using the name "Maryland" for the main character as well as the state in which the play is set seems a little clichéd, but its significance should not be overlooked. Historian Nina Silber notes that "several authors exploited the feminine names of southern states to make the analogy between femininity and southern geography explicit."[35] That, however, is not the only analogy Belasco made in his play. "Maryland" as both setting and protagonist not only provides a convenient metaphor for the state during the war but also enlightens Maryland's status in popular Civil War memory during the late nineteenth century. This simple literary device allowed Belasco to demonstrate the unresolved conflicts of both girl and state. Throughout the play, the multiple divided loyalties in and among the various families highlight the much larger theme of an identity-confused border state torn between opposing sides. By infusing the divisions of Civil War Maryland with the character in his play, Belasco added an important element to the postbellum feminization of the state.

FIGURE 3.1. Poster for *The Heart of Maryland*
(courtesy of the Library of Congress).

Maryland Calvert's loyalty to the southern cause and her relationship
with those who support the Union, including members of her own family,
is established very early in the play. A young Confederate officer pursuing
the affections of a young relative of Maryland's inquires, "However does a
rabid little abolitionist like you manage to get along under the same roof
with Miss Maryland?" Knowing Miss Maryland's deeply held sentiments,
the young girl replies, "I reckon it's just as well not to rouse her secesh."
The Confederate spy, Thorpe, also states fairly early on to Maryland's
brother that "your sister, Miss Maryland, one of the most loyal women in
the South, and your local knowledge makes you invaluable. That's why
you were sent to me."[36] The confidence in Miss Maryland's loyalty to the
South expressed by various characters in the play not only foreshadows
the confusion the protagonist will soon face in deciding on which side
her loyalty lies; it also reflects the state's divided house during the war.
Furthermore, the intensity of Maryland Calvert's loyalty to the Confederate cause was indicative of the already prevalent process of southernizing
the border state during the late nineteenth century.

Not long after these initial cues, Belasco begins to draw out more explicitly the significance of the state's loyalty to the play and the narrative
he wants to tell. Miss Maryland receives a letter from General Robert E.
Lee thanking her for her contribution to the Confederate war effort,
which Maryland's aunt, Mrs. Gordon, reads aloud with pride:

> Headquarters, Southern Army
>
> My dear little Miss Patriot:
>
> Your last contribution of tobacco, coffee, and shirts, is hereby gratefully
> acknowledged. Were all hearts in Maryland as loyal as yours, she would
> stand with her sister states, ovo'hthrowin' her present shamblin'
> indecision.
>
> Yours with most grateful regards,
> Robert E. Lee

Colonel Thorpe concurs with Lee's assessment by saying, "Miss Calvert
is known to be the fiercest Southerner of us all," but, much like Lee,
Thorpe questions the state's loyalty and is aware of its indecisiveness. He
asks Mrs. Gordon, "Do you know, I find a strong tide of sympathy for the
North amongst the people here?" Mrs. Gordon replies, "Ah, but there's
an undercurrent of love for their native state. Were it not fo' those Northern soldiers at Cha'lesville—stationed there to ove'awe the people—they
would rally to our ranks."[37] Mrs. Gordon's lines are particularly interest-

ing in that, unlike Thorpe and Lee, she assumes the Confederate identity of her state and argues that only the presence of Union troops gives a misleading impression of the state's population as predominantly sympathetic to the North. These subtle few lines seem insignificant to the larger plot, but they would have resonated with a crowd still wanting to believe a certain memory and legacy of the war. They also mirror the argument Lost Cause devotees employed to justify Maryland's non-secession by citing militaristic and authoritarian rule on the part of Abraham Lincoln and the Union army to prevent the state from joining the Confederacy.

As the play progresses, Miss Maryland, the most loyal of all Confederates, realizes the struggle and timidity of not only her own loyalties but those of all Marylanders. In a dramatic scene with Kendrick, Miss Maryland exclaims, "Oh, you don't know how we feel—we women of the South! How our hearts are torn by this divided duty." She continues: "on one side, our country" and "on the other, our very own turned to foes." Maryland's role in aiding Kendrick's escape harms not only her own reputation and legacy but also that of her family. Mrs. Gordon notes remorsefully that she "can see our name trailing in the dust—the wiping out of our proud record of loyalty" and the fact that she is "ashamed to look the neighbors in the face."[38] Mrs. Gordon seems unaware that many of her neighbors view loyalty as adhering to a completely different cause and that many of them would support a Confederate-turned-Union supporter. In her eyes the state of Maryland is firmly entrenched in a Confederate ideology, and she fears that her family will come to represent a misfortunate anomaly.

Maryland's Civil War identity was defined by its loyalty in Belasco's play, but there is also, and more subtly, its history as a slave state. That is brought to life in the character of Uncle Dan'l, an overtly racist and stereotypical loyal slave. Belasco introduces him in the script as a "lovable old darky" with "a large watermelon" lying nearby. Although he only appears in a few instances, Uncle Dan'l fits more broadly within an idealized and romanticized image of Maryland and the South. In a moment of distress, Miss Maryland calls out for Uncle Dan'l, whispers instructions in his ear, and asks him to hurry. He responds to the ardent secessionist with a simple and polite, "Yes, Miss Maryland." Again, through the script of Belasco's drama, we see the influence of Lost Cause ideology on popular culture and how that influence further affected the Civil War memory of the Old Line State. Similar attempts to solidify a white, Confederate identity for Maryland several decades later faced growing opposition from those fighting for equality.[39]

Many critics were quick to point out the distorted, romanticized view Belasco painted of the South and the entire Civil War period. One noted in the *New York Tribune* that "the enormities which he puts on the stage as perpetrated by military men of high rank were never committed by officers who wore the recognized uniform of the Confederate Army" and took issue with the play's "wild shrieking melodrama." A southern reviewer concurred. Under the lukewarm heading "It Is Not Altogether Good Nor Altogether Bad," he groused, "If it had been an attempt to burlesque the army, it could not have been better done." Another critic recalled, "As is usual in plays of this sort, the heroine is a loyal Southern girl, and the hero a soldier of the North." George Bernard Shaw sarcastically remarked, "I infer from the American war plays that most of the Northern officers acted as spies for the Southern army, and that the Southern officers acted as spies for the Northern army."[40]

Yet, as Glenn Hughes and George Savage point out, although the play "was treated rather severely by the critics . . . its popular appeal was enormous."[41] Local newspapers across the country raved at each stop on the play's cross-country tour. A Nebraska newspaper referred to the production as the "most memorable triumph in dramatic work" and "unequalled." Others commented that it had "few compeers" and "is a masterpiece of intense dramatic power." The belfry scene received particular applause. A critic from the *St. Paul Globe* wrote that the scene was "said to be the acme of realism" as well as "a striking spectacle." In commemoration of the play's two hundredth performance at the Herald Square Theatre, souvenirs for the night were "solid silver, gold-lined bon-bon boxes in the shape of a heart." The response in London was equally enthusiastic, with widespread pronouncements that *The Heart of Maryland* was "interesting and thrilling" and reports of record-breaking numbers at the Adelphi box office.[42]

The reaction, popular and critical, to *The Heart of Maryland* reveals a significant aspect of late nineteenth-century depictions of Maryland during the war. The overwhelmingly positive response to the play demonstrates that few took issue with the production as partisan or favoring a particular side. Unlike the attempt to place a Maryland Confederate monument on the Gettysburg battlefield a decade earlier, in 1886, few objected to *The Heart of Maryland* for attempting to stake a claim for Maryland's position during the war. Some questioned the play's historical accuracy, but as a theater critic for the *New York Times* contended, its representation of Maryland's loyalty was fair in that "the people of that State were about equally divided."[43] Few other narratives that described the role of Maryland confessed to, let alone emphasized, its fractious society and culture in the Civil War era. The widespread acclaim for the play also affirms the willingness of many, particularly in the North, to view the Civil War South as gentle and benevolent, even in a time of great division and conflict. As a period in American history that solidified the legality of "separate but equal" in *Plessy v. Ferguson*, *The Heart of Maryland* provides another example of the passivity with which many viewed some of the war's more troubling legacies and consequences.

Barbara Frietchie (1899)

Another Civil War play set in Maryland premiered a few years after *The Heart of Maryland* and provoked a strong reaction, though in a much different way. *Barbara Frietchie*, by Clyde Fitch, originated from a poem of the same name penned in 1864 by John Greenleaf Whittier. The poem depicts a local legend of the small town of Frederick, Maryland, in which Barbara Frietchie, an elderly Unionist woman, proudly flew the U.S. flag from her house as Confederate troops commanded by Stonewall Jackson marched past. As legend and poem have it, the marching soldiers grew angry, but Jackson, impressed with the woman's bravery, demanded that she not be harmed.[44]

The play debuted and ran for eighty-three performances at the Criterion Theatre in Manhattan from October 1899 to January 1900. Fitch was harshly criticized for turning the story of Frietchie, an elderly woman, into one of young romance. In Fitch's hands, Barbara is a young Confederate sympathizer living in secessionist Frederick who is engaged to Union captain Trumbull. After Trumbull is wounded and dies in Frietchie's home, out of devotion to him she displays the Union flag as the Confederate soldiers march by and is the only one in Frederick to do so. Despite Jackson's order that anyone who harms Barbara will be shot, a bitter former admirer and suitor, Jack Negly, shoots her. Negly's own father, Colonel Negly, is forced to ensure that Jackson's command is carried out.[45]

Like Mrs. Gordon in *The Heart of Maryland*, many of the characters in *Barbara Frietchie* assume a Confederate and southern identity for the state of Maryland. In an expression of love and assurance to Trumbull, Barbara cries out, "and Maryland and all the South, the blessed, sweet, dear South, still you, you Northerner—you *Yankee!*—you, my soldier lover—I love *you most!*" Jack Negly celebrates a Confederate victory by shouting,

"Three cheers for Maryland and Stonewall Jackson! Hooray!"[46] In one of play's silent film adaptations there was a reference to the secession of Maryland that, of course, never occurred. Although coming from the mouths of fictitious characters, these lines embraced and promoted a Confederate identity for Maryland.

Loyalty was a central topic in responses to the play, but the reactions focused not on the loyalty of Maryland explicitly but instead on the loyalty of Barbara Frietchie. For months after the play's initial performance, the *New York Times* ran a series of letters to the editor that included exchanges not only on the question of whether or not Frietchie existed, but whether she was a Unionist or a secessionist. The nature of the discussion inevitably came to characterize Barbara Frietchie as indicative of the state of Maryland's loyalty at large. Two weeks before the play debuted in New York, Fitch anticipated criticism from the license he had taken in reinterpreting the legend and the poem Whittier had written more than thirty years earlier. A *New York Times* reporter opined that the "heroine of the play will be found to be a new Barbara Frietchie" and "Mr. Fitch makes his Barbara a beautiful Southern girl instead of an old woman." Fitch felt free to manipulate the legend as he saw fit because he had "delved into all available data to discover if Whittier's heroine had a real existence" and had concluded "the burden of proof against that assumption."[47]

Those claims, of course, did not go unanswered. The first letter came just two days later with the line, "I regret that 'his delving into available data' has not given me the pleasure of meeting Mr. Fitch and of assuring him of the very real existence of Barbara Frietchie." The writer, Emily N. Ritchie McLean, claimed that her "grandfather was the executor of her [Frietchie's] husband's will" and her "father came into possession of some of her household furniture after her death." McLean approved of Fitch paying tribute to "the aged heroine" but felt that her existence "should not be denied."[48]

C. E. Hudson took issue with McLean's conclusions. Hudson asserted the existence of a letter, written by Whittier, in which the poet supposedly "stated that his poem was absolutely without foundation in fact; that he never heard of a person of the name 'Barbara Frietchie' or of the name itself until he used it; and that the whole incident was simply imaginary." He thought, "Whittier must be recognized as an authority on the subject," and thus the case was closed.[49]

Hudson's reply prompted a wave of letters to the *Times* from those declaring some sort of "authority" over the real story of Barbara Frietchie. For many, denying Frietchie's existence was to take a point of pride away from Marylanders who were loyal to the Union during the war and believed that the legend of her heroics served as a justification for claims that Maryland was an ardent supporter of the North and its cause. McLean responded to Hudson: "I can consider myself an authority on the existence of Barbara Frietchie, as I was born in Frederick, Md., my father's home was opposite Mrs. Frietchie's, and her 'attic window' was a familiar daily sight to me."[50]

Others, including Clyde Fitch himself, chimed in. John Jerome Rooney knew a friend who had been acquainted with Frietchie, and he was confident that she "really was an ardent Union sympathizer." In response to the letters criticizing his denial of Frietchie's existence, Fitch claimed that the initial article that represented his voice was false and "probably originated from an exuberant press agent or enthusiastic correspondent." He stated emphatically, "Barbara Frietchie, of course, existed." Although Fitch agreed with Rooney that Frietchie existed, he did not come to the same conclusion about her loyalty to the Union. Fitch contended, "I have it on the authority of relatives of Barbara that her patriotism was very much to question" and "had she been able to wave any flag before the rebel troops, they fear it would have been a Confederate one." Jesse W. Reno took issue with that and stated, "Barbara Frietchie was loyal to her heart's core." Henry Goddard claimed "that no more loyal soul to the Union cause ever existed in Frederick."[51]

This lengthy exchange reveals the importance of Maryland's Civil War loyalty in memory. Nevertheless, the heated back-and-forth over Barbara Frietchie's loyalty was about the actual individual and not the character in the play. The impetus for the discussion was the *Times* article in which Fitch supposedly denied that she once existed and then questioned her loyalty. Her loyalty, as depicted in the play, did not strike any of the responders as unfair or incorrect; it was only when the claims of historical truth were made outside the parameters of a fictitious production that individuals attempted to check the narrative being put forth. This important qualification will gain additional significance when we examine the state song controversy.

The passionate debate also evidences the fact that the legend of Barbara Frietchie embodied the Civil War legacy of Maryland. Establishing her true loyalty was akin to making a case for the true loyalty of Maryland. In this respect, Maryland was feminized not only in the legend of a female heroine but through individuals who jumped to her defense and attempted to protect her name. Denying the existence of Frietchie altogether was another strategy that former Confederates and Lost Causers

FIGURE 3.2. Photograph of Barbara Frietchie, ca. 1862
(courtesy of the Library of Congress).

used in an attempt to southernize Maryland. If Barbara Frietchie did not
exist, she could not be a source of pride for Unionists in Maryland who
delighted in telling of her noble wave of the American flag.

Fitch's play would not be the last time debates would swirl over the
legacy of Barbara Frietchie and her place in the memory of Civil War
Maryland. Only a few months after the exchange in the *New York Times*, a
columnist in the *Confederate Veteran*, J. William Jones from Richmond, Virginia, contributed an article titled "The 'Barbara Frietchie' Myth." In his
article, Jones presented an argument that denied the fact that Frietchie
ever waved a Union flag in the face of Confederate forces under Stonewall Jackson. He referenced several individuals, including Frietchie's
nephew, and laid out several factors that would have made the action
impossible. Jones realized that the legend "has been so often refuted it

FIGURE 3.3. Photograph of actress Julia Marlowe, ca. 1890
(courtesy of the Library of Congress).

would seem useless to do so again," but he deemed it worthwhile to "preserve in the VETERAN the facts" because southern teachers were "unwise enough" and southern parents "careless enough" to allow their students and children to use readers that included the story of Barbara Frietchie.[52]

In 1914, the Barbara Frietchie Memorial Association dedicated a monument to her in Mount Olivet Cemetery in Frederick, Maryland. While Unionists in the state rejoiced with the dedication of the monument, members of the Maryland United Daughters of the Confederacy (UDC) vigorously opposed the placement of the monument. The president of the Maryland Division of the UDC, Cordelia Odenheimer, expressed the frustration of the Maryland branch at a national gathering of the organization. She prefaced the state report by noting the "outrage which had been perpetrated in the erection of the monument to Barbara Frietchie at Frederick, Md." The UDC report featured in the *Confederate Veteran* also noted that the monument "was fought by the Daughters of Maryland in every way possible, but in vain" because it "now stands a monument to falsehood." Barbara Frietchie represented a point of fracture in Maryland society, and attempts to sanctify her in memory challenged those who were intent on the southernization of the border state.[53]

For Maryland's Honor: A Story of the War of Southern Independence (1922)

Although Lloyd T. Everett's novel *For Maryland's Honor: A Story of the War for Southern Independence* did not garner as much attention as *The Heart of Maryland* or *Barbara Frietchie*, it nonetheless represents an important aspect of Maryland's Civil War loyalty in popular memory. Everett was the son of a Maryland Confederate veteran and, appropriately, a member of the Sons of Confederate Veterans. This inevitably influenced the story he told in *For Maryland's Honor*, but he did not shy away from commenting on his state's divided sympathies even though he proclaimed the moral correctness of the Confederate cause.[54] The rising membership of the Ku Klux Klan, the frequency of lynching in the South, and increased segregation also undoubtedly affected Everett's narrative.

Everett's plot mirrors that of *The Heart of Maryland* with the notable difference that the loyalties of the main characters are inverted. In Everett's narrative, the male protagonist and young Confederate Marylander Phil Elliott seeks the affection of a Unionist woman, Marion Palmer. When we meet her, she is engaged to a Union soldier from Boston named Guy Hancock. As the story progresses, the relationship of Elliott and Palmer evolves from initial timidity because of their opposing views on the war to their eventual marriage and Elliott's untimely death at the novel's end. All the while Everett underscores Maryland's Confederate heritage. *For Maryland's Honor* is more than the novel's title; it was the author's purpose in writing it.

Everett was aware of the criticism Maryland received from those who supported the former Confederacy, and he makes a point to address it. Early in the novel, a public debate is held concerning the issue of secession, and the audience, made up primarily of Marylanders, "was Southern in sentiment" but moderate in their view, favoring "the continued union of the States so long as possibly compatible with the welfare of their several people." Phil Elliott stands in front of the crowd and makes his case with a keen knowledge of the sentiments of those gathered. He "knew that they were true Marylanders—hence patriotic Southerners—and were deeply resentful at the persistent crusade of aggression and abuse waged against their section."[55] Everett's use of the phrase "true Marylanders" to describe those who supported the Confederate cause was an interesting, subtle claim for him to make regarding the state's loyalty. In Everett's eyes, Marylanders with Confederate sympathies were the norm, whereas a Maryland Unionist was anomalistic. In this respect, Maryland assumed a Confederate identity because of the rarity of Unionism within the state's borders.

Not only did Everett contend that "true Marylanders" were Confederates, but throughout the book he also attempted to justify the state's course during the war. As Elliott explains to Marion Palmer, "we are always ready to stand by our comrades when assailed in their just rights" and the "cause of one of our sister States or colonies in peril or suffering, is the cause of ourselves—of Maryland." Claiming that after several instances of injustice had played out, Maryland finally resolved "upon rolling back at her threshold the tide of invasion," Everett used his novel to make partisan claims about Maryland's "true" character during the Civil War.[56]

Not only did Everett attempt to establish a strong Confederate identity for Maryland, he also tried to explain the perceived shakiness of the state's wartime loyalty to the Confederate cause. Throughout the novel, Everett combined fiction with real historical events taken mostly from the years just before the war began. It is within these discussions of events that we can extract the more pertinent features of Civil War memory in mass culture. Early historians of the Lost Cause called forth many of the same reasons Everett did for the ambiguity of Maryland's loyalty. He pointed to Governor Hicks as a central factor in Maryland's inability to break away from the Union. His description of Hicks was brief and pointed: "After a course of dalliance and delay," Hicks "was eventually to go over body and soul to the Northern invaders." Everett argued that Hicks's slight delay in convening the legislature to vote on secession put Maryland in the position of a "helpless victim" when "*Habeas Corpus*, free speech, the freedom of the press, were taken away from the people" and the "most honorable and influential citizens and members of the State Assembly were cast into prison." Many postbellum writers had certainly portrayed Maryland as a "helpless victim," but Everett was more explicit.

He attempted not only to dissolve Maryland of its culpability in its failure to secede but also to generate sympathy for the state by feminizing it and characterizing it as a victim.[57]

Frequently using lines from a popular Confederate song to describe what Maryland faced during the war, Everett wrote that "Maryland found the despot's heel indeed upon her shore" and that other southern states viewed her "as a beautiful maiden bound in chains." He also believed "the despot's heel" provided incentive for "redemption of their beloved State" and led to the creation of the song—"Maryland, My Maryland."[58] Everett was hardly the only one who remembered the song more than sixty years after it first appeared in the form of a poem. Seventeen years after the first copies of *For Maryland's Honor* began to circulate, Maryland's General Assembly adopted "Maryland, My Maryland" as the official state song. The assembly's act would have ramifications for many years to come.

Even though it did not garner tremendous success or notoriety, *For Maryland's Honor* was reviewed in the *Confederate Veteran*. The review was positive and acknowledged Everett's knowledge of the topic as a Marylander, a son of a veteran, and a veteran of the Spanish-American War. The reviewer stated that because Everett was a "Marylander by birth" he wrote "as one familiar with the facts of Maryland's history during the stirring period in question." The critic then went on to ascribe the characteristics of the novelist with qualities he also attributed to the Old Line State. Everett wrote "with the temperament and habits of thought of the people of his State," the review stated.[59]

While not explicit in describing what kind of temperament or habits of thought Maryland possessed, the reviewer undoubtedly saw the positive feminine qualities of the state in Everett's writing. The reviewer noted that the novel was "a story of love and war, of daring deeds and 'impetuous wooing' between fights and across the lines" and "a story of life and love." All of this, concluded the satisfied reader, was set in one of the most "beautiful" sections of the country. Everett's poised and elegant writing style mirrored, in the eyes of the columnist, the feminine nature of the author's home state. Additionally, his title, *For Maryland's Honor*, implies a book that was written to defend the honor of a feminine Maryland. Even nearly sixty years after the war, Marylanders felt compelled to take up the pen in order to protect the identity and dignity of their home state.[60]

Although no other novelists focused as intently on Civil War Maryland, Everett was not the first to turn his eye to the divided border state. Novelist Thomas Dixon also touched on the Old Line State's Civil War loyalty. Dixon was prolific during the first few decades of the twentieth century, and his 1905 work *The Clansman* served as inspiration for D. W. Griffith's film *The Birth of a Nation* (1915). Before *The Birth of a Nation* reached American audiences, Dixon wrote *The Southerner: A Romance of the Real Lincoln* (1913) and *The Victim: A Romance of the Real Jefferson Davis* (1914). Both cast a brief gaze on Civil War Maryland, its identity, and its loyalty.

In *The Southerner*, a book he dedicated to President Woodrow Wilson, Dixon portrays Lincoln as southern at heart, in particular with regard to issue of race. In his portrayal of Lincoln's reaction to the Baltimore Riot, he presented a president who was more gentle and patient to Maryland than other postwar writers did. Dixon's Lincoln resisted calls from northern senators to punish the border state's secessionists more harshly and simply ordered that his troops avoid Baltimore on their way to the capital. He wrote that the president's "careful and friendly treatment of the Marylanders quickly proved its wisdom" because it generated a "reaction in favor of the Union . . . and the State remained loyal to the flag." Hardly in line with those who characterized Lincoln as a despot or tyrant based on his policies toward Maryland in the spring of 1861, Dixon attempted to use the border state as a backdrop from which he could appropriate the legacy of Lincoln for the narrative of the Lost Cause. In Dixon's account, Lincoln's gentle touch and the chivalrous nature with which he dealt with the delicate fabric of Maryland society and his sternness toward the ardent Unionists in the North created the image of a man who was, in a way, southern and respected the Confederate identity of numerous Maryland citizens.[61]

The following year Dixon published *The Victim*, and this time he centered his attention on the Confederate president, Jefferson Davis. The only place, however, that Maryland featured prominently in the text was in his discussion once again of Lincoln's response to the Baltimore Riot of 1861. This time he was not as extolling of the president's actions. He began with a view similar to the one he presented in *The Southerner*. "The shrewd, good-natured, even-tempered President at Washington used all his powers of personal diplomacy to pour oil on the troubled waters of Maryland," he stated. He then quickly shifted to a more negative analysis of the subsequent attempt Lincoln made to quell the secessionist sentiment in Maryland. Dixon wrote that the "steps he took were all clearly unconstitutional" and that they "were the acts of a dictator." Given that the primary subject of this manuscript was Davis, Dixon's analysis of Lincoln was more critical but still acknowledged his political skill. Nevertheless, in this narrative, Maryland was still a passive participant while Lincoln and the federal government actively controlled the suppressible state.[62]

While biographers, writers, playwrights, and novelists attempted to cultivate a Confederate identity for Maryland, Union and Confederate veterans (both from and outside Maryland) put forth their own interpretations of the border state. The romanticized and southernized image of the state that emanated from mass cultural depictions existed alongside portraits of the state from those who fought on its behalf, marched through its landscapes, or felt their own Civil War experiences were affected in one way or another by Maryland's wartime loyalty and actions. Many veterans were influenced by the image of Maryland that came from early Lost Cause histories and literary works, but their own personal investment in the popular memory of the American Civil War led them to draw their own conclusions about the Old Line State and the soldiers who called it home.

CHAPTER 4

Two-Front War

Marylanders' Dual-Identity in Memory

Americans discussed Maryland's legacy not only on scenic battlefields or on Broadway but also in Grand Army of the Republic (GAR) halls, in national encampments, at Woman's Relief Corps (WRC) conventions, in United Daughters of the Confederacy (UDC) conference rooms, and on the pages of veteran newspapers and magazines. At the 1920 National Convention of the WRC, the Department of the Potomac president Mary M. North nominated a Maryland woman, Anna Belle Roberts, for the position of junior vice president. North reminded the women gathered, "The Department of Maryland is south of the Mason and Dixon line," and Roberts works in this region. When she works, she often "has a hard time to do it; but she does well," North stated. After the Department of Maryland seconded the nomination, Isabel Worrell Ball, also from the Potomac branch, made a more forceful speech in favor of Roberts. "You women don't know anything about what you have to deal with. This little Department of Maryland stands right there between Secession and Union. You don't know anything about the laws of Maryland," she insisted. Roberts was working hard on behalf of Union memory in a place that was "simply infamous" in terms of its loyalty.[1]

Roberts was elected junior vice president and shortly thereafter gave an acceptance speech. In her address, she affirmed North's and Ball's characterizations of Maryland. "Only those who know what the border states are, really know what we have to contend with," she observed. Most of her brief speech, however, centered on the loyalty of the Maryland Department of the WRC. "Our Department is very loyal, but it is small," she said. She reinforced this point, making clear that the department "does work loyally." The loyalty of Maryland and its citizens was a focal point of those who lived through the Civil War, and they often drew different conclusions about the merits of the state's wartime contributions.[2]

It was not just pride that was at stake for veterans both inside and outside the state, although pride was certainly a factor. It was also a matter of identity. Marylanders, like other veterans, possessed a dual-identity that included their allegiance and ties to their home state as well as their loyalty and contributions to their respective causes. Maryland veterans attempted to drag their state identity alongside their own personal Civil War military identity. They faced challenges from veterans outside the state who maintained dual-identities but expected Marylanders to shed their state identity. Outside veterans did not think Maryland's ambiguous legacy was reconcilable with larger sectional causes. The unique position of Maryland, however, made this a more challenging task but one they felt compelled to tackle. They faced a two-front war in postwar memory. They had to perpetuate their respective cause, and they had to defend their position within those causes. In a word, Marylanders struggled to maintain this dual-identity while other veterans did not.[3]

Union Memories

By far the largest, in terms of membership, postwar fraternal organization north or south was the Grand Army of the Republic. The GAR formed in 1866 and grew into a powerful Union veteran organization throughout the late nineteenth century. Because of its size, historian Stuart McConnell notes that the organization was influential in shaping identity and political policies. McConnell speculates that "the GAR was perhaps the single most powerful political lobby of the age." The GAR, however, was not just a political lobby. The organization engaged in various "symbolic acts" in order to preserve the legacy of the Union in American memory and affirm their postbellum community. Parades, national campfire events, monument dedications, battlefield ceremonies, anniversary celebrations, and Memorial Day services all provided avenues through which the GAR could shape its own memories of the war. The GAR also shaped Union identity more explicitly through the publication of its newspaper the *National Tribune*. In 1900, the Maryland Department of the GAR claimed 56 posts and 2,613 members. These were modest numbers when compared to those of more northern states. Compared to other states, however, the participation of Maryland African American veterans within the GAR was high. Historian Barbara Gannon identified 23 African American GAR posts in Maryland.[4]

The Military Order of the Loyal Legion of the United States (MOLLUS) formed in 1865 but never enjoyed the same level of membership as the GAR. Nevertheless, the organization had branches and members throughout the North and engaged in its own commemorative activities. Additionally, papers that MOLLUS members read at their meetings were often published. Therefore, through speeches and their subsequent publications, members of the Loyal Legion could also shape Union identity and memories. In 1905, MOLLUS claimed 9,009 members and of that number, the state of Maryland claimed only 51, including 37 original members.[5]

The Woman's Relief Corps was the official auxiliary to the GAR. A group of Massachusetts women helped organize the WRC in 1883, and by 1900 the organization claimed almost 120,000 members. According to the 1901 national roster of the WRC, Maryland possessed just 17 corps and 553 members—again, a small number of members when placed beside many other states within the national organization. While the WRC occasionally reflected on the contributions made by women during the Civil War, it was not the organization's primary mission. Historian Nina Silber notes, "For the most part, the WRC spent its money, and its time, paying tribute to men." As the history of Maryland and its relationship with the WRC reveals, the narrative of the organization is far more complicated.[6]

Through their various commemorations, speeches, and publications, these three organizations grappled with the identity and legacy of Civil War Maryland. Several Unionists recalled the loyalty of Maryland citizens when they read about their reaction to Robert E. Lee's 1862 proclamation to Maryland in an 1898 edition of the *National Tribune*. In his reprinted piece, "The American Conflict," editor, politician, abolitionist, and non-veteran Horace Greeley recalled "no enthusiastic response" on the part of Marylanders. The New England native cited the relative indifference on the part of Maryland natives not only to Lee's overtures but also to choosing sides. "The Marylanders had no gluttonous appetite for fighting on the side of the Union; still less for risking their lives in support of the Confederacy," he wrote. In Greeley's eyes, Maryland did not resist Lee because it was full of ardent pro-Unionists but because it had no fervor for taking up either side. Marylanders also lacked enthusiasm for Confederate persuasion in 1862 because, he argued, "All who were inclined to fighting on that side found their way into the rebel lines long before." He noted the relative ease with which Confederate sympathizers could find their way into Virginia, especially "from the intensely disloyal, slaveholding Counties of southwestern Maryland."[7]

Another *Tribune* piece, published in 1909, recorded a similar analysis of the proclamation to Maryland but gave more credit to the state. The author, John McElroy, was a survivor of the Andersonville prison camp and editor as well as co-owner of the *National Tribune*. He chastised Lee and the Confederate leadership for how "little any of them realized that the great heart of Maryland was inflexibly and overwhelmingly Union." The "men who had really any heart in Secession had long ago slipped across the Potomac to join the Confederate army" and those left espousing rebel rhetoric were simply "a little circle of society dudes in Baltimore," he chided. McElroy stated that these "dudes" were secessionists but "had not the slightest idea of imperiling their precious dollars nor their personal safety for an instant in support of Secession." Greeley and McElroy believed that by 1862 the majority of secessionists in Maryland were gone and that what remained in the border state were strong-willed, determined Unionists and faux-Confederates.[8]

Other Union veterans outside the state, although not the majority, also defended Maryland as a loyal state during the Civil War. Former Civil War officer and governor of Illinois John L. Beveridge made a subtle case for Union Maryland in his address before the Illinois MOLLUS. He recounted arriving in Maryland "on loyal soil" and characterized the Old Line State as a respite from "twenty long, and weary months" on the "slave-accursed, and God-for-saken soil of Old Virginia." An 1893 article in the *National Tribune* also made an understated argument on Maryland's behalf. The author conceded that "the secessionists had triumphed for a moment" in Baltimore but countered that "in Western Maryland, at Frederick and Hagerstown, the Union men were running up the stars and stripes" and, in the end, "the hearts of the people were beating loyally and true for the Union."[9]

Many advocating on behalf of Maryland took more forceful approaches in defending its Unionist sentiment and character. The front page of the June 10, 1882, *National Tribune* featured a discussion of Maryland during the war and concluded that Maryland was Union at its heart. The author asked, "Is it too much, then, to claim for Maryland that her fidelity to her obligations in the early days of secession preserved the National capital for the installation of the lawfully-elected President" and possibly determined the outcome of the war? The column concluded that "when other States are honored, let her not be despised" and "when others are mentioned with affection and gratitude, let her name not be left out." Similarly, an editor for the same newspaper penned a piece titled "The Loyalty of Maryland" with the subtitle "The Reception of the Two Armies in This Border State was Decidedly in Favor of the Union." The editor estimated that "probably 90 per cent of them [Marylanders] were for the Union."[10]

Some Union veterans were not content to simply claim Maryland as a Union state; they also wanted to confront the narrative of a Confederate Maryland. The *Carrolltonian*, a newspaper printed out of Westminster, Maryland, confronted General Bradley T. Johnson's characterization of the state as Confederate in his appeal to the state legislature for a Confederate Soldiers' Home for aging veterans. The *Carrolltonian* recorded that Johnson assumed, erroneously, not only the southern loyalty of Maryland but also that its "people were, and still are, in sympathy with the Lost Cause." The Maryland newspaper retorted: "The truth is, that, outside of a degraded minority of slaveholders and usurers; outside of a number of Baltimore merchants courting a Southern trade for revenue only; outside of a few hot-headed youths and romantic young women, the Confederate soldier had few friends in Maryland." Union veterans from the state also challenged the Confederate legacy of the state in its most entrenched city, Baltimore, and through the most public form of memory-making, monuments. A multi-decade effort came to fruition when Union veterans gathered in Baltimore's Druid Hill Park to dedicate a monument to Maryland's loyal sons.[11]

Union veterans from the Old Line State were more direct in their remembrances because it was their personal legacies that were at stake. Specifically, their dual-identity represented an important part of this legacy. It was their identity as Old Liners and Union veterans that was at risk. With debates swirling among Union veterans about the true character of the state, it was imperative to Maryland Union veterans that they establish their Unionism within their state through the form of prominent monuments.

The majority of Union veterans outside the state, however, chose to emphasize the actions of specific Marylanders, both positive and negative. This was an attempt at severing Marylanders' dual-identity. By emphasizing individuals and groups, rather than the entire state, outside veterans could accept Maryland Union veterans into their postwar community based on their Unionist identity while stripping away their state affiliation. Conversely, those who possessed negative memories of Maryland's citizenry focused their resentment on those who threatened their Unionist identity both during and after the war.

Several members of MOLLUS highlighted loyal Marylanders but painted them more as victims of Confederate control. At a meeting of the Michigan Commandery, veterans gathered and listened to a reading from the diary of Ziba Graham, a first lieutenant from the Sixteenth Michigan. Those in attendance heard Graham's entry that recorded the "loud cheers" Union veterans received when they arrived in Maryland. He also mentioned that "a flag which had been carefully concealed during the rebel stay was proudly waving on the principal house of the town." "The rebels have stolen nearly every horse in the neighborhood, also levying upon the citizens for everything they wanted," Graham wrote. Similarly, at the twenty-fifth anniversary of the formation of MOLLUS in 1890, major general and former attorney general of the United States Charles Devens recalled the honor displayed by Maryland's Union citizens and soldiers but dismissed the state for being southern. "If I could properly give a warmer welcome to any about others, it should be to the gallant soldiers of Kentucky and Tennessee, of Maryland, West Virginia, Missouri, and other States of the South, who came to rejoice our hearts and strengthen our hands," Devens stated.[12]

The narratives of Civil War Maryland offered by Graham and Devens represent those who chose to separate the loyal from the disloyal. To many Union veterans, such separation was necessary in order to honor only those who deserved to be remembered and commemorated. Accepting Maryland unequivocally into Unionist memory was a form of disloyalty because it forgave the treasonous element within the state. Therefore, Union Marylanders deserved to be enumerated from the ambiguity of their home state.

Other outside veterans, however, took this a step further, arguing that Maryland's Unionist efforts redeemed the state from its more heinous regions and people. A contributor to the *National Tribune* referenced the Baltimore Riot of 1861 but argued, "The stern, unyielding loyalty of the noble sons of Maryland to the General Government should be permitted to atone for the insane fury of a senseless mob." The author also noted that it "is customary to speak of a State as though it was an individual and reckon the degree of its loyalty by the proportionate number of troops contributed by it to the two contending armies." This particular writer agreed that states should be analyzed in more depth rather than making blanket generalizations. He departed from veterans who dismissed the state, however, by contending that the loyal merits of Maryland were what should be emphasized when reflecting on the war. Although this writer did not dismiss Maryland for its disloyal element, he still denied Union Marylanders state identification by pointing to the complexity of state loyalty.[13]

Union veterans who chose to highlight loyal Maryland were not doing so because they embraced reconciliation; rather, they remembered loyal Maryland in order to subsume the Confederate legacies of the state. By commemorating Union Maryland and Marylanders, northern veterans denied former Confederates a point of pride in their own memories of the war. In many respects, it was a counterpoint to some of the Lost Cause interpretations of the state covered in the previous chapter. Claiming Maryland became common as Union and Confederate veterans debated the memory of the war. Many Union veterans did not emphasize the loyal element in the state to prove their point; instead, they acknowledged disloyal Marylanders only to dismiss them for their insignificance.

McElroy fit into this latter category when citing a controversy over "Maryland, My Maryland" in the early twentieth century (a controversy that would not end in the near future). He sardonically wrote, "The bark of Baltimore Secessionists proved to be much worse than their bite for comparatively few of them entered the Confederate army and actually fought for the Confederacy." While Maryland secessionists made their voices heard early in the war, according to McElroy, the true character of Maryland was Union through and through.[14]

Not all Union veterans agreed with McElroy. Many outside veterans questioned whether or not Maryland was truly loyal. James S. Anderson reminded his Wisconsin brethren of their experiences in the Old Line State. "We had passed out of Maryland into Pennsylvania, and we were in the land of our friends," he recalled. Anderson implied that Maryland was not the land of friends for the Union soldier. Similarly, Ohio veteran George M. Finch stated that the "authorities at the National Capital watched the development of the rebellion in the neighboring States of Virginia and Maryland with the keenest anxiety." Finch did not simply allude to Maryland's rebellious sentiments but lumped the state together with Virginia, rather than with other border states.[15]

GAR, MOLLUS, and WRC members discussed not simply the loyalty of Maryland during the Civil War but also the current climate in trying to commemorate Union contributions in the state in the present day. An April 17, 1890, column in the *National Tribune* reported on the growing resentment of Maryland Union veterans toward the state legislature "for its failure to recognize the Union soldiers in any way, and especially for its failure to complete the record of those soldiers." The veterans, meeting in Baltimore, gave the Maryland state government "a well-merited rebuke." They noted that the government had "been generous to ex-rebels," especially through its donation of the Confederate Soldiers' Home in Pikesville. The article recounted the sizable contribution made by Marylanders to the Union compared to the much smaller number of soldiers who went south to fight on behalf of the Confederacy and concluded that there "is no excuse for this partiality for rebels." Moreover, the fact that these soldiers left their home state to fight for the Confederate army denied the state government the excuse that they "were in the service of the State." Confederate-sympathizing Marylanders "joined the rebellion simply because they preferred rebellion and slavery to loyalty and freedom." Maryland Union veterans were frustrated that disloyalty was being officially honored by their home state while their loyal deeds were omitted. There was not a Union equivalent to the Confederate Soldiers' Home in Pikesville. This frustration was not simply derived from jealousy or bitterness, although both were certainly present among Union veterans in the state; it was also an outgrowth of their concerns over the larger Civil War identity of their state.[16]

Similarly, Maryland GAR members who gathered in Baltimore to celebrate Memorial Day made sure to distinguish between loyal and disloyal Maryland veterans. One of the main orators of the day began his speech with "Comrades of the Grand Army, Citizen-soldiers of the Republic, Loyalists of Maryland." Such a distinction was an attempt by a Maryland native to affirm Union Marylanders' dual-identities amid growing skepticism about their home state from other Union veterans.[17]

Maryland Union veterans struggled to distinguish themselves from their disloyal neighbors throughout the first half-century following the Civil War. For some, this meant lobbying or criticizing their state government for greater recognition. For others, it meant reminding fellow veterans of the importance of loyal Marylanders. Numerous GAR and WRC members outside the state realized the challenges Union Marylanders faced in their wartime activities as well as in their postwar battles over legacy and memory.

At the 1890 National Encampment of the GAR, the nomination of a Marylander for a junior officer position within the organization sparked a discussion of the difficulty in being loyal in Maryland. Several state delegations put forth names to fill the position of junior vice-commander-in-chief. A Comrade Lang made the formal nomination of Marylander Comrade George W. Creamer to the GAR. In the course of his nomination speech, Lang stated he wished "to present one of Maryland's loyal sons, who resisted the insult that was given to our flag and to the Sixth Massachusetts on the 19th of April, 1861." He knew the hesitancy that many GAR members would exhibit in appointing a Marylander to such a lofty position within the organization and the custom that "territory should be taken into consideration." Given the differing opinions among outside Union veterans of the border state, it is not surprising that the GAR would express insecurity about such a proposition. "I claim, comrades, that there is no territory within these United States that is entitled to greater consideration when honors are to be given than that territory along the border . . . and those states who then bore the brunt of the battle," he assured them. Lang then once again guaranteed that the individual being nominated was "a loyal Marylander."[18]

Most state representatives supported the nomination of Creamer, and in so doing they also reflected on Civil War Maryland and its loyalties. A member of the Texas contingent was a veteran of the Sixth Massachusetts regiment that fought the rebel mob in the streets of Baltimore. In light of his experiences in Baltimore, he said it was his "pleasure to cast a vote for any loyal man in Baltimore or in Maryland." One Vermont man claimed he was in Maryland in 1862 and knew "what it cost to be a loyal citizen of the United States there, and a soldier, meant something more than to face the rebels who were in arms, it meant to be ostracised by many of his own neighbors; it meant to be spat on, and reviled as one who was a sympathizer with the Yankees."[19]

Representatives from border states, in particular, enthusiastically supported the nomination of Creamer and reflected on the difficulties in being Unionist in divided states. During his seconding of the nomination of Creamer, Comrade Walker of West Virginia made clear that he spoke on behalf of "the loyal element of those border states that not only helped fight the battles of the rebellion, but fought the battles at their own firesides and in their homes, standing by the flag of this country." The Delaware contingent informed the GAR members in attendance that the nominated individual from Maryland "not only fought the battles of his country, but he had to fight all the days from '65 to the present, and moreover battled in the Grand Army of the Republic in that state." The spokesman from Kentucky gave the lengthiest speech in the nomination process. He conceded that he only represented "part" of his state because Kentucky was not "united." The bitter divides of the war were still present in his state, and they had "kept up that fight considerably since" the war, the Kentuckian remembered. He wanted to nominate

Comrade Creamer not because Maryland was a border state or because
he himself came from a border state but because he wanted "to abolish
the distinction" between border states and northern states altogether.
"We are all Yankees now," he declared. The representative of Kentucky
rejected a border state identity, but through his speech, he revealed empathy with Creamer based on their shared experiences on the border
of the war. In this respect, abolishing the distinction between border
states and Union states would help protect the dual-identity of veterans
from border states because they would no longer have to defend their
home states. George W. Creamer was subsequently elected as junior vice-
commander-in-chief of the GAR.[20]

The responses to the nomination of a Marylander to a nationally
elected position within the most powerful postbellum fraternal organization sheds light on the status of Maryland during the late nineteenth
century in the minds of Union veterans. For most outside Union veterans, Creamer was worthy of praise by the GAR for his contributions not
simply as a Union veteran but as a Unionist living in a deeply divided
border state. His state's loyalty was questionable at best, but his own personal devotion to the Union was not debatable. The election of Creamer
did not represent a movement toward reconciliation or a slackening of
loyalty to the Union on the part of the GAR; rather, it underscored the
importance of distinguishing the loyal from the disloyal so the glory of
all Union veterans could be preserved. Remembering the devotion of
border state residents bolstered Union memory of the war by showing
that even in the most questionable regions, such as Maryland, individuals worthy of praise emerged despite all odds, namely, in spite of their
identity as Marylanders.

As the veteran from Kentucky demonstrated, however, not all wanted
to qualify the dedication of Union veterans. Some border state veterans
did not want the loyalty of their home state to lessen their Civil War
deeds. "We are all Yankees" was a popular sentiment among those who
were forced to overcome their divided homes and neighborhoods in
carving out their postwar memories. Union Marylanders faced a two-
front war in which they battled to preserve the Unionist memory in general and Maryland Unionist memory in particular. Despite the wishes of
some border state Unionists, the experiences of Maryland WRC members reveal being pro-Union both during and after the war was a challenge to overcome.

Many national WRC conventions that referenced the Department of

Maryland mirrored the sentiment that was present during the nomination of Anna Roberts. At an earlier convention, the chairman of the executive board, Lizabeth A. Turner, presented her board-mandated report of the Maryland Department of the WRC. "We, of the Northern States, hardly realize what it was for the loyal women of Maryland to define their position in 1861, and stand boldly up for the Stars and Stripes and for the men who dared defend them," she remarked. During the report to the national convention, national president of the WRC Florence Barker remembered fondly the efforts of Anna Ella Carroll who, as an advisor to the Lincoln administration, "did more than any other by her writings and personal efforts to hold Maryland true to the Union." At the 1920 convention, the national press correspondent noted that "Maryland is in the hard-to-be-worked belt," but the work the department was doing was "exceedingly gratifying."[21]

Maryland women also reflected on their own experiences and relayed them to WRC members at the national conventions. Marylander Henrietta E. Briscoe informed her peers that in a border state "where southern sentiment is prevalent it takes brave women with loyal hearts to go on with our work." Mary North reported to the national organization: "Away down here, on the eastern shore of Maryland, I am trying to help along your good work and ours by teaching the salute to the flag among the school children." "We cannot rush against the prejudices which still exist and so must work with care to overcome them," Baltimorean and schoolteacher Mary Cadden wrote of lingering Confederate sympathies in the city and the state. North accepted the questionable Civil War identity of Maryland, but hoped that through diligent work, the dual-identity of loyal Marylanders and that of the state more broadly could be preserved.[22]

The WRC, both inside and outside Maryland, viewed Unionism as a challenge in the Old Line State. More northern members offered support to their border state colleagues by noting the intense loyalty and patriotism they displayed not only during the war but also long after its conclusion. Maryland members used the ambiguous legacy of the state to their postwar advantage, not unlike the defendants on trial for conspiring to assassinate Abraham Lincoln in the immediate aftermath of the war. Highlighting the oppression and opposition they faced was meant to prove how incredibly loyal they were to the cause of Union and the WRC. This also allowed loyal Maryland women to retain their dual-identity as native Marylanders and active supporters of the Union. They worked in a climate hostile to Union memory, but they did not let that stop their efforts. Rising from Maryland's divisive past became a point of pride rather than one of shame.

WRC members from other states were, however, not entirely full of praise for the WRC Department of Maryland. A common criticism leveled against the Maryland branch, often by Marylanders themselves, was that the department was too "colored." The racial makeup of the WRC had become a much-discussed topic within the organization by the turn of the century. African American women were active participants within the organization. Many joined out of commitment to the Union veterans, others possibly enlisted in the organization as a way to network and gain information for successful pension collection, and some saw the WRC as a potential launching point for civil rights activism. The national organization reported that the Maryland Department complains of "too many colored Corps that care little for the real purpose for which they are organized." To these women, the African American corps were not focused on the task of commemorating Union soldiers. At the fifteenth national convention in 1897, the Kentucky WRC put forth a petition "for a division of the white and colored members of this Department, and request you to make the colored members a Detached Corps; believing it be for the best good and advancement of this Department." Mary Cadden quickly moved that Maryland be included in the petition given the racial makeup of their department.[23]

Several prominent women within the organization then offered their opinions on the resolution and the merits of segregating the border state departments. A Massachusetts woman, Harriette L. Reed, regretted that "most of the colored women in these Corps have come out of the depths of slavery" and deduced, "We should not expect too much of them." "Ladies it is not Ohio, it is not Massachusetts, it is not Maine that were are considering," she reminded her audience. She concluded her endorsement of the separation, asserting that "they are not yet ready; but I trust the time will soon come when the negro race will come up and take its place among the best people of the land."[24]

Other members challenged the resolution, none more eloquently and forcefully than Julia Mason Layton, an African American from the Department of the Potomac. She started her address by emphatically stating, "I have come this morning, not as a representative of a despised and ignorant race depicted to you this morning, but I come to you as a member of the Woman's Relief Corps." Layton believed that the WRC was "the one organization on the face of the globe that accorded a woman her right, be she black or white." She challenged the notion that ignorance was only present in the black corps by alluding to the fact that there "are ignorant women" in both the white and black corps. In her own corps, she counted nearly thirty women who were high school or college graduates. Layton informed the women gathered that she was married to a black veteran of the Civil War who "fought all the way through" as a part of the U.S. Navy and for his service "is today a helpless man." She went on to inquire why, if the black corps were so deficient, the white women from Kentucky and Maryland did not offer assistance and cited the GAR and WRC motto of "Fraternity, Charity, and Loyalty," implying the real deficiencies within the organization. She ended her speech with a warning: "Now, Mrs. President, I thank you very much, and I want to say this one thing: sisters, be careful what you do with these ignorant people."[25]

Layton's speech put Reed and others who favored the petition quickly on the defensive. Reed answered in a subtly condescending tone that mirrored the sentiment of her initial speech. "It is very evident that our colored sisters are coming forward and are improving their opportunities, as evidenced in the eloquent speech by our sister from the Department of the Potomac," she stated. She insisted that the point she was trying to make was "that the majority of the membership composing the colored Corps are much older women and have not had these advantages." Layton did not let this comment go unanswered and quickly interjected, informing Reed and the rest of the WRC that she "was born a slave in 1859, in the State of Virginia."[26]

Alice Scott of Missouri also made an impassioned plea against segregation on behalf of the colored corps in all border states and the South. She reminded the convention that "the negro men . . . worked for you." They also "worked for the Union" and "were loyal to the Union." In light of this sacrifice, Scott asked the women if they were still willing "to voice the disloyalty" and say to the African American veterans who fought so ardently for the Union "that you are too ignorant to go with us." "The negro has been loyal in every word in every war of America," she concluded before offering a word of caution to "be careful what you are talking about."[27]

Much like Harriette Reed, Marylander Mary Cadden felt personally affronted by those challenging the petition. In reference to her "teaching in a colored school," she stated, "I have even done for some of them what their own color refused to do." She cited her grandfather, a Maryland slaveholder, freeing his slaves when they turned thirty as "personal sacrifice" and represented her family's progressiveness "much in advance of Mr. Lincoln." Cadden responded to those opposed to the petition by arguing that it was they who "raised the 'color line'" and the people "of Maryland have not so done."[28]

To Scott and Layton, as African American women in the WRC, loyalty extended far beyond memory of Civil War border states but was, rather, linked with postbellum conceptions of equality. In this way, their goals diverged from those of the Unionist white women from Maryland. They pointed to the loyalty they demonstrated throughout the war as justification for their equal status within the WRC and American society more broadly. They had their own dual-identity that required defending. As Unionists from Maryland they labored for the Union memory of their state, and as African Americans they fought for equality in the age of Jim Crow. Anna V. Thompkins of the Potomac Department asked the white WRC members in favor of detaching the black corps of Kentucky and Maryland, "How can you forget what my people did for yours,—your boys, your husbands and your sons?" As the WRC was an auxiliary to the GAR, women within the organization often made claims of pride based on the actions of the men from their home states.[29]

Maryland African American GAR members also made their own claims of loyalty. As historian Barbra Gannon states, "black GAR men seemed to have been more likely to own and wear their GAR uniforms." She also notes that the entire membership of the black GAR Charles Sumner Post located in Chestertown, Maryland, owned GAR uniforms. Gannon concludes, "Given the poverty of black veterans, purchasing a uniform required great sacrifice and indicated their devotion to the GAR." To African American GAR members from Maryland, the necessity of the sacrifice was even greater. Not only did they want to show their devotion to the GAR as individual African American Union veterans, they also wanted to maintain their dual-identity by demonstrating their devotion as Union veterans who mustered into service from Maryland.[30]

These claims of pride struggled against a climate of racial tension in Maryland. In 1884, the Maryland General Assembly approved legislation that banned "marriages between white persons and persons of negro descent." Ten years prior to the controversy, African American Baltimoreans were making similar pleas for integration, this time for schools. The *Cleveland Gazette* commented on the conditions of African American schools by using a Baltimore-area newspaper report. The article stated that the schools were "the poorest and most miserable" and that if the teachers at these schools were not white "they wouldn't give the colored children any walls; just put up a tent, or some temporary structure of the kind." Baltimore African Americans argued, "Nothing but mixed schools will assure us equal advantages with the whites in both learning and accommodation; then, the teachers would be of the best and the buildings the same." The debates over the integration of the Maryland Department came just one year after the U.S. Supreme Court's ruling of separate but equal in *Plessy v. Ferguson* (1896). Challenging segregation and arguing for integration was not new to African American Marylanders. The debate over the direction of the WRC was but one moment in a much longer civil rights struggle.[31]

African American women recounted the devotion of Union African American men in their quest for equality not just socially but also in memory. The history of the Maryland WRC points to the larger significance of Civil War memory for many living in the unresolved aftermath of the conflict. Commemorating and remembering was not just about pride but also had larger tangible effects. If African American women could affirm their contributions and the contributions of their husbands, they could extend the argument of equal standing beyond mere commemoration. Their fight to remain attached to the main regional divisions was critical fifty years after the Civil War. As chapter 5 demonstrates, the fight for racial equality and Civil War memory often went hand in hand, particularly for Marylanders.

Past national WRC president and current executive board member Annie Wittenmyer relayed the advice of a former junior vice president. "Don't disturb the Department of Kentucky. They would manage; and also that Maryland be allowed to go on as she has," she stated. Wittenmyer also noted that in Pennsylvania "we elect a colored woman and she serves and there is no fuss about it" and that the "best commander in one of the Posts there is a colored man." She then moved that the issue of detaching the black corps of Kentucky and Maryland be tabled. Several members seconded the motion and it was voted on and carried. The black corps of Kentucky separated later while the Maryland black corps most likely remained attached to their regional branches.[32]

The testimony of WRC members Layton and Scott reveals an important distinction for those living in or near the border region. They fought ardently against further segregating the WRC by detaching the black Kentucky and Maryland units. This is a departure from other branches of the WRC outside the boundaries of border states. Segregation through detachment not only meant a step in the wrong direction socially; it also meant a subordination of their own memories and legacies of the Civil War. Similar to Maryland veterans who wanted equal claims to memory at

Antietam and Gettysburg, African American WRC members in the state wanted equal claims but with a different long-term goal. Additionally, the fight to remain integrated by the WRC mirrored the efforts of African Americans within the Maryland GAR. Gannon notes that the all-black John Logan Post in Maryland "demanded by their actions that 'Colored Troops' be integrated into the larger history of the Civil War." Although they accepted their "all-black associations," they still longed for an integrated memory of the war much like their female counterparts.[33]

Union veterans and citizens did not reach a consensus during the late nineteenth and early twentieth centuries regarding Civil War Maryland or its loyalty. Some chose to highlight the devotion of the state to the righteous cause of Union while others refused to forget the disloyal rebels who lived in the Old Line State. Union-sympathizing Marylanders struggled to overcome their divided state's past in order to commemorate their efforts alongside their comrades. Both sides of the Maryland debate used the state's loyalty in the larger struggle over reconciliation. Characterizations of Maryland as Union helped bolster the righteous cause of the war while simultaneously taking a point of pride away from advocates of postwar Confederate identity. Conversely, dismissing the state as Confederate or singling out disloyal Marylanders ensured due credit was reserved for the truly loyal, not the ambiguously or dividedly loyal. Both sides of the debate, therefore, contributed to arguments against reconciliation, even though they ran counter to each other on the surface. The debate also called into question Union Marylanders' dual-identity. Postbellum Unionists were not the only ones, however, who had strong opinions on Maryland. Confederate veterans and the United Daughters of the Confederacy reflected deliberately on Maryland's place in the narrative of the Civil War.

Confederate Memories

The first issue of the *Confederate Veteran* magazine appeared in 1893, and the magazine ran continuously until 1932. It served, represented, and promoted the voices of various postwar Confederate organizations, including the United Confederate Veterans, the United Daughters of the Confederacy, the Confederate Southern Memorial Association, and the Sons of Confederate Veterans. Through the issues of the magazine, these organizations attempted to not only promote their own Civil War memories but also counter northern interpretations of the war. Additionally, the magazine provided opportunities to discuss and debate the place of particular states in the legacies of the conflict, namely, deeply divided Maryland.[34]

The majority of the essays in the *Confederate Veteran* as well as the speeches and reports of the Maryland division of the UDC focused on the positive contribution Marylanders made to the Confederacy and its cause. These reflections appreciated the sacrifice Confederate Marylanders made in spite of the Unionist status of the state. They did not shy away from remembering the "tyranny" of northern policies toward the border state and the Unionist sentiment within the state. In many ways, praising Confederate Maryland and regretting Union Maryland bolstered the growing ideology of the Lost Cause by confirming the arguments put forth in the early Confederate histories of the late 1860s. Nevertheless, during the late nineteenth and early twentieth centuries, the ability of the truly heroic citizens of the state to rise above and beyond Unionist impulses bolstered Confederate Maryland while diminishing the legacy of the rest of the state. Through this process, Confederate Marylanders maintained their dual-identity, but their status as Confederate veterans was uplifted while their Maryland ties were subsumed.

Native Baltimorean and New York attorney H. Snowden Marshall touched briefly but pointedly on Civil War Maryland at the dedication of Confederate Memorial Hall in Richmond, Virginia, in 1921. The hall was known as the "Battle Abbey of the South" and designed to maintain archives and a portrait collection donated by the R. E. Lee Camp of the United Confederate Veterans. Marshall was one of the event's featured speakers, and in his speech he covered a variety of Civil War topics. During the course of his address, he recounted the roles of various states in the conflict, including two border states. "Maryland and Missouri were overrun before state action could be taken," he said. He continued by stating that the two states "have nothing to be ashamed of" because the "best people of each of these states found their way to spend their lives and fortunes in the great cause in which their people were engaged." Marshall's remarks were some of many that characterized Maryland and its citizens in this way.[35]

Numerous outside veterans and essayists commended the Maryland Confederate soldiers who cast their lot with the South and the Confederacy. The *Confederate Veteran* reported favorably on an 1894 Confederate Memorial Day service in Maryland. "Maryland sent 20,000 of her best and bravest, the scions of families representing her gracious aristocracy, and her equally honorable yeomanry, into the armies of the Confederacy," the article stated. The author went on to write, "The history of the war abounds in honorable mention of the Maryland 'rebels'" and the "loyalty and patriotism of the 'southern sympathizers' of this prostrate border state of 1861 cannot be questioned now." Similarly, Jefferson Davis wrote in an 1889 letter to Captain William L. Ritter, a veteran of the Third Maryland Artillery, that "Maryland though not a member of the Confederacy, sent many of her best sons to support the cause of State rights, and they contributed very greatly to give the Confederate flag its immortality." "The blood of the old Maryland Line might well be relied upon to tell in a forlorn hope," he wrote. Virginian governor and Civil War major John W. Daniel also offered a tepid endorsement of those Marylanders who made their way south during a Confederate veteran reunion held in Richmond. He stated, "They were not many, but they were much, these men of Maryland." Davis and Daniel remembered fondly the Marylanders who joined them in their cause. In their eyes, those who served nobly on behalf of the Confederacy deserved to be honored in the postbellum period alongside other Confederate veterans.[36]

Many former Confederates outside the state viewed Maryland through the same lens as Davis and Daniel but with a slightly different focus. Rather than simply acknowledging the wartime actions of the state's soldiers, they emphasized the sacrifice Confederate Marylanders offered in their southward-leaning loyalty and devotion. At a 1909 Baltimore celebration of Robert E. Lee's birthday, Alabama congressman William Richardson spoke on behalf of the most southern states and their views of Civil War Maryland. The *Confederate Veteran* reported that Richardson contended that "the men in the Far South regarded the Maryland Confederate soldiers as the greater heroes." "The Maryland man had at his door our distinguished friends, the Yankees; and when they wanted to get in a Confederate regiment, they almost had to go through the woods to do it," he said. Richardson admitted that "there was no division in the Far South" but the divisions within Maryland made their sacrifice to the Confederate cause all the more inspiring and heroic. This group of outside veterans accepted the dual-identity of Marylanders because their status as Old Liners strengthened their Confederate bond and legacy.[37]

Maryland veterans themselves also embodied this concept of Maryland sacrifice in their postwar reminisces. Veterans of the First Maryland Regiment (CSA) offered their regimental flag to Jane Claudia Saunders Johnson, the wife of Maryland general Bradley T. Johnson. The Johnsons were paramount in shaping the Confederate heritage and legacies of

Maryland. Bradley Johnson, a Maryland native, was a general during the Civil War and commanded the First Maryland Infantry (CSA). After the war, he was paramount in promoting a Confederate identity for Maryland. He organized Confederate veterans in Maryland, was crucial in the dedication of the first Confederate regimental monument at Gettysburg, and published several books and delivered countless speeches on Civil War topics, including Confederate Maryland. In their letter to Jane Johnson, the regiment informed her that under the flag "Maryland's exiled sons have fought and bled in a holy cause." Many Maryland Confederate veterans acknowledged and accepted the Union sentiment of their home state but contrasted it to their own devotion. On the surface, this may seem like an attempt of Maryland Confederates to shed their dual-identity and simply enter the postwar Confederate community as fellow Confederates. This strategy, however, demonstrated pride on the part of Confederate Marylanders in their state identity because it allowed them to acknowledge the turmoil of their state but underscore their devotion. In this respect, Confederate Marylanders were martyrs for the Confederacy because they gave up their homes to fight on behalf of secession.[38]

Baltimorean-born Randolph McKim made a similar argument of Marylanders' sacrifice but was more empathetic toward the state as a whole. During a reunion speech, he laid out the internal political divisions that pervaded Maryland, and he believed the state "would have seceded if allowed to follow its inclination." He went on to argue that "the condition of the Maryland soldier was particularly pathetic, for practically when he cast his fortunes with the South he erected a wall bristling with camps and armed men between himself, his home and his kindred." McKim also emphasized the incomparable sacrifice of Maryland soldiers but he also made a subtle endorsement of his own state's loyalty by arguing that it was forced into the Union fold and that its inability to secede was the result of those outside the border state.[39]

Confederate general Isaac Trimble, a native Virginian who lived in Baltimore following the war, echoed this sentiment in an 1883 speech before the Society of the Army and Navy of the Confederate States in Maryland. He recalled the words of Robert E. Lee, who told him on multiple occasions that the men from Maryland were "unrivaled soldiers." Trimble also offered his own thoughts on the First Confederate Maryland in which he said the men of the regiment "were the dandies of the army, better dressed, better shod, better drilled, and in gayer spirits than any in the whole army, and never one deserter." Throughout his address,

Trimble walked a fine line between praising the Old Line's Confederate soldiers and not dealing directly with the overall Civil War loyalties of the state.[40]

A significant number of outside Confederate veterans reflected on the Maryland citizenry, its loyalty, and its interactions with southern military forces. A veteran from South Carolina penned an essay that detailed his experiences under Lee in 1862. He recalled that they "entered Maryland with grand éclat, amid flying banners, the playing of the bands, and the huzzas of an enthusiastic crowd of sympathizers in beautiful Frederick City." Confederate veterans under Lee often reflected on their experiences in particular Maryland towns. "Hagerstown was strongly Union in sentiment, so all along the streets could be heard female voices singing Northern war songs," one wrote. The women changed their tune, he recalled, when they caught a glimpse of General Lee. "The female population nearly went wild over him. All along the street through which he passed there was a perfect wringing of hands with these exclamations, 'O what a grand man he is!' and 'Don't you wish he was ours?'" This veteran did not so much give credit to the Maryland population as he remarked condescendingly on the inability of northern women to escape the charm of Confederate leadership, in particular Robert E. Lee. An Arkansas man remembered Hagerstown differently. Although he believed the town's sympathy to be "fifty-fifty," the "hospitality of the people of Hagerstown was equal to that of Virginia, and the ladies of Virginia were the most hospitable on earth, so we did not have to beg them for bread; if they had anything to eat, they gave it freely." One Maryland veteran wrote that when he returned home to Maryland before the war, he "found a number of my old companions, with sympathies like my own, who were as enthusiastic to enter the Confederate army as myself."[41]

Marylander Bradley Johnson took this positive interpretation further when he explained the righteousness of the his state's Confederate soldiers and sympathizers in a speech delivered in front of the Confederate Association of St. Mary's County, Maryland. "I want posterity to consider us as sound-headed as well as warm-hearted, and I want them to understand that our source in leaving our native State was dictated by reason as well as by enthusiasm," he remarked. After noting that the failure of the Confederacy "was no fault of ours" and defending the merits of the institution of slavery, Johnson outlined the heroism of his Old Line comrades. He emphasized the fact that they "never ceased to maintain a Maryland organization under a Maryland flag in the army of the Confederate States" as well as the fact that they "succeeded in writing the name of the State on the brightest pages of American history." Subsequently, he regretted that all of these contributions were ignored "by the powers that have controlled Maryland" throughout the postwar era. Johnson had spent and would continue to spend a significant portion of the rest of his life attempting to rectify this omission. Johnson, more than any other, argued ardently on behalf of Confederate Marylanders' dual-identity.[42]

Not all outside Confederates agreed with Johnson's enthusiastic endorsement of his home state. In fact, many questioned Maryland's devotion to the Confederacy, and some dismissed its contributions to the southern cause entirely. Ex-Confederates criticized Maryland in different ways, with some analyzing the state as a whole and others focused on individuals or groups operating within Maryland's borders and on behalf of the state. To this group of veterans, Maryland did not deserve an equal place in Confederate memory because it did not contribute equally when compared to other more southern states. Honoring Confederate Maryland would mar their own identity as true Confederates because those who were less worthy were receiving undeserved admiration.

While many outside veterans reminisced favorably about their experiences in the Old Line State, others viewed Maryland through the lens of more negative experiences they had while in the border state. Veteran of Hood's Texas Brigade and postwar writer Joseph Benjamin Polley recalled a chilling reception in Maryland. After traversing the cold Potomac waters and entering Maryland, Polley wrote, "The coldness of the water, however, was more than equaled by the frigidity of the welcome extended." He said that the band's playing of "Maryland, My Maryland" did not help soften the response of the Maryland citizenry. "No arms opened to receive, no fires blazed to warm, and no feast waited to feed us, as wet, shivering, and hungry, we stepped out of the water and set our feet on Maryland's soil," he wrote. Polley did not go on to castigate the state for its cold welcome, but the implications of his narrative left little doubt in any reader's mind of his opinion of the state. Those who had negative experiences attributed their memories of the state not to its veterans, but to its citizens and its home front. This represented yet another obstacle Confederate veterans from Maryland had to confront. They not only had to defend their honor as Confederate soldiers. If they were going to redeem their state, they also had to defend Maryland's Civil War home front.[43]

Many Confederate postwar writers and commentators who lived throughout the South spoke in more general and less personal terms of Maryland, but they still managed to subtly condemn the loyalty of the state, specifically by noting its population's resistance to the secession movement. This also served as a way of severing Maryland from Confederate memories and commemoration. Carolina teacher Kate De Rossett Meares authored a piece titled "Opposition to Secession in the South." In it, she traced anti-secession impulses throughout southern states, but she saves her most blunt analysis for the border states. She believed "the really valiant fight against secession" occurred within the border states and agreed with the common perception that the citizens within the border states "shrank from a dissolution of the Union with real horror." In particular, "Maryland took no steps at all toward secession." Former Confederate officer and U.S. Court of Claims judge Charles B. Howry came to a similar conclusion on the population's views toward secession. "The three border States of Maryland, Kentucky, and Missouri had within their confines a largely preponderating number of people who were averse to the secession movement then going on," he deduced.[44]

Even those outside Maryland who were not as explicit in their condemnation of the state still managed to clearly express their unfavorable views of Civil War Maryland. One column reprinted in the *Confederate Veteran* traced the inherent advantages the North had over the South and devoted several lines to comparisons of population numbers. Within these lines, the author enumerated the contributions the border states made to the respective sides of the conflict. He recorded that "from the border Southern States and communities of Missouri, Kentucky, East Tennessee, West Virginia, Maryland, and Delaware she [the North] got more men and supplies for her armies than the Confederacy got for hers." While not an overly aggressive denunciation of the border states, the line on the contributions they made to the North implies that their Unionist impulses played a role in the victory of the Union and the defeat of the Confederacy.[45]

Some postwar Confederates reinforced the concept of Maryland as a Union-leaning, northern state, but they reflected more specifically on why this was the case and on the role certain individuals and institutions played in keeping Maryland out of the Confederacy. Specifically, these southerners placed the blame on the Maryland governor and the oppressive policies of the federal government. A frequent contributor to the *Confederate Veteran* during the first decades of the twentieth century, Reverend James H. M'Neilly of Nashville, noted, "The border States of Maryland and Delaware were in the grasp of Federal power." M'Neilly made sure to note this unfortunate reality in his recounting of the various opinions of how to proceed during the early stages of war, specifically in his discussion of the hesitancy on the part of the border states.[46]

Southerners alone did not constitute the entire category of postwar writers who documented the obstacles that impeded Maryland's secession. English writer Percy Greg wrote, "Gov. Hicks, of Maryland, refused to convoke the Legislature or appeal to the people" and "in so doing he betrayed his trust." Greg concluded that it was not up to Governor Hicks "to decide the course of Maryland, but to obey her will as it should be declared by the sovereign people." Through this phrasing, he implied that the true character and "will" of Maryland longed to join the Confederacy, but that because of the indecisiveness and the conniving of Hicks, the state could not follow the wishes of the majority citizenry.[47]

Others outside the state placed Maryland a rung below other Confederate states by taking its troublesome Civil War history into account. In this way of approaching the memory of Maryland, outsiders inferred that the state deserved recognition but not equal recognition. The dual-identity of Confederate Marylanders was accepted but not necessarily for the benefit of Old Line Confederate veterans. Outside veterans, and even some inside the state, would use Confederate Maryland veterans' dual-identity as justification for placing the border state's soldiers in a lower position of remembrance.

Approbation for Maryland often had a condescending and patronizing tone. Hagerstown, Maryland, native Reverend W. D. Barger recounted the events at the Battle of Gettysburg, and during his analysis he noted, "The little State of Maryland had sent some twenty thousand men to the ranks of the Virginia Army." Although he himself was a Marylander, Barger realized the modest size of the state. This did not overtly detract from Maryland's Confederate legacy, but instead he tried to make the case that proportionally, the border state devoted a great deal to the Confederacy. While emphasizing and praising Confederate Marylanders, Barger knocked Maryland down a few pegs in popular Civil War memory.[48]

Some Confederate Marylanders hoped that through their postwar institutions and affiliations they could demonstrate their true loyalty and identity. William H. Pope, superintendent of the much-lauded Maryland Line Confederate Soldiers' Home in Pikesville, made clear to his comrades in the first issue of the *Confederate Veteran* that fraternization between Union and Confederate Marylanders was not a common occurrence. He wrote, "We have never mixed in any manner with the other side—have not joint reunions, no joint banquets, no decoration or memorial days in common." To Pope and many other Confederate Marylanders, resisting reconciliation was a point of pride and demonstrated their continued loyalty to the Confederacy. Pope wanted to put to rest any notion of appeasement on the part of Confederate Marylanders because he realized that many former Confederates would be suspicious of such actions coming from veterans who lived next to such a large Unionist population. "In fact, we do not mix, we go our way and they go theirs, and we find we gain more respect by so doing," he continued. He then attempted to assert the true loyalty of the Old Line State's Confederates, stating, "We do not belong to that class of Confederates that believed they were right. We *knew* we were right in 1861, we *knew* we were right when the war closed, and we *know* today that we were right." By affirming the righteousness of the Confederacy, Pope hoped to solidify his state's positive contribution in southern memory.[49]

The Confederate Soldiers' Home in Pikesville that Pope served as superintendent was a point of pride in and of itself for the state's southern sympathizers. The home was featured in numerous issues of the *Confederate Veteran*, and veterans often remarked that it was among the best veteran homes in the United States. When the Association of the Maryland Line, a veteran organization of Maryland Confederate veterans, honored Mrs. Bradley Johnson as an honorary member of the organization, the article that covered the story featured photographs of the Confederate Soldiers' Home in Pikesville as a symbol of Confederate Maryland devotion. The home became a symbol of Maryland Confederate identity as much as any monument the state could erect.[50]

To some former Maryland Confederates, city monuments, protests, and veterans' homes were not enough to salvage Maryland's Civil War memory. Reflecting on a visit to the home in Pikesville, Baltimore librarian Wilbur F. Coyle appreciated the splendor of the home but stated, "In some way Maryland has let slip the credit that should be hers for the prominent part that many of her sons played in the great conflict on the side of the South." He acknowledged the existence of Confederate Marylanders on "the pages of history" but also understood that "everybody does not read history." "It takes such evidence as one sees at the Home to make an everlasting impression," he wrote. Coyle believed that the full devotion could not be understood through words but through personal experiences within Maryland. This obstacle to recognition, Coyle believed, hindered Maryland in occupying an equal and shared place in southern heritage.[51]

The organization that was perhaps the most active in commemorating the deeds and heroics of the Confederacy during the late nineteenth and early twentieth centuries was the United Daughters of the Confederacy. The UDC engaged in various commemorative efforts, including monument building, fundraising, school content monitoring, essay contests, and annual gatherings. The UDC was also active and engaged in the debates of Civil War Maryland and efforts to situate Maryland within the war's broader context and history. Although the Maryland UDC claimed only a few posts and fewer than one thousand members by 1907, members of the Maryland UDC labored intensely on behalf of their home state's identity and memory.[52]

Maryland women reminded their colleagues of the Old Line State soldiers' sacrifice. At the 1916 national UDC convention, Maryland UDC president Ellen Emmerich Mears made a bold claim on behalf of Maryland Confederate soldiers. "Greater, far greater, were the sacrifices made by the men of Maryland than by those in the States that seceded from the Union," she said. She contended that being a Confederate soldier from Maryland "meant, in addition to hardship and danger, exile from home and kindred." Mears noted the divisions within Maryland and understood why there was "no star in the Confederate flag to represent Maryland," but she did not let that undermine the devotion of her state's soldiers in remembering them. Mears's claim of "greater" sacrifice is made all the more striking when we realize that she was addressing a group of mostly southern women whose two-part driving purpose was to promote the memorialization of the Confederacy and to promote the legacies of their native states. Such bold steps were deemed necessary by Marylanders operating in the commemorative landscape of the postbellum period, for they had to overcome their divided history and the conceptions of many in the South in order to maintain their dual-identity as Confederate Marylanders. In this same context, the Maryland women of the UDC, in some ways, challenged the simplicity of the feminization of their home state. While facing oppression during the war, Maryland contributed to the Confederate war effort in heroic and incomparable ways. The choice of Maryland UDC members to highlight this demonstrates resistance to other voices from the outside concerning their own state's Civil War memory.[53]

Maryland UDC members also sought to justify their position and that of their state by citing the federal policies they faced. In a prize-winning essay titled "The Services of the Women of Maryland to the Confederate States," Laura Lee Davidson of the Baltimore UDC attempted to explain why the Confederate women of Maryland had "little written history" when they "suffered more bravely or labored more indefatigably for the cause in which they believed with all their souls and loved with all their hearts." The reason for this oversight was simple, in Davidson's estimation. "Maryland was under Federal control during the whole term of the war, and all expression of sympathy for the South was sternly repressed," she wrote. With the "iron heel" of the North pressed firmly on the state, "the work of the Confederate women of Maryland was perforce done in secret." The remainder of the essay detailed the oppressive federal policies Maryland faced and the previously undocumented heroics of Confederate Maryland women. In concluding her piece, Davidson wrote that "the women of Maryland sent their sons, their husbands, and their lovers to die for the Confederacy" because they "went to the aid of a free people fighting for the right to govern themselves in safety and in honor."[54]

Many members of the Maryland UDC worked to ensure that their more southern colleagues did not forget the sacrifice of Maryland women. Louise Wright, president of the Baltimore chapter of the UDC, welcomed her fellow Daughters to Baltimore for the fourth annual meeting of the national organization in 1897. In her opening speech, Wright briefly noted "the bravest knights" from Maryland in their support of the Confederacy but quickly turned to the hardships faced by the women left behind. "In the record of the suffering of our women during those awful years of the war, no words can adequately tell what the women of Maryland endured," she said. The conclusion that Wright drew from the endurance and perseverance these women displayed was that "the love which yielded up such an awful sacrifice" was remarkably strong and "the sympathy with a cause" must have been incomparably "deep." In the opening lines of her welcome to the entire UDC, Wright made a case for the Confederate devotion of Maryland. Baltimore as the site of the national annual meeting represented a rare opportunity to enshrine Maryland's place within Confederate canon in a direct and clear fashion.[55]

In a report by the national UDC on the creation of a museum in the Confederate White House in Richmond, one woman documented that "every Confederate state, also Kentucky and Maryland," aided in the establishment of the museum. Therefore, the report of the UDC fell in line with the prevalent pattern of applauding Maryland's participation but characterizing the state separately from the true, most loyal Confederate states. The process of ranking and evaluating Maryland's postwar memory-making and commemorative efforts was not confined to this one instance.[56]

In line with the report of the UDC on Maryland's role in the Confederate museum, many UDC members evaluated the space Maryland occupied in postbellum commemoration activities. Marylanders themselves were also involved in this process, and they tried to carve out a space in the growing Confederate legacy for their home state. Specifically, the Maryland UDC was active in the commemoration of the border state and promoting its wartime contribution and sacrifice. The Maryland UDC faced opposition from those who challenged the Confederate loyalty of the state.

The women of the Maryland UDC were constantly reporting and having their activities reported to the *Confederate Veteran*. Such reports offered Maryland Confederate women the opportunity to share their continued and undying loyalty to the rest of the South. Early Maryland UDC reports included the reburial of Maryland Confederate dead, Confederate charity fundraising, and Confederate monuments. The front page of the October 1902 issue was devoted to the Maryland UDC's monument to the defeat of the Confederacy and the South in Baltimore. In 1909, the Maryland UDC made plans to erect a Confederate monument on the Monocacy battlefield; five years later, on the fiftieth anniversary of the battle, they dedicated a small monument "in the memory of the Southern soldiers who fell in the battle fought July 9, 1864 which resulted in a Confederate victory." A few years later, in 1918, the state dedicated a monument in Baltimore to Confederate women specifically. On one side the inscription read "To the Confederate Women of Maryland, 1861–1865. The Brave at Home" and on the other side,

> In difficulty and danger,
> Regardless of self,
> They fed the hungry,
> They clothed the needy,
> They nursed the wounded,
> They comforted the dying.[57]

Most frequently, however, Maryland Confederate women reported their activities and efforts directly to the national UDC during the annual meeting. At the 1907 meeting, Maryland UDC president Cordelia Powell Odenheimer reported with pride on the activities of the Maryland branch. She noted that there was a "steady progress and liberal dispensing of relief" along with ceremonies bestowing "Crosses of Honor" and "indefatigable efforts made to establish correct histories." After highlighting the year-long efforts of various local branches, Odenheimer made

FIGURE 4.1. Spirit of the Confederacy Monument, Baltimore, Maryland
(courtesy of the Library of Congress).

special mention of the unveiling of a portrait of "Maryland, My Maryland" author James Ryder Randall in the Old Senate Chamber where
the Continental Congress convened in late 1783 through 1784. As the
portrait was unveiled, "verses of Maryland, My Maryland, were sung softly
as a requiem of Maryland's Confederate poet." By emphasizing the dedication of a portrait of a Maryland Confederate sympathizer within the
walls of an important state building, Odenheimer hoped to demonstrate
the inroads the Maryland UDC was making in formally solidifying the
Old Line State's southern identity.[58]

Ten years later, Maryland UDC president Helen Beauregard Parr reported on a similar commemorative effort made on the part of the Baltimore UDC. "For many years we have wished to place a tablet in memory
of Mrs. Mary E. Surratt, of Maryland, an innocent woman who was tried
and condemned by the Federal Government," the Baltimore chapter
president wrote. She continued by satisfyingly acknowledging that within
the past year the goal was completed "and the beautiful tablet of golden
bronze, the work of Maxwell Miller, a young artist of Baltimore, is hanging

in the Maryland Room in Richmond." Parr mirrored the technique employed by Odenheimer, now president of the national body, of making a deliberate point to underscore commemoration of Confederate-minded Marylanders in more formal venues and organizations. Entrenching a Confederate Maryland identity in government buildings and museums represented a significant victory for UDC women operating within the confines of a border state. Furthermore, commemorating an individual who was convicted of conspiracy by a U.S. military tribunal underscored the effort Confederate Marylanders exerted and the lengths they were willing to go to retain their dual-identity.[59]

Promoting a Confederate Maryland was only one side of what the state's UDC branch was doing to affect Civil War memory. The Maryland UDC devoted a substantial amount of its time and effort to challenging northern encroachments through commemorative or educational means to Confederate legacies. In 1911, for example, the state division as well as the Baltimore branch offered a formal protest and resolution challenging the use of Henry W. Elson's *History of the United States of America* in schools and colleges throughout the United States with particular attention to the South. The resolution asserted that Elson's textbook contained "gross calumnies against the South and her institutions and misrepresentations of the causes that led to the War between the States" and through these misrepresentations the honor of southerners' parents was "grossly impugned." In response to this wrong, the Maryland division resolved to register "an indignant protest in the name of truth and justice against the use of Elson's so-called history in any of the schools, colleges, and universities of our land." The Maryland UDC called on Confederate veterans to aid in their cause so that "the youth of the country no longer be taught as facts untruths which are slanders on the fair fame of the South, her institutions, and her people."[60]

President Odenheimer also weighed in on the issue. "I have read paragraphs taken from Elson's history which made my blood boil," she wrote. She cited the fact that Elson referred to the Civil War as "The Slaveholders' War" and his "falsified" portrayal of the relationship between southerners and slaves "in a language unfit for print." After making clear she would attempt to challenge the text's use in schools and colleges across the United States, she detailed the direction school textbook selection should take. "It is high time that no history should be admitted into any school of the South until every sentence and word has been carefully scrutinized by competent and faithful Southern men," Odenheimer wrote.[61]

By putting itself on the frontlines of battles over memory and legacy, the Maryland UDC showed its devotion and loyalty to the Confederacy. The Maryland UDC joined other state divisions in protesting the awarding of an essay prize to a Minnesotan girl for a paper on Robert E. Lee. The Maryland branch took issue with her characterization of Lee as a traitor and his subordinate officers and other southerners as ignorant. It was clear from the written protest that the girl's status as a citizen of the North was a strike against her qualifications for writing the essay. "A Northern schoolgirl writing an essay on the South during the War between the States, with the limited knowledge necessarily hers . . . could hardly be expected to write with better knowledge of her subject or to succeed in her pose as an expert military critic of General Lee's campaigns or of the skill and competency of his generals!" the Maryland UDC exclaimed. The state UDC aligned with other southern states to defend their leader and their legacy. The Maryland UDC exerted similar opposition efforts throughout the early twentieth century. For example, the Maryland Daughters helped prevent prints of "St. Gauden's equestrian statue of General Sherman" from "being placed in public schools in Baltimore." Combating northern memory of the war in their own backyard highlighted their persistent devotion. Some of the most ardent challenges made in support of Confederate Marylanders came, however, in response to the proposed exclusion of three border states from an important Confederate memorial.[62]

Plans to erect a monument to Jefferson Davis in Richmond, Virginia, commenced shortly after his death in December 1889. At a mass meeting in late December of that year, those in attendance resolved to organize an association that would be charged with the task of establishing a monument to the late Confederate president. The Jefferson Davis Monument Association was charted in January 1890. The organization secured the right to bury Davis in Richmond, and by 1892 they had the support of the United Confederate Veterans in erecting a monument to Davis in Richmond. In 1895, the association contacted the UDC in order to enlist its help in raising funds and the planning process. Four years later the United Confederate Veterans agreed to hand over the process to the UDC completely, and in 1901 the Jefferson Davis Monument Association, UDC took over the operation. The new directors of the organization decided to hold a bazaar in the spring of 1903 in order to raise funds for the project. It is more than likely that the attention that the bazaar brought to the proposed monument exposed J. Randolph Smith of North Carolina to the intended design of the structure.[63]

In an essay titled "Eleven Columns for Davis Memorial," Smith unequivocally expressed his opinions on who should be honored in the
memorial and who should not. The plan for the monument was to have
thirteen columns that surrounded the central monument to Davis and
the Confederacy. The thirteen columns would represent the eleven states
that seceded and the two border states that sent representatives to the
Confederate Congress, Missouri and Kentucky. Smith took exception with
the proposed inclusion of the two border states in the monument to the
leader of the Confederacy. "Think of what the President of the Confederacy would say to having these States honored equally with his own eleven
Confederate States!" he wrote. He asserted that "no State could serve the
Confederacy and the Federal government, and Kentucky and Missouri
had Federal Governors." He continued by noting that Kentucky and Missouri had representation in the U.S. Congress and the protection of the
federal government throughout the duration of the conflict. Smith then
added Maryland to the list of states that sent "some of the bravest men"
to the Confederacy but should not be included in the monument. He implored his fellow Confederates to shun these three states. He wrote, "Let
us erect no columns to these States, stepsisters to the Confederacy . . . let
no State be represented in it that did not give its *all* to the Confederacy,
and certainly let no States that by government and arms fought against
us and put indignities upon our President be represented."[64]

Confederate veterans and UDC members from these three states certainly did not approve of the label "stepsisters to the Confederacy," nor
were they willing to accept their omission from the Jefferson Davis Monument. A Missouri UDC member responded in the subsequent volume
of the *Confederate Veteran* with her own rebuttal as well as objections she
compiled from like-minded individuals. She chastised Smith's views on
the monument in her own piece "They Want More than Eleven Columns." "For shame! He should not express such sentiments. Only eleven
columns! No! no! a thousand times no!" she retorted. The Missourian
advised Smith "to read up on the history of Kentucky and Missouri previous to and during our great war and see how Gov. Magoffin positively refused men and ammunition to subjugate her Southern sister states—not
stepsister—when Lincoln called for 75,000 men." Sam Box, a resident of
Indiana, claimed Smith was "living in delusion" and made sure to include
Maryland in his defense. He believed Smith's plan "would do a great injustice to thousands of good, patriotic citizens and soldiers in Maryland,
Kentucky, and Missouri, whose loyal devotion to the South was never
questioned and who have stood the test of time." While Marylanders

FIGURE 4.2. Jefferson Davis Monument, Richmond, Virginia
(courtesy of the Library of Congress).

often struggled for their own state identity, border states often faced similar obstacles and defended their contributions collectively.[65]

The Jefferson Davis Monument was dedicated on June 7, 1907, in front of a large crowd. Smith's vision for the monument was unrealized as thirteen columns surrounded the central component. The columns represented the eleven states that seceded as well as Kentucky and Missouri, which set up Confederate governments and contributed congressional representatives to the Confederacy. Although Maryland was not represented in one of the columns, the monument included fourteen bronze seals that surrounded the monument representing the eleven states that seceded and the three border states—Kentucky, Missouri, and Maryland—that mustered in regiments in support of the Confederate military. Although Maryland received recognition in the monument, it was not equivalent to that of other Confederate states or even other border states. Second-class status in commemorative enterprises was not new for Marylanders in 1907 and contributed to the forcefulness with which they promoted Confederate legacies and Confederate identities for their home state.[66]

Periodicals from both Union and Confederate veterans served as a medium to analyze, praise, or condemn Civil War Maryland. WRC and UDC meetings gave Maryland women a platform to make their cases for their state. Monuments made public and permanent legacies that Marylanders believed needed to be remembered. All of these mediums were central in identity formation both within and outside the state. Marylanders were forced to defend their dual-identity, especially when linking their efforts to the greater community of veterans and women who supported the same causes. Those outside the state did not accept Marylanders' self-proclaimed identities at face value. As the following chapter demonstrates, sectional and state identities were not important for legacy alone. Debates over identity often reflected society at large and played an important role in social change.

CHAPTER 5

Maryland, My Maryland

The Old Line State's Struggle for Civil Rights and Civil War Memory

Jack L. Levin expressed his dire concern over the education of Maryland youth in a 1993 article featured in the *Baltimore Sun*. Levin was deeply troubled with what he heard as he walked by an elementary school class-room. He heard children singing of a "despot's heel" and the necessity to "gird thy beauteous limbs with steel" and "avenge the patriotic gore that flecked the streets of Baltimore." The disconcerting song continued with lines that called for bursting "the tyrant's chain" and praised the spurning of "the Northern scum." This was a controversial melody for an instructor to be teaching ten-year-olds and a lesson that would assur-edly bring reprimands of some form. Nevertheless, the "hateful song," as Levin characterized it, was the official state song of Maryland, "Mary-land, My Maryland." Adopted in 1939, the song originated from a poem penned by James Ryder Randall in 1861. Randall wrote the poem in re-sponse to the Baltimore Riot, and it called for the secession of Maryland. The poem was set to the tune of "O, Tannenbaum" and became popular throughout the South during the Civil War.[1]

The adoption of "Maryland, My Maryland" as the state song in April 1939 was an attempt at affirming a white, Confederate identity in a growing climate of black activism and civil rights in Maryland during the 1930s. Maryland's search for a usable past became imperative and des-perate during the twentieth century. Civil War memory was not simply a matter of legacy. It became a social and cultural tool used in an attempt to organize society and maintain the racial status quo. The struggle over Maryland's Civil War memory was not just a struggle of sectionalism, but also one of race. African Americans in the Maryland challenged the ri-gidity of Jim Crow throughout the oppressive system's history. When Af-

rican Americans began to break down the system, some white Marylanders tried to resist these changes by asserting a Confederate identity for
the state. These attempts at institutionalizing a Confederate identity for
Maryland did not go unchallenged. As Marylanders debated the place of
African Americans in society, they also debated the Civil War identity of
their native state.

Maryland's unique status during the war contributed to its racialized
memory of the Civil War. The earnestness of the struggle over a divided
memory of the war developed alongside the intense struggle over race
relations in the state. The divides over Civil War memory and race in
Maryland formed into a symbiotic relationship that intensified as the
twentieth century progressed. In particular, the racial antagonisms and
civil rights efforts of the 1930s in Maryland created a culture in which
race was the defining lens of Marylanders' memories of the Civil War.
During the late nineteenth century, sectionalized memories of the war
dominated American society, but by the 1930s in Maryland race joined
these sectional memories in defining the state's collective memory of the
war. The volatile relationship between memory and race in the Old Line
State during the twentieth century, in many respects, corresponded with
broader American conversations. Maryland reflected larger patterns of
racial struggle and memory that characterized the United States as a
whole rather than most individual states.[2]

The border state was distinctive, in some respects, because of its approach to the question of race. Maryland was split over policies of racial equality, and this split was most evident in comparisons between the
Eastern Shore and western Maryland. The Eastern Shore featured lynch
mobs and ardent segregationists, while many in western Maryland viewed
the Eastern Shore as a backward, troublesome region within the state.
Compared to southern states that more easily adopted Confederate identities and Jim Crow legislation, Marylanders clashed over how the state
should remember the Civil War and the status of African Americans residing in Maryland.

The civil rights movement of the 1960s provided an additional challenge to the Confederate, white Civil War memory of Maryland. The
Maryland Civil War Centennial Commission tried to put forth an unbiased and neutral commemorative program for its state, but controversy
and divisions still emerged during the height of the centennial and the
civil rights movement. Border states, but in particular and to a greater extent Maryland, were the frontlines for the divisions over identity during
the war, and the history of Maryland's postwar memory reveals that it

continued to embody those struggles well into the twentieth century. Civil War memory thus provides a window through which to view the social and cultural divisions of Maryland and the nation more broadly throughout the twentieth century.

Jim Crow in Maryland

In the late nineteenth century, the Maryland legislature enacted numerous laws that sought to curb the racial progressivism facilitated by the Civil War and Reconstruction. In 1884, the Maryland General Assembly added a provision to unlawful marriage by "forbidding marriages between white persons and persons of negro descent to the third generation." One 1904 law required that railroad companies "provide separate cars or coaches for white and colored passengers" while another called for the "separate accommodation of white and colored passengers in the sitting, sleeping and eating apartments of all steamboats plying in the waters within the jurisdiction of the State of Maryland." Maryland also approved funds in 1910 for the creation of separate hospitals and schools for African Americans in the state. With the constitutionality of state racial segregation affirmed in the U.S. Supreme Court's ruling on *Plessy v. Ferguson* (1896), Maryland moved quickly to entrench and institutionalize racial segregation.[3]

Perhaps the most controversial attempts at institutionalizing Jim Crow came in proposed amendments to voting registration laws. Most notably, in 1909 the attorney general of Maryland, Isaac Lobe Straus, proposed an amendment to the Maryland Constitution that sought to disenfranchise African American voters living in the state. The amendment generated outrage not just in Maryland but also throughout the nation. The Grand Army of the Republic's (GAR's) national newspaper, the *National Tribune*, featured several articles that detailed the provisions of the amendment and expressed disdain for its contents and what it represented. The *Tribune* referred to the proposal as the "most infamous proposition ever offered to disenfranchise the voters of the State" and characterized it as "worse in many essential respects than any vote-suppressing provision in the Southern States." African American civil rights activists in Maryland organized opposition to the amendment that ultimately led to the bill's defeat.[4]

Maryland African Americans did not just work to challenge voting rights infringement. They actively challenged Jim Crow legislation and practices throughout the system's history. Several African Americans attempted to break down the restrictive policies of their home state through political activism and even political campaigning. Harry S. Cummings was elected as the first African American city councilman in Baltimore in 1890. Cummings was forced to walk a fine line in terms of his activism, but he was still able to improve the condition of blacks living in Baltimore through education. Given his approach, it is not surprising that he had a relationship with Booker T. Washington, who also valued education as a tool of social advancement for African Americans. Cummings and Washington collaborated in response to a disenfranchisement amendment, and Washington donated money "which made possible the distribution of anti-disfranchisement literature." Cummings was undoubtedly influenced by the approach Washington endorsed of fighting discrimination through African American education, and he attempted to implement it through his position in the Baltimore city government. Cummings's moderation, however, was not always appreciated by African Americans living in Maryland, and his obituary featured in the *Baltimore Afro-American* stated, "it must be said in all fairness that he is one colored man whose political activities did not arouse the prejudices of the Southern white element." While noting Cummings's limitations in his activism, the *Afro-American* conceded that he nevertheless remained a "leader among the colored people of Maryland."[5]

Seven years after Cummings successfully ran for city council, black Baltimoreans again pushed for political office. In 1897, African Americans in Baltimore were becoming disillusioned with the Republican Party. They felt that the Republicans in power who benefited from their support had consistently broken their campaign promises to the African American community in Baltimore. They also did not see the Democratic Party as a practical alternative that would be sympathetic to their cause. Subsequently, a group of African Americans organized a committee to form their own independent party and run on their own ticket. They created a list of candidates to run in the fall city and state elections with George M. Lane leading the group as their candidate for mayor of Baltimore. Lane was accustomed to breaking down barriers, as he was "one of the first African-Americans in Maryland to be admitted to the bar." The political group and its candidates garnered a great deal of attention but were ultimately disappointed in their results. Lane's campaign was unable even to reach Election Day because on October 21, 1897, the Board of Election Supervisors determined that more than half of the signatures secured for Lane's nomination were invalid. There was only one day to gain the rest of the signatures, resulting in the end of Lane's campaign for mayor.[6]

In the years following the attempt to change voting registration laws in Maryland in 1909, William Ashbie Hawkins continued the fight against segregation in the Old Line State. Hawkins was an African American attorney who challenged the constitutionality of segregation laws on numerous occasions. He brought the Baltimore, Chesapeake and Atlantic Railway Company to court for poor conditions and treatment of African Americans on ferryboats. While the Maryland state legislature attempted to take advantage of the *Plessy v. Ferguson* ruling, Hawkins joined those throughout the country who strived to confront its ramifications on a local level. He defended John H. Gurry, who was charged with breaking a segregation law. Hawkins also successfully defended an African American man who experienced violence from a group of white residents who did not approve of the man moving into their neighborhood. In the aftermath of his trial, the court deemed the segregation law unconstitutional.[7]

The legal efforts of individuals like Hawkins faced stiff opposition from many individuals in Maryland's legal system. For instance, in 1920, Judge James Murray Ambler of the Baltimore City Court affirmed the legality of segregation in his decision on a lawsuit brought forth by African American Lewis H. Davenport against the Baltimore and Annapolis Electric Railway Company. Davenport had sued the company for $5,000 worth of "damages for alleged assault by preventing him from riding in a car that the company had set aside for the use of white passengers." Judge Ambler "declared that the Supreme Court had recognized the lawfulness of segregation of the races on the railways."[8]

Opposition to Jim Crow segregation in Maryland was often closely connected to memories of the Civil War. As noted before, the *National Tribune* extensively covered the proposed change to Maryland's voter registration. The commentary that accompanied the coverage was highly critical of the aims of the amendment and sought to generate opposition to its implementation. The *Tribune*, as the newspaper of the GAR, reached veterans across the country. As they read of reminiscences of battles and campaigns, they saw attempts to limit gains achieved through the Civil War. In other words, the Maryland disenfranchisement amendment was an assault on Union memory of the war because it restricted its emancipationist legacy as well as the Fourteenth and Fifteenth Amendments, which secured the status of African Americans as citizens and granted them the right to vote. The *National Tribune*'s coverage of the Maryland voting amendment is indicative of the "Won Cause" articulated by historian Barbara Gannon. The interracial comradeship displayed in the ranks of the GAR ran through the pages of its most important publication. The newspaper entrusted with preserving and delineating Union memory also endorsed attempts to fight Jim Crow in Maryland.[9]

The *National Tribune* was not the only newspaper that had connections to both the GAR and anti–Jim Crow ideology. The founder of the *Baltimore Afro-American*, John Henry Murphy Sr., was an African American veteran of the Thirtieth Regiment Infantry United States Colored Troops organized out of Maryland and a member of the GAR. He founded the *Afro-American* in order to create a newspaper that would challenge Jim Crow practices in Maryland. Although the paper did not cover commemorative events as intently the *National Tribune*, it did feature stories on major Civil War anniversaries. The stories of the Civil War that were included in the *Afro-American* were often used to remember pivotal moments in African American history as well as show the progress that still needed to be made in a deeply segregated and unequal society. The paper also often reported on commemorations and anniversaries that celebrated the life of Abraham Lincoln. Anniversaries of Lincoln's birthday, the Gettysburg Address, and the Emancipation Proclamation were often noted in the newspaper. As an active member of the GAR, Murphy saw an opportunity to cultivate a connection between Civil War memory and civil rights activism.[10]

Resistance to Jim Crow in Maryland through Civil War memories faced opposition from competing memories of the war and its era. In 1927, Charlotte O. Woodbury, historian general of the United Daughters of the Confederacy (UDC), sent out a letter to former Confederates and their families to acquire materials requested by an author for a book on Reconstruction. The author wished "to consult old letters, diaries kept and not published, touching upon the conditions, the hopes and fears of the people, their social life, etc." Many individuals responded to this call for materials and crafted their own narratives of the war from their personal memories of the war. Several Confederate Marylanders answered the request. They wrote of the challenges they faced and many even took time to describe the status of Civil War Maryland in popular memory. A Hartford County resident noted that his county was underappreciated for the service it played in the war. Another claimed that Maryland soldiers were not given their due credit during the many reunion and commemorative events occurring across the country in the early twentieth century.[11]

A response penned by Theophilus Turing touched on the issue of Civil War Maryland in memory as well as the condition of slaves in Maryland.

Turing wrote that Maryland's "position was never clearly understood by her neighbors of either the South or the North." It was, however, his tacit endorsement of Maryland slavery that held the most significance for battles over race relations in the twentieth century. Turing based his credibility to speak to the issue of Maryland slavery on the fact that he was "the son of a mother of a slave holding family for generations." "I speak from first hand knowledge of the kindly relation between the whites and blacks," he wrote. Turing claimed that slaves were treated well and asserted that the institution had little to do with the Civil War. By recalling the benevolence of slavery, he simultaneously upheld the so-called benevolence of Jim Crow. While slaves were treated differently, they were treated justly in his eyes. Through his response, Turing not only reinforced the narrative of the faithful slave in which slaves were depicted as unflinchingly loyal to their masters and exhibited affection toward them; he also demonstrated how Jim Crow was able to adopt and inherit the same ideology put forth before the Civil War. Jim Crow legislation operated in a fashion similar to slavery by making distinctions based on race, but according to the logic put forth by Turing, those distinctions were appropriate, balanced, and fair.[12]

Turing's memory of slavery was undoubtedly affected by the Jim Crow society in which he lived. As David Blight posits of the July 1913 Gettysburg anniversary reunion, "Jim Crow, only half-hidden, stalked the dirt paths of the veterans' tent city at Gettysburg. He delivered supplies, cleaned the latrines, and may even have played tunes at the nation's feast of national memory." By the 1920s, Jim Crow was in plain sight and had his hands firmly grasped on Maryland's memory of the Civil War. Historian Kathleen Ann Clark points out, however, that African Americans throughout the South continued to cultivate their own memories of the Civil War and emancipation and that these memories weakened Jim Crow's grasp on Civil War memory. Marylanders' struggles over race and Civil War memory reveal that the experiences Blight and Clark reference not only occurred simultaneously but also clashed with one another in one border state.[13]

Perceptions of Jim Crow and Civil War memory went hand in hand in postbellum Maryland. Those challenging the legality and morality of Jim Crow often combined their attempts with reminiscences of the war or, at the very least, placed their own ideological stance alongside broader memories and legacies of the Civil War, such as John Henry Murphy Sr., the *Baltimore Afro-American*, and the *National Tribune*. Likewise, those who sought to uphold Jim Crow in an attempt at reaffirming the racial status quo in Maryland did so through Civil War narratives and occasionally through narratives set in Civil War Maryland. The tactic of evoking a particular aspect of the Civil War in order to either maintain or topple the racial status quo was employed with even more earnestness in the tumultuous decade of the 1930s in Maryland society.

The Turbulent 1930s

The year 1939 served as a catalyst for the official adoption of "Maryland, My Maryland" as the state song because it marked the centennial year of the birth of James Tyler Randall. It was not, however, the first time that Maryland tried to pass legislation to adopt "Maryland, My Maryland" as the state song. In 1935, a bill passed "both houses of the Legislature, with only one dissenting vote." The governor at the time, Harry Nice, vetoed the bill and refused to accept it until "the offensive verses were removed." The verses that Nice referenced included lines of spurning "Northern scum" and the "despot's heel," representing Abraham Lincoln and the federal government. The Maryland Federation of Music Clubs, under the leadership of B. S. L. Davis and Louise Criblet, helped push the bill through in 1939 to make the longtime unofficial song of Maryland official with the "offensive verses" intact. Although David O. Selznick did not release the film version of *Gone with the Wind* until December 1939, Margaret Mitchell's novel was already a few years old. Both the novel and the film helped popularize the ideology of the Lost Cause for many Americans and contributed to the memorialization that the UDC was promoting during the 1930s. The culture that *Gone with the Wind* helped create undoubtedly influenced the passage of "Maryland, My Maryland" as the state song at the end of the 1930s.[14]

Additionally, the social and cultural context of 1930s Maryland played a central role in the timing of the song's adoption. The Great Depression, as in the rest of the country, struck a devastating blow in Maryland, and blacks experienced a higher rate of unemployment in the state. Additionally, the "tensions that accompanied economic hard times often exploded in racial prejudice and racial violence." As a result, the 1930s was a significant decade in the history of Maryland civil rights. The lynching of Matthew Williams in 1931 garnered widespread attention both in Maryland and nationally. Williams, an African American man who lived on the Eastern Shore in Salisbury, Maryland, shot and killed Daniel J. Elliot, his employer and a prominent citizen of Salisbury, over a wage dispute on December 4, 1931. Williams unsuccessfully attempted to commit suicide after he shot Elliot, and he was eventually shot by Elliot's son when he tried to escape. As a result of his wounds, Williams was taken to Peninsula General Hospital. That same evening a large mob formed in town and marched on the hospital. The mob was able to trick Williams's guards, and they subsequently dragged him out of a hospital window. The *Philadelphia Record* reported that while "the two guards were parleying with the main mob at the front door of the hospital a smaller group sneaked in the rear and dragged Williams out, his head and face covered with bandages." They paraded him through the streets and hanged him from a tree in the courthouse yard. The mob cut down his body from the tree and set it on fire in a neighboring lot.[15]

Newspapers were quick to pick up on the story. Baltimore newspapers in particular turned a critical eye to the incident and the Eastern Shore as a whole. An editorial the following day in the *Baltimore Post* exemplified the frustration of many Marylanders over the lynching. Under the title "Maryland's Disgrace—The Shame of the Eastern Shore," the author began the piece by stating, "The blood lust of the Eastern Shore has claimed a victim." The editorial concluded by asserting that the "lynching yesterday was a disgrace to the Eastern Shore; another lynching there would be the shame of Maryland." Several newspapers included editorial cartoons as responses to the lynching, including one with the title "Maryland, My Maryland."[16]

The image from the *Baltimore Sun* in particular depicted the relationship between Maryland's Confederate memory and identity and the mob violence that plagued the state. By portraying a victim of lynching under the heading "Maryland, My Maryland," the sketch directly linked efforts of Confederate memorialization with racial, vigilante violence. The cartoon also demonstrates that Randall's words were still relevant to Marylanders living in the 1930s and that it continued to polarize the citizens of the border state.

Additionally, the proliferation of images depicting lynchings in Maryland occurred at a time when spectacle lynching was growing because of the rise in consumer culture. Historian Grace Hale notes that "consumer culture created spectacle lynchings" and that "the incorporation of cars and trains, radios, phones, and cameras" played a crucial role in this process. The extensive coverage that the Eastern Shore lynching received was part of a national trend that was closely connected to the evolution of consumerism in the United States, and it reflected an irony

FIGURE 5.1. "Maryland, My Maryland!" *Baltimore Sun*, December 6,
1931 (MSA s1048-1, 2/31/3/14, Maryland State Archives).

that technology helped spread news of and to socially backward places
like the Eastern Shore.[17]

The *Baltimore Sun* also reproduced several editorial comments from
Eastern Shore newspapers in the immediate aftermath of the lynching.
One commenter in the *Salisbury Times* said that residents of the Eastern Shore should "pay little heed to the overdrawn pictures that will
be painted by metropolitan newspapers, who have no obligation to this
peninsula and whose only purpose is that of preparing news as to increase their own circulations." An editorial in the *Cambridge Daily Banner*
asserted that the editorial in the *Baltimore Sun* furthered "its campaign
of misrepresentation of the Eastern Shore of Maryland . . . to the point
of being insulting to every resident of this peninsula, although we do
not suppose this makes any difference to the publishers of that paper."[18]

The tensions between Baltimore and the Eastern Shore point to an

FIGURE 5.2. "In the Land of the Free and the Home of the Brave," *Jeffersonian*, December 12, 1931 (MSA 1048-1, 2/31/3/14, Maryland State Archives).

important change that had developed in Maryland society by 1931. By the twentieth century, Baltimore, as well as the rest of the Western Shore, had become fully urbanized and industrialized. This contributed to a dichotomous relationship with the Eastern Shore, which had remained predominantly rural. Through this process, Baltimore became more aligned with western Maryland, leaving the Eastern Shore relatively isolated as a bastion of Confederate memory and creating a different geographical dividing line within the state than during the war. The polarized regions divided not only along economic lines but also on issues of race. According to the 1930 U.S. Census, Baltimore was the eighth largest city in the United States with a population of 805,000, and approximately 18 percent of the population was African American. Baltimore civil rights had made inroads both politically and racially by the 1930s, but the Eastern Shore possessed a much different history of racial affairs than the rest of the state.[19]

The *Afro-American* placed the lynching of Williams in the larger context of the Eastern Shore's racial history. "Since 1882, Maryland has had 31 lynchings," and of those, "28 were colored and 3 were white," the *Afro-American* stated. It also offered an alternative name for Salisbury: Lynchtown. Another article in the *Afro-American* characterized the entire Eastern Shore as the "Lynching Shore." The article noted that the "recent lynching on the Eastern (Lynching) Shore of Maryland was not a flash in the pan." The *Afro-American* not only placed the lynching in its historical context but it also analyzed the societal context of the Eastern Shore. After laying out the disparity between white and black teachers in Eastern Shore counties, the newspaper added, "A lynching area can be depended upon not only to murder colored people but to rob them of school funds." The *Afro-American*'s portrait of the Eastern Shore was not hyperbole. Maryland's Eastern Shore had a particularly sordid past regarding race relations and lynching. As legal scholar Sherrilyn A. Ifill points out, as far as "matters of race were concerned, the Eastern Shore of Maryland was not, in 1931, very different from the rest of the South," and for "the last 150 years, Maryland has been characterized by a kind of racial schizophrenia." The "racial schizophrenia" that plagued Maryland mirrored the divisiveness brought on by memories of the Civil War. The passivity with which many residents of the Eastern Shore viewed the lynching and the history of lynching in the region contributed to the tensions between western and eastern Maryland.[20]

In the immediate aftermath of the lynching, Maryland governor Albert Ritchie faced intense pressure to bring those responsible to justice. "The crime of this negro was a shocking thing, but he should have paid the penalty for it through the established legal machinery," Governor Ritchie stated. He continued by saying that the lynching "must bring the blush of shame to every law-abiding Marylander, whether on or off the Eastern Shore." In his comments, Ritchie noted that the state attorney said he intended "to prosecute the case with vigor, stopping not at the leaders, but carrying it to every other person who took part, who can be identified."[21]

Unfortunately, the task of the identifying those involved in the mob proved more difficult than originally thought. A Wicomico County grand jury aided by Attorney General William Preston Lane conducted a probe. After examining 128 witnesses, the jury found "absolutely no evidence that can remotely connect anyone with the instigation or perpetration of the murder" of Matthew Williams. The case therefore concluded and not a single individual was tried in the lynching of Williams. The lack of justice for those responsible for the lynching created a sense of frustration among many Marylanders, including the author of a column in the *Baltimore Sun* that called for a state anti-lynching law.[22]

Despite the national attention and calls for new legislation, the Eastern Shore was once again under the spotlight after the lynching of George Armwood not even two years after the lynching of Matthew Williams. On October 16, 1933, Mary Denston reported an attempted assault on her as she walked to the post office in Princess Anne, Maryland, ten miles south of Salisbury. Denston was not injured, but she described her attacker as George Armwood, a twenty-two-year-old African American laborer from Somerset County. Authorities were able to track down Armwood, and, after they moved the prisoner to and from multiple cities for fear of mob action, he was imprisoned on the Eastern Shore in Princess Anne. After ignoring warnings from Judge Robert F. Duer of Somerset County and enduring the firing of tear gas, a mob launched an assault on the prison. The crowd of nearly one thousand, composed of citizens from Princess Anne and Salisbury, assaulted the officers guarding the prison and took keys from Deputy Norman Dryden. The mob dragged Armwood from his cell and out of the prison while they beat, stabbed, and kicked him. Before hanging Armwood from a tree, the mob cut off his ears and removed his gold teeth. After he was dead, the mob dragged his body to the local courthouse and there hanged and burned it from a telephone pole. As in Matthew Williams's case, no one was convicted for the lynching of George Armwood.[23]

The lynchings of Matthew Williams and George Armwood in eastern Maryland and certainly racial injustices throughout the South, such as the Scottsboro case in 1931, provided motivation for African American memories of the Civil War era. Several former slaves who labored in the Old Line State shared their experiences in the form of slave narratives in the waning years of the nineteenth century as well as through slave narratives from the Works Progress Administration (WPA) Federal Writers' Project during the 1930s. In a WPA interview, former slave Caroline Hammond, recalling her life under slavery in Anne Arundel County, noted that her owner Thomas Davidson "was very good to his slaves, treating them with every consideration that he could, with the exception of freeing them." His wife, however, was another story. "Mrs. Davidson was hard on all the slaves, whenever she had the opportunity, driving them at full speed when working, giving different food of a coarser grade and not much of it," she said. Although this is hardly a direct condemnation of Jim Crow Maryland, the fact that a former slave living in Baltimore was willing to share the cruelty she faced under the institution of slavery is significant. Hammond's narrative takes on more significance when one considers the time period in which she offered it. The 1930s was a tumultuous decade for race relations in Maryland. Therefore, the fact that Hammond's narrative was offered during this time frame allowed her to place her own struggle against racial oppression alongside those who were fighting racial oppression more than seventy years later.[24]

Hammond also leveled her harshest criticisms at a time when the UDC was dominating a substantial portion of the nation's Civil War memory. In 1932, Virginia chapters of the UDC and others throughout the South successfully campaigned against a proposed peace monument at Appomattox under the banner of white supremacy. As W. Fitzhugh Brundage points out, by the 1920s elite white women in the South created "an infrastructure for the dissemination of a collective historical memory at a time when few other groups were able to do so." While southern white women assembled and unified in order to speak with a strong voice on behalf of an unmitigated Confederate memory of the Civil War, Caroline Hammond offered a bold alternative from a state that fostered competing memories like her own and that of the UDC membership. In the wake of the lynchings, the clashing memories of Maryland's black and white citizens resonated louder as they emanated from a culture that was equally divided over race. These memories of the war took on more importance as they melded with social politics to cultivate a usable past.[25]

Caroline Hammond was not alone in her effort to thwart Confederate memorialization and memory in the Old Line State. Throughout the 1930s and beyond, African American Marylanders challenged those who tried to narrow the divided border state's history to a solely Confederate and white one. As early as 1931, the *Baltimore Afro-American* was challenging Maryland's participation in Confederate memorialization, specifically the dedication of the Heyward Shepherd Memorial. Heyward Shepherd was an African American man and the first victim of John Brown's raid on Harpers Ferry in 1859. The purveyors of the monument, the UDC, dedicated the monument in 1931 to commemorate the narrative of a faithful slave and uphold the benevolence of slavery. The Baltimore newspaper protested the dedication of the Heyward Shepherd Memorial, citing that "these Confederate dames are as busy today fighting for the 'lost cause' as their ancestors were from 1861 to 1865" and that the United Daughters of the Confederacy was also "seeking to justify secession by blackening the character of the abolitionists and glorifying slavery." The article made no attempt to hide its position, asserting, "The AFRO-AMERICAN not only condemns the whole procedure but deprecates the fact that any Baltimorean or any of our college presidents had a share in it." Historian Caroline Janney notes that the location of the monument within the border state of West Virginia "was quite symbolic, representing a literal border between white and black memories of Brown and his raid." It is equally symbolic that some of the harshest criticism of the memorial would come from another border state that remained deeply divided over the Civil War.[26]

The lynchings also helped launch "intense activism on the part of black and white residents in Baltimore." Shortly after the lynching of Armwood, the Baltimore branch of the National Association for the Advancement of Colored People (NAACP) re-formed and began to pursue opportunities to push for equality, in particular striving for desegregation in public education. After several years of struggle and opposition, the efforts at reform through legislative and judicial means came to fruition in the landmark *Murray* case.[27]

In December 1934, Donald Gaines Murray wrote to the University of Maryland requesting information about the institution's law school. Murray was a native Marylander, a graduate of Amherst College, and African American. The president of the University of Maryland, Raymond A. Pearson, responded to Murray's request less than a week later. "Under the general laws of this State the University maintains the Princess Anne Academy as a separate institution of higher learning for the education of Negroes," he wrote. Pearson also informed Murray that partial scholarships were created "at Morgan College or institutions outside of the State for Negro students who may desire to take professional courses or other work not given at the Princess Anne Academy."[28]

Despite Pearson's letter, Murray applied to the University of Maryland School of Law. The registrar then wrote to Murray to inform him on how the university planned to handle his application to the law school. After attaching the original letter Pearson wrote, the registrar, W. M. Hillegeist, delivered the news. "President Pearson instructed me today to return to you the application form and the money order, as the University does not accept Negro students, except at the Princess Anne Academy," he wrote.[29]

Murray was not content with the president's decision, nor was he satisfied with Hillegeist's explanation. In March 1935, he wrote to the University of Maryland board of regents and made a forceful argument on behalf of his admittance to the law school. "I am a citizen of the State of Maryland and fully qualified to become a student of the University of Maryland Law School," he wrote. He added that "no other State institution affords a legal education," an argument that would hold merit in the subsequent legal battle. He then became more critical of the specific actions the university took regarding his application. Murray said that the "arbitrary actions of the officials of the University of Maryland in returning my application was unjust and unreasonable and contrary to the Constitution of the United States and the Constitution of this State." He said that he was appealing to the board of regents as the governing body of the university to rectify the situation and accept him based on the fact that he was a qualified applicant. President Pearson once again replied to Murray, and on this occasion he recommended that Murray look into Howard University and its law school.[30]

With his appeal being unsuccessful, Murray opted to pursue legal action in order to secure his admittance into the University of Maryland Law School. The attorneys who represented Murray were Charles Hamilton Houston and Thurgood Marshall, who were both affiliated with the Baltimore NAACP. Murray brought a suit against the president, the registrar, and the board of regents. The case went to the Baltimore City Court in June 1935 with Judge Eugene O'Dunne presiding, and on June 18, 1935, the court ruled in favor of Murray and instructed the defendants that they were required to admit Murray as a student to the University of Maryland Law School.[31]

The university appealed the decision, and the opinion by the Court of the Appeals was filed in January 1936. It affirmed the doctrine of separate but equal and applied this concept to Murray's case. The opinion read, "And as in Maryland now the equal treatment can be furnished only in the one existing law school the petitioner in our opinion, must be admitted there." The state of Maryland provided no alternative for African Americans seeking a law degree in the state, so the University of Maryland was required to admit any qualified African American candidates. With the ruling of the Baltimore City Court and the confirmation of the Court of Appeals, Donald Murray and the Baltimore NAACP struck a blow against Jim Crow policies in Maryland. It also helped launched the career of a young Thurgood Marshall.[32]

In the conflicted racial environment that saw the lynchings of Matthew Williams and George Armwood and the admittance of Donald Murray to the University of Maryland Law School, Confederate memorialization in Maryland occurred at an expeditious pace. In 1938, the Pointe Coupee Book Club of Louisiana dedicated the James Ryder Randall Oak and Tablet to commemorate where Randall supposedly penned his famous poem. The dedication of the tree along with the adoption of a Confeder-

ate song as the official state song in 1939 were responses to the successful
and momentum-building efforts of the NAACP and other civil rights activists in Maryland during the 1930s. By combating legislation with their
own legislation, a portion of the white population living in Maryland
could hope to maintain at least some small version of the status quo
and southern heritage in an ever-changing racial and cultural society. As
historian Anne Marshall points out, "in the hands of white conservatives,
mass culture proved a very powerful tool to reiterate white versions of
history and to solidify racial hierarchy of whiteness and blackness." In
other words, Confederate memory and white southern identity were not
only inseparable but also relied on each other for survival. Confederate
Marylanders struggled to maintain this relationship more so than other
white southerners. Living in a state that was divided over both the memory of the Civil War and issues of race made Marylanders sympathetic to
Confederate memories fight more ardently for what they viewed as the
correct legacy of their state. One of the ways they attempted to do this
was through commemorating Maryland native James Ryder Randall.[33]
The words of his nine-stanza poem that reverberated for decades after
the peace at Appomattox were as follows:

I

The despot's heel is on thy shore,
   Maryland!
His torch is at thy temple door,
   Maryland!
Avenge the patriotic gore
That flecked the streets of Baltimore,
And be the battle queen of yore,
   Maryland! My Maryland!

II

Hark to an exiled son's appeal,
   Maryland!
My mother State! to thee I kneel,
   Maryland!
For life and death, for woe and weal,
Thy peerless chivalry reveal,
And gird thy beauteous limbs with steel,
   Maryland! My Maryland!

III

Thou wilt not cower in the dust,
   Maryland!

Thy beaming sword shall never rust,
  Maryland!
Remember Carroll's sacred trust,
Remember Howard's warlike thrust,—
And all thy slumberers with the just,
  Maryland! My Maryland!

IV
Come! 'tis the red dawn of the day,
  Maryland!
Come with thy panoplied array,
  Maryland!
With Ringgold's spirit for the fray,
With Watson's blood at Monterey,
With fearless Lowe and dashing May,
  Maryland! My Maryland!

V
Come! for thy shield is bright and strong,
  Maryland!
Come! for thy dalliance does thee wrong,
  Maryland!
Come to thine own anointed throng,
Stalking with Liberty along,
And chaunt thy dauntless slogan song,
  Maryland! My Maryland!

VI
Dear Mother! burst the tyrant's chain,
  Maryland!
Virginia should not call in vain,
  Maryland!
She meets her sisters on the plain
"Sic semper!" 'tis the proud refrain
That baffles minions back again,
  Maryland!
Arise in majesty again,
  Maryland! My Maryland!

VII
I see the blush upon thy cheek,
  Maryland!
For thou wast ever bravely meek,
  Maryland!
But lo! there surges forth a shriek,

From hill to hill, from creek to creek—
Potomac calls to Chesapeake,
  Maryland! My Maryland!

VIII
Thou wilt not yield the Vandal toll,
  Maryland!
Thou wilt not crook to his control,
  Maryland!
Better the fire upon thee roll,
Better the blade, the shot, the bowl,
Than crucifixion of the soul,
  Maryland! My Maryland!

IX
I hear the distant thunder-hum,
  Maryland!
The Old Line's bugle, fife, and drum,
  Maryland!
She is not dead, nor deaf, nor dumb—
Huzza! she spurns the Northern scum!
She breathes! she burns! she'll come! she'll come!
  Maryland! My Maryland![34]

James Ryder Randall was a point of pride for Marylanders who wanted to preserve a Confederate heritage for their state and also wanted to maintain the racial hierarchy embedded in the state's society. Although the Pointe Coupee Book Club of Louisiana was the primary organizer of the dedication of the Randall Tablet and Oak and both were dedicated in Louisiana, Maryland was prominent during the ceremony. The Louisiana club organized the commemorative effort that included a bronze tablet in front of the large oak tree that would henceforth be known as the Randall Oak. The club placed the tablet on the roadside prominently in front of the oak. The inscription read: "Randall Oak. Near this tree within the walls of Poydras College, were written the Immortal lines of 'Maryland, My Maryland' by James Ryder Randall. Born in Baltimore Maryland, Jan. 1, 1839. Died in Atlanta, Georgia Jan. 14, 1908." During the ceremony, held on April 26, 1938, three flags flew over the marker: a U.S. flag, a Louisiana flag, and "a Maryland flag donated by the Maryland Chapter of the United Daughters of the Confederacy." Even though the commemoration took place well beyond the borders of Maryland, the state's UDC managed to make its imprint on the commemoration that honored one of its Confederate heroes.[35]

The featured speaker at the dedication was Louis Henry Gosserand. Gosserand was "reared near the oak tree" and was considered a "student of history." In his speech, like so many before him, Gosserand attempted to paint a picture of a passive Maryland and dictate the state's Civil War memory on his own terms. Given the fracturing of Jim Crow in Maryland during the 1930s, the New Orleans native was even more empowered to appropriate Maryland's heritage. At one point during his address, he mentioned his experience of knowing Randall and hearing him lecture while he attended Tulane University. Gosserand described Randall "as so very retiring and benevolent in manner and appearance that one wonders whence he had summoned the vim, the force and the belligerence in his vigorous call to arms." In these lines, Randall's personality is indicative of the larger narrative of Civil War Maryland as indecisive and timid. To Gosserand, it was remarkable that Randall was able to write such aggressive prose given his personality and the personality of his home state. Even in Gosserand's description of Randall courting his wife, Randall's "retiring" personality was mentioned to demonstrate the "progressive" nature of his approach. Gosserand also pointed out that "Randall was never strong physically and it was on account of his health that he never joined the Southern Army." Much like his native state, Randall could not muster the strength to fight on behalf of the Confederate cause. Gosserand even concluded his speech by speculating on how the Louisiana landscape might have played a decisive factor in the cultivation of "Maryland, My Maryland." "Indeed the gentle poet of Poydras College possessed the linguistic talent and the lyric ardour that were necessary to mould his exalted and soulful theme into song, but when we glance athwart this beautiful countryside . . . we must pause to inquire," he stated. He continued, "Yes, we do wonder just what part all of it played, in the spirit, the imagery, the melody, and the sublimity that were conjured up by the poet in the fullness of his sincerity."[36]

Although Gosserand was probably not attempting to take away credit from the state of Maryland and Randall for his poem, his speech represented a recurring theme in the collective Confederate memory of Civil War Maryland. In the eyes of many Confederates who lived through the Civil War, Maryland was not strong enough to secede during the war and therefore was not strong enough to proclaim its legacy after the war. To Gosserand, Louisiana deserved perhaps as much credit as the author of "Maryland, My Maryland," and it certainly deserved more credit than the conflicted border state. The need to protect and, occasionally, appropriate Confederate Maryland memories was exacerbated by the progress made by Maryland civil rights activists. The racial hierarchy that existed in Maryland during the Civil War was falling away, and it was up to residents of southern states to try and salvage the Old Line State's legacy. By the end of the 1930s, other southern states felt forced to claim the Confederate identity of Maryland on their behalf as individuals like Donald Murray struck at Jim Crow.

White Marylanders themselves tried to retain some semblance of their Confederate identity through the adoption of "Maryland, My Maryland" as the state song in 1939. Maryland was not alone in this process. Several southern states adopted slave and minstrel songs during the same period. As much of the South confronted a growing civil rights movement, songs that upheld a racial hierarchy and Confederate identity for their home states were powerful tools.[37] None, however, had the direct connection to the Civil War that "Maryland, My Maryland" possessed. The sponsor of the bill to make "Maryland, My Maryland" the state song was Delegate Charles F. Argabright, a Virginia native and resident of Baltimore. The immediate response to the adoption of "Maryland, My Maryland" as the state song was mostly positive. Although the news of the adoption was not met with widespread fanfare, newspapers that did cover the story expressed satisfaction and contentment with the legislative result. The headline for the story authored by Virginia Y. McNeil in the *Baltimore Sun* read, "State Song is Now Official: Maryland, My Maryland at Last Adopted by the Legislature and Approved by Governor Completing Symbols."[38] To McNeil, the adoption was long overdue and marked the end of an inevitable legislative process. Much like the rest of the Maryland's Civil War memory, the state song would soon be swept up in a storm of debate and controversy over the identity of Civil War Maryland during the mid-twentieth century.

Maryland's Civil Rights Movement and Civil War Centennial

In 1958, Martin Luther King Jr. delivered the commencement address at Morgan State College, a historically black college in Baltimore. King encouraged the graduates to strive to be good at whatever career they pursued and outlined the struggles that the United States faced. As he concluded his speech, he asked that those in attendance "go out, not as detached spectators, but as individuals involved in the struggle, ready to cooperate with God, ready to cooperate with the forces of the universe, and make the new world a reality." "Go out determined to make the ideals of brotherhood a reality for your generation and for your children and for your children's children, and this will be the great day in our world with this attitude and with this work, we will be able, by the grace of God, to create a new America," he said. King ended his speech with words that would become famous when he would recite them five years later. "Freedom must ring from every mountainside," he said. When this finally occurred, King remarked, "all men will be able to stand together, black men and white men, Jews and Gentiles, Protestants and Catholics, and sing a new song—Free at last, free at last, great God Almighty, we are free at last! (Thunderous applause)."[39]

African Americans in Maryland were active in fighting segregation and inequality years before King delivered his address to the students at Morgan State College. Civil rights activists founded the Congress of Racial Equality (CORE) in 1942, and Baltimoreans formed their own chapter in late 1952 and early 1953. The Baltimore chapter launched several sit-in movements and anti-segregation campaigns that achieved notable successes and led to significant desegregation action on the part of Maryland businesses.[40]

Maryland African Americans were also protesting against Confederate memorialization throughout the 1940s. In particular, the dedication of the Lee and Jackson double-equestrian statue in Baltimore generated a vigorous response from African American Marylanders that saw the monument as an affront to not only their race but also their country. The Lee and Jackson monument was dedicated on May 1, 1948. J. Henry Ferguson left $100,000 to the city of Baltimore upon the death of his sister, Ella Ward, for the creation of a monument to honor Robert E. Lee and Thomas J. "Stonewall" Jackson. Lee and Jackson were childhood heroes of Ferguson, and he hoped that the monument would serve as a reminder to the people of Maryland of their Christian character. Ward died in 1934, and during the following year a competition was held by the Municipal Art Society of Baltimore to select a sculptor to complete the project. Laura Gardin Fraser won the competition and began working on the monument. The project developed slowly, partly because of Fraser's methodical approach and partly due to limitations of resources during World War II. Italian clay and metal were difficult commodities to come by during the war, and the thought of using these precious materials during wartime for the purpose of aesthetics would be unpopular among many. The monument was completed in 1948 and depicts Lee and Jackson, both on horseback, parting ways in May 1, 1863, before the Battle of Chancellorsville.[41]

The monument was dedicated on May 1, 1948, before a crowd of three thousand people. The potential divisiveness of the occasion was perhaps made apparent weeks before the dedication. The *Free Lance-Star* published out of Fredericksburg, Virginia, included an article in its April 29, 1948, issue titled "Baltimore Wants Confederate Flags." The article began, "This city is advertising for Confederate battle flags—but hold your fire, Yanks." It continued by asserting, "There's no rebirth of the Civil War in prospect, it's just the monument city getting ready to dedicate another statue." The *Free Lance-Star* indicated that officials from Baltimore wanted to decorate the city with Confederate flags for the unveiling and dedication of the monument on May 1. Although the reigniting of war was unlikely, the thought of Baltimore being festooned in Confederate iconography was problematic for some, including many African Americans living in the city.[42]

In addition to the large crowd that gathered to witness the unveiling, the dedication on May 1, 1948, included the governors of Maryland and Virginia, cadets from the Virginia Military Institute, and the editor of the *Richmond News Leader* and biographer of Robert E. Lee, Douglas Southall Freeman. Freeman served as the primary speaker for the occasion, reflecting on the lives and legacies of Lee and Jackson. The *Free Lance-Star* noted that Baltimore "revived some of its Confederate loyalties today" and "gave its Southern characteristics full play for today's ceremonies." The newspaper also recognized the impact the dedication had on the businesses in the city. "Hotels and public buildings flew Confederate banners and menus bristled with hominy grits, spoon bread and corn sticks. . . . The mint in the juleps was crushed, of course," the newspaper reported.[43]

In the days following the dedication, not everyone relished the nostalgic view of the Confederacy and its leaders that took over the city. African Americans began to voice their frustrations with the monument and the ceremonies that surrounded the dedication. An op-ed piece featured in the *Baltimore Afro-American* reflected this frustration in an essay titled "Why Not Benedict Arnold?" The author of the editorial noted that the governor of Maryland, William Preston Lane, stated in his speech at the dedication, "the scars of the Civil War have long since been healed." The author wondered what he meant by this and continued his essay by stating, "The governor is president of a conference of governors of 17 Southern States whose chief goal now is to keep all existing college, university, and professional schools 'for whites only.'" To the editorialist, the scars of the war were still very much open, and the dedication of a Confederate monument while southern leadership was opposing desegregation only underscored this troubling reality. The author of the piece quoted the mayor of Baltimore, Thomas D'Alesandro, when he commented that Lee and Jackson served as reminders for "us to be resolute and determined in preserving our sacred institutions." The essay reminded the readership of the *Afro-American* that the "sacred institution" Lee and Jackson "sought to preserve was slavery." The racially divisive environment of Maryland in the 1940s also served as a visceral example of the continued impact of that very institution.[44]

In addition to domestic struggles, the author of the essay also made connections to international circumstances that were fresh in the minds of Americans living in the aftermath of World War II. The letter made a direct connection between Americans' enemies in the 1940s and the enemies of loyal Americans in the 1860s. "Hitler killed Jews. Lee and Jackson exploited colored people as animals and property," the author stated. To look to such people for "inspiration" was, in the words of the letter writer, "pure drivel and tommyrot." The notion of honoring enemies of the American government was more problematic in times of war than in times of peace. Fighting against honoring disloyalty and racial injustice went hand in hand for many African Americans.[45]

Marylanders also did in fact "go out" in the years following 1958 and attempt "to create a new America," or at the very least, a new Maryland. One such individual was Robert Mack Bell, a black high-school class president from Baltimore. Bell was arrested in 1960 for his role in the sit-in protest movement against lunch-counter segregation in Baltimore. On June 17, 1960, Bell and several other students organized sit-ins at local restaurants, forcing four to close their doors, including Hooper's restaurant that "asked Chief Magistrate Joseph Kalodny to issue warrants against the protestors" because the restaurant claimed that they "refused to leave the place" after it was ordered closed.[46]

The Baltimore sit-in movement produced immediate results as several restaurants changed their policies on segregation in the weeks immediately following the actions of the local students. Twelve students involved, however, faced trespassing charges as a result of their actions. The case of the restaurant against the students eventually reached Maryland's highest court, the Maryland Court of Appeals, and the court concluded that the student demonstrators were not permitted to "invade or remain upon the property of private citizens so long as private citizens retain the right to choose their guests or customers." The appeal of the students eventually reached the U.S. Supreme Court in 1963 with Robert Bell lending his name to the appeal because it was first alphabetically. The justices were divided over the case eight months after it was argued, and by the time a decision was reached, Congress had already answered the question of segregation through the Civil Rights Act of 1964. Despite the hesitation of the U.S. Supreme Court justices, the case of *Bell v. Maryland* helped put pressure on the federal government to take action against segregationist policies in the United States. More than thirty years after Bell participated in the Baltimore sit-in movement, he rose to the position of the chief judge of the Maryland Court of Appeals.[47]

In the divided racial environment that characterized Maryland and amid the competing memories that existed within the state, the Maryland Civil War Centennial Commission attempted to commemorate the Civil War. Historians, such as Robert Cook and David Blight, have examined the complexity in commemorating the Civil War during the height of the civil rights movement.[48] No one, however, has examined how Maryland tried to navigate the troubled waters of commemoration while it was still grappling with the remnants of Jim Crow segregation and memories of the Civil War that were still bitterly debated. The Civil War forged divisions in Maryland society that ran deeper than in any other state and made Maryland's Civil War centennial all the more complicated. The Maryland Civil War Centennial Commission tried to stay as neutral as possible in its activities, but that remained a difficult task throughout the centennial celebration, and controversy erupted throughout the decade. The commission operated under the supervision of J. Millard Tawes, the governor of Maryland, and included prominent members of Maryland society appointed by the governor who maintained an active interest in the American Civil War. George Radcliffe, a former U.S. senator, served as the commission chairman, and Park Loy served as the executive director. Loy previously served as the secretary and treasurer of the National Antietam Commemoration Commission, the organization tasked with commemorating the seventy-fifth anniversary of the Battle of Antietam in 1937.[49]

At the outset of the Civil War Centennial, the Maryland commission crafted "A Manual for the Observances of the Civil War in the Counties and Cities of the State of Maryland." In the opening pages, the commission laid out what ideas and results it hoped to foster in Maryland through the centennial. The members of the commission were clearly aware of the divides that persisted in Maryland society over the memory of the Civil War when they crafted their manual. They hoped to "stimulate interest in this period and to encourage further study of the Civil

War" because they believed "that honest research will heal old wounds, giving us better understanding of the causes that led to conflict." The centennial commission saw the anniversary as an opportunity to alleviate the tensions that still existed over competing memories inside the border state. Marylanders were conscious of competing Civil War memories because of their persistence and entrenchment within their society. This, in many ways, made Maryland unique. For instance, Virginia and South Carolina as well as New York and Massachusetts only saw a single Civil War narrative. Therefore, their centennial commissions did not have to walk as fine a line as the Maryland commission. Along these same lines, the commission wanted to "point out the common heritage and to emphasize the unity of this State and of the Nation that has developed since the dreadful conflict of 1861–1865." The members of the commission thought that by remembering the divisions of Maryland society during the war, it would make its citizens appreciate the strides they had made since the final shots of the Civil War. This, of course, needed to be performed with "vision, patience and tolerance" because there was the obvious potential for controversy in remembering the war in such a complicated state.[50]

Throughout the centennial, the Maryland Civil War Centennial Commission attempted to maintain in practice the guidelines it set forth in theory. The commission tried to remain unbiased in terms of favoritism toward Union or Confederate commemorations and expressed this sentiment in its invitation to other state governors and centennial commissions. It noted that "the position of Maryland, both geographically and sentimentally, was unique, with historical backgrounds of such character to make possible commemorative programs with dignity and unbiased in the form presented." The Maryland commission noted the state's position "immediately south of the Mason and Dixon Line and north of the Potomac River" as well as its struggles "between 'Secession' and 'Non-Secession.'" The commission took pride in the fact that its state contributed soldiers to both sides and that "Marylanders supported whichever side their consciences dictated." The commission members also proudly noted, "The Maryland Monument on The Antietam Battlefield is the only one dedicated to the memory of the fallen sons of both the North and the South." The Maryland Civil War Centennial Commission was characterizing the divisions that had plagued Maryland society for a century as a positive for the state's Civil War history and legacy. It attempted to seize a moment in which Maryland's unique position in the Civil War could actually benefit the state's legacy.[51]

The governor of Maryland for the entire centennial of the Civil War was J. Millard Tawes. Tawes fully supported the middle road that the Maryland commission attempted to remain on throughout the hundred-year anniversary of the conflict. "The members of the Maryland Commission for the Civil War Centennial have wisely not attempted to decide who was right and who was wrong regarding the Civil War, nor to settle other controversial issues," Tawes wrote. He was aware of the potential blowback that could occur during the centennial in Maryland because he was cognizant of the intensity of the memories Marylanders possessed of the Civil War in the twentieth century.[52]

In 1962, the Maryland commission issued a progress report of the centennial commemorations occurring in the state. One of report's categories was an examination of the commission's effort to remain impartial. Once again the commission reinforced its guiding principle that the centennial must honor all of Maryland sons. The report stated the policy of the commission was "that of paying tribute to the valor and sacrifices of those (both Union and Confederate) who fought and died in support of principles which they thought to be right." The report also mentioned commemorative efforts that sought to alleviate tensions that might have still existed with other states, namely, Massachusetts. The commemoration of the Baltimore Riot of 1861 included speeches delivered by both the governor of Maryland and the governor of Massachusetts and governors also were "entertained at a dinner at the Hotel Belvedere preceding the commemoration program."[53]

One of the most public attempts of the commission to honor both Union and Confederate Maryland soldiers was the dedication of a plaque to both in the Maryland State House in Annapolis, Maryland. The plaque was dedicated on October 5, 1964, in front of a crowd of 250 attendees. Under the title inscription "Maryland Remembers," the plaque read, "By the dedication of this plaque, she leaves for posterity evidence of her remembrance of her nearly 63,000 native sons who served in the Union Forces and the more than 22,000 in those of the Confederacy in The War between the States." The decision to refer to the conflict as "The War Between the States" rather than the "Civil War" was an interesting one. The commission's choice reflected a characterization of the war that many Confederate sympathizers preferred, and it perhaps served as a form of appeasement on the part of the commission toward Confederate proponents. This, however, would not be enough for some advocating on behalf of Confederate memories.[54]

Governor Tawes spoke at the dedication ceremony and once again reiterated the goal of the commission to remain neutral and unbiased. He said that the Old Line State "experienced the tragedy of fratricide— brother against brother—'probably with more intensity than any other part of the nation.'" Tawes was aware that such a divisive conflict undoubtedly "breeds hatred and bitterness and leaves behind it wounds that are long in healing." "Some of the scars are visible even today, after the passage of a hundred years," he remarked. He contended, however, that "most of the rancor and hostility has vanished." While "most of the rancor and hostility" might very well have "vanished," the governor would soon discover that a significant amount remained present in Maryland. As Tawes had throughout the Civil War centennial, he spoke carefully about Maryland's place in the Civil War and encouraged his state's commission to act in a similar fashion.[55]

Unfortunately, for Tawes and the commission the State House plaque that was intended to be a beacon of reconciliation and impartiality received criticism, notably from Ruby Duval. Duval was a member of the Maryland Civil War Centennial Commission and past president of the Maryland division of the United Daughters of the Confederacy. When Duval learned of the proposed plaque in the State House, she expressed her frustration to the commission executive director, Park Loy. Unmoved by the use of the phrase "The War Between the States" in the inscription, she said that she was "surprised to learn" from Loy's letter of the proposed plaque and that she and the "Commission Representatives of Anne Arundel County" were not consulted about the wording of the plaque as Loy had previously indicated. Duval had suggested to Loy the possible placement "of a bronze plaque in memory of" Confederate soldiers, sailors, and marines from Maryland. She was disappointed that the commission decided to dedicate a plaque to the memory of both Union and Confederate Marylanders. She concluded her letter by once more reminding Loy of his mistake. "As a member of the Maryland Civil War Centennial Commission from Annapolis, Anne Arundel County, the seat of our State Government; as well as a Maryland historian, I again remind you that you failed to keep faith with your statement of January 10th mentioned above," she wrote.[56]

Duval's letter to Loy advocating on behalf of Confederate Maryland memories was not an anomaly. Duval expressed her aims in being a part of the Maryland commission in her report to the UDC at the beginning of the centennial in 1961. She stated, "The centennial observance of the War of 1861–65 ties in with our own objectives and as a member of Maryland's Civil War Centennial Commission, I use every opportunity to bring our Confederate history to the fore." Duval was also behind the establishment of James Ryder Randall week in Maryland. She saw the centennial and her official role within it as a prime opportunity to cultivate Maryland's Civil War identity. She viewed the State House plaque as a disappointment because it promoted Maryland's dual Civil War identity. Duval not only represents the persistence of competing memories in Maryland, her protest also underscores a continued resentment of reconciliationist overtures inside the state. Duval's words echo the same sentiment of reconciliation representing disloyalty that many soldiers expressed on the Antietam and Gettysburg battlefields decades earlier.[57]

The dedication of the State House plaque was not the only act during the centennial that proved controversial, and it was also not the only time that Executive Director Park Loy received criticism. The Antietam–South Mountain Centennial Association stated its frustration with Loy at a board of directors meeting in which Loy was an attending guest in 1962. The president of the association, W. H. Shealy, "stated that the Association feels that Mr. Loy has not been cooperative." Shealy pointed to Loy's "failure to take our brochures to Columbus," the site of the annual Civil War Centennial Meeting. He also expressed his disappointment with Loy for neglecting to give Governor Tawes a prospectus of the events to take place at Antietam and requested that the governor "send letters of invitation to the governors and the state commission of each state represented at Antietam."[58]

Loy defended himself and in so doing embodied the Maryland centennial commission's primary aim of avoiding controversy. The minutes of the board of directors meeting noted, "Due to the emphasis on the re-enactment in our brochures Mr. Loy did not take them to Columbus because the National Commission and the Ohio Commission are opposed to re-enactments." The board, however, believed that since the commemorative plans "were in effect before the National Commission's ruling against re-enactments that it should have been Mr. Loy's primary concern for the success of our commemoration." Loy did not pass along the commemoration prospectus because he did not want to place Maryland in a controversial position with the larger centennial commissions, but in so doing he inadvertently caused discontent within the state of Maryland. In Loy's eyes, the already complicated process of commemorating Civil War Maryland during the 1960s was challenging enough without placing the state under a discerning national microscope.[59]

Honoring another Confederate poet from Maryland besides James Ryder Randall also proved controversial. Abram J. Ryan was born in Hagerstown, Maryland. Ryan was a priest and served as a chaplain in the Confederate army. He also was a gifted poet and the works he published immediately following the war were highly influential in Confederate memorialization of the war throughout the South well into the twentieth century. Ryan was known as the "Poet-Priest of the South," and one of his most famous poems was "The Conquered Banner" (1865). The opening stanza read:

> Furl that Banner, for 'tis weary;
> Round its staff 'tis drooping dreary;
> Furl it, fold it, it is best;
> For there's not a man to wave it,
> And there's not a sword to save it,
> And there's not one left to lave it
> In the blood which heroes gave it;
> And its foes not scorn and brave it;
> Furl it, hide it—let it rest![60]

In July 1964, Loy wrote to Francis X. Gallagher, a member of the Maryland state legislature, concerning a proposed monument to Abram Ryan. He noted that the General Assembly of Maryland passed a resolution in 1959 calling for the erection of a monument to Ryan, but the Maryland Civil War Centennial Commission contacted Monsignor McGrath of St. Mary's Parish of the Roman Catholic Church of Hagerstown and he expressed no interest in the monument. The church in Hagerstown was considered the natural place for such a monument because it was the site of Ryan's christening. Due to the lack of interest exhibited by Monsignor McGrath, the commission deferred further consideration "until sometime later during the life and functioning of the Commission." As the official duties of the Maryland commission were winding down, Loy thought the time was right to once again attempt to settle the issue of a monument to the "Poet-Priest of the South."[61]

In the process of trying to more fully ascertain the circumstances surrounding the proposed monument, Loy received a letter addressed to a member of the General Assembly of Maryland by Edward A. Egan of Chicago. Egan took a keen interest in the proposed monument, as he had given talks across the country on Abram Ryan and was also working a "chapter of a long-researched and well-documented biography of Father Abram J. Ryan." He noted that his chapter would also cover monuments to the Confederate poet. Egan stated that both Tennessee and Alabama had or were planning to dedicate multiple memorials to Ryan while Maryland, his home state, still did not have a single memorial to him. "In writing the chapter on the memorials to Father Ryan, I will inevitabl[y] detail what Maryland and Hagerstown have done," he said. He informed the representative that it would "not be a pleasant task . . . to say that Father Ryan has been refused even a token of recognition in the place of his birth, Hagerstown."[62]

Upon receiving the forwarded letter, Loy and the Maryland commission once again approached Monsignor McGrath to discuss the prospect of a monument to Ryan. The commission learned that "the predecessor of Monsignor McGrath had expressed an opinion that Father Ryan was a controversial figure and that his war-time activities had no ecclesiastical significance in so far as St. Mary's Parish was concerned." Given the circumstances, Loy concluded, "it is my opinion that we should take no steps leading to the possible development of an undesirable local controversy," but he wanted to learn the views of Gallagher before the commission decided because he introduced the resolution urging the placement of a monument to Ryan.[63]

Egan received a copy of Loy's letter and offered a strongly worded rebuttal to his opinion. He agreed with Monsignor McGrath that the monument did not belong in St. Mary's Parish but believed that the monument should instead occupy a more public place in Hagerstown. He also did not understand why McGrath was entrusted with making the final decision regarding a monument to Ryan. Egan stated, "No justifiable reasons exist for basing public recognition of Father Ryan by the citizens of Maryland, Washington County and Hagerstown solely and mainly on the unproved assertions of Monsignor McGrath." He also took exception to Loy's phrase "an undesirable local controversy." Throughout his letter to Loy, Egan tried to prove that no controversy would result. He cited the fact that the Maryland legislature passed the resolution calling for a monument to Ryan and Governor Tawes approved it. He also recalled his experiences speaking about Father Ryan to residents of the Hagerstown and how well his speech was received and how widely covered it was in the local newspapers. He encountered no such controversy during his trip. Unfortunately for Egan, his efforts were for naught as no monument was erected to Father Abram Ryan in his hometown or his home state.[64]

The earnestness displayed by Egan and the response of Loy and the Maryland commission revealed a central struggle that existed throughout the Civil War centennial. Many Marylanders were not content with unbiased or middling commemorations. Even in 1960, they displayed an intensity and attachment to the process of establishing a clear Civil War identity for their state. The commission wanted to maintain a balance for the state to avoid controversy, but the divides that characterized the citizenship of Maryland throughout the years following the war continued as the state tried to commemorate its Civil War contributions in the mid-twentieth century. Maryland was a state that continued to wrestle with its Civil War identity, and that identity was deeply conflicted in the 1960s.

The divides over commemorating Maryland's Civil War history during the centennial were not simply formed over Union and Confederate memories. Race also played a factor in how individuals viewed the unfolding of the centennial and how Maryland should remember its contributions. In fact, many of the most divisive issues related to commemorating a particular side of the war were also deeply connected to the divisions over white and black memories of the Civil War. One of the most noteworthy examples of how the civil rights movement influenced Maryland's commemoration of the centennial was the Calvert County Civil War Centennial Commission's boycott of commemorative programing because of President John F. Kennedy's demand that the events be desegregated.

Throughout his administration, Kennedy strived to make sure Civil War centennial events did not limit the participation of African Americans. In the lead up to its annual meeting, the National Civil War Centennial Commission "capitulated to President Kennedy . . . and agreed to avoid segregated hotels at Charleston, S.C." Kennedy "urged that Negro delegates from state Civil War Centennial Commissions be accorded equal treatment," and he put the commissions on notice that the "Administration would not condone racial segregation at any federally sponsored meetings." To Kennedy, the Civil War centennial was an opportunity to highlight the racial progress that was made over the past century and segregated ceremonies undercut his objective.[65]

The members of the Calvert County Civil War Centennial Commission did not approve of this policy put forth by Kennedy and accepted by the national and Maryland state commissions. Calvert County is located in southern Maryland, and its eastern border is the shore of the Chesapeake Bay. Park Loy had sent invitations to the local Maryland Civil War commissions for a ceremony on Veterans Day in Annapolis, Maryland, and he received an RSVP from the chairman of the Calvert County commission, John Parran Broome, which indicated he would not attend. Loy decided to write the chairman and ask if there was anyone else from the county's commission who could attend as a substitute because it was Loy's hope that Calvert County would be represented at the proceedings. The response that Loy received was so troubling that he decided to pass it along to former U.S. senator and present chairman of the Maryland Civil War Centennial Commission George L. Radcliffe. Broome wrote to Loy, "I am sorry to report that none of our committee has much interest in this organization since President Kennedy has insisted that it must be de-segregated." He continued by surmising "that if we are to relive the Civil War as it was, this issue should not have come into matter." Broome then expressed his regret but confessed, "that is the way I feel." In his letter to Radcliffe, Loy deemed it "unfortunate that the members of the Calvert County Committee should be so influenced and by this reply practically eliminating Calvert County from active participation in any future action." The response of the Calvert County Civil War Centennial Commission to Kennedy's policy of desegregating the centennial high-lighted the struggle of commemorating Civil War Maryland during the 1960s. The members of the Calvert County committee had such a clear idea of how they wanted to remember the Civil War that if they could not do so on their terms, they would boycott the entire process. The need to create a sectional identity for Maryland was mirrored by the need to establish a white identity for the state and its Civil War legacy.[66]

The culture and legacy of the civil rights movement also undoubt-edly influenced the environment in which Maryland African American protests to Confederate commemoration took place. In 1952, the *Washington Afro-American* reported on the abundance of Confederate regalia among the Dixiecrats with an article subtitled "Flags, Caps, States' Rights Talk Smoke Screens to Hide Opposition to Truman's Civil Rights Pro-gram." The same newspaper also outlined a story in which a group of 130 African American students attempted to change their high school's use of Confederate symbols, including Confederate uniforms for the band, "Dixie" as the school song, and the *Rebel Review* as the title for the school newspaper.[67]

As the centennial concluded and the civil rights movement secured landmark legislation, the state song of Maryland came under scrutiny. The initial reaction to Maryland's new state song did not mirror the sen-timents toward it a few decades later. African Americans who opposed the song were joined by white citizens of the state who felt that "Mary-land, My Maryland" did not represent the Old Line State's true identity. The *News American* reported on a movement to replace "Maryland, My

Maryland" as the official state song. Tom Wason, author of the reporting article, recalled that in the song's "first verse, the federal government is called despotic and in the final verse northerners are called scum." Wason also reported that county delegate Werner Fornos was contacted by members of his constituency "who felt that the song is an inflammatory holdover from the Civil War." Fornos suggested that the state of Maryland hold a contest in order to find an alternative to the current state song. History professor John W. Baer also suggested changing the state song and remarked that the first and last verses were indeed the "most outrageous" and that there existed a "widespread ignorance about the song among Marylanders."[68] The debate over the song did not end in 1970, and almost ten years later another Maryland government official, state senator Howard Denis, attempted to change the song by encouraging a statewide contest. Denis argued that the song was "very offensive" and that he could not "see how any self-respecting citizen of the state can sing the lyrics."[69]

As before, however, many came to the defense of the song and cited the history and heritage of the tune. The Senate Constitutional and Public Law Committee killed the bill sponsored by Denis with a vote of six to two. Denis expressed his frustration and dissatisfaction by calling the song "a hate song" and noting that it "distorts history and is an insult to Marylanders who were loyal to the Union." Others believed that it was a waste of the state government's time and that if they contemplated the bill their constituents would question, "is that what they're doing in Annapolis?"[70] Many notable columnists chimed in against the efforts of Denis to whitewash Maryland's history. Richard Cohen authored a column titled "Tidying Up Our History With Aid of the Eraser," and George Will concurred, asserting that "attempts to sanitize what the past has passed on to us are disloyalties disguised as fastidiousness, disloyalties to our parent, the past."[71]

At the very least the culture of the civil rights movement influenced the move for a change of the song. Some prominent historians of Civil War memory, including Robert Cook and David Blight, have made a connection between remembrance of the divisive conflict and the civil rights era.[72] In her article on race and memory in early twentieth century Kentucky, Anne Marshall implores "historians to reconsider the nature of black and white contests over white and African American Civil War memory and to broaden the arenas in which we look for them."[73] A simple song reveals that even more than a century after the war concluded, Americans, black and white, continued to harbor strong ties with the Civil War and its memory. For Marylanders, establishing the Civil War identity and loyalty of their state was of the utmost importance because of the Civil War's centrality in American society throughout the second half of the twentieth century.

EPILOGUE

During a heated exchange in Robert Redford's 2010 film *The Conspirator*, General August Kautz admonishes and mocks Maryland native, former attorney general of the United States, and Surratt defender Reverdy Johnson. In the course of his tirade, Kautz questions Johnson's credibility: "Sounds to me like the enemy is among us. I recall Maryland was not among our most loyal states during the war. I think its Senator ought to certify his allegiance to this court." *The Conspirator* depicts the trial of Mary Surratt and fellow conspirators involved in the assassination of Abraham Lincoln. While the subject of Maryland's loyalty occupies only a small part of the film, the decision to include it is significant. Nearly 150 years removed from the trial of the Lincoln conspirators, the Civil War loyalty of Maryland still holds a grip on our collective imagination of the war. Just as the attorneys involved in the trial of the Lincoln conspirators attempted to use the state's sectionalism to make their arguments, Redford, along with writers James D. Solomon and Greg Bernstein, uses the Old Line State's conflicted Civil War identity for dramatic effect. A state that is not easily defined in Civil War scholarship or memory studies continues to grab us.[1]

The reference to Maryland in *The Conspirator* was not an anomaly. Long after the fanfare of the centennial subsided, the struggles over Maryland's Civil War memory continued. In March 1984, Daniel Berger submitted an editorial to the *Baltimore Sun* titled "Whose Maryland!?" that set off a firestorm. Berger took issue with the fact that "Maryland, My Maryland" was the state song of Maryland. "That song is as American as the Ku Klux Klan and as patriotic as the Communist 'International,' which is no reason to compel anyone to sing it," he wrote. He continued by stating that the song's "adoption in 1939 as the official state sentiment was an act *against* history."[2]

Brice Clagett, former chairman of the Maryland Historical Trust, offered a forceful response to Berger's column. He contended that Berger's argument "that Maryland had a pro-Union majority during the Civil War . . . is a fashionable view, but it does not accord with the evidence." Clagett's rebuttal generated a wave of letters that flooded the *Baltimore Sun* both in support of and in opposition to his remarks. One claimed that "Maryland stood for the Union and helped save the indivisibility of this nation" and that it was regrettable that "present-day Confederate sympathizers try to perpetuate their myths in the state." Another suggested that it "took a Union Army to keep Maryland in the Union" and concluded his piece stating, "Keep 'em honest, Brice." Hebert Howard wrote, "Abraham Lincoln did more to destroy constitutional liberty than any president we have ever had" and "to call him 'scum' and a 'despot' in our state song is to treat him too kindly." It was, however, the comments made by Goucher College history professor Jean Baker that caught Clagett's attention. Baker posited that Marylanders wanted neutrality in 1861 and "throughout the war, a much larger group of Marylanders were pro-Union." The exchange of letters eventually developed into a back-and-forth between Clagett and Baker. After a series of responses featured in the *Sun*, Clagett and Baker agreed to a public debate in November at the Enoch Pratt Free Library over the status of Maryland in the Civil War. Baker presented "The Case for the Union," and Clagett delivered "The Case for the Confederacy."[3]

The arguments featured in the debate were primarily rehashing those made in the letters to the editor, including discussions over the election of 1860, the question of secession, Union occupation of Maryland, and troop numbers. These topics of course were representative of the debates over Maryland in Civil War memory that were more than a century old. In 2017, Jean Baker recalled her experience with the debate. She remembered being booed by hecklers when she mentioned having "relatives on both sides of the Civil War" and one man "shouted you talk like you are from New England." Baker summarized the experience "as thoroughly unpleasant . . . with Clagett incredibly patronizing and a hostile crowd and subsequent harassing phone calls at odd hours from Maryland's neo-confederates." The internal debate over Maryland's place in Civil War memory raged on in the 1980s.[4]

The reference to Maryland in *The Conspirator* and the letters printed in the *Baltimore Sun* as well as the public 1984 debate not only demonstrate the continued struggle over the state's Civil War identity but also reflect the central components that characterized Maryland in Civil War memory: the importance of border state identity to American memory of the war and the role of loyalty in the postbellum period. Throughout the nineteenth and twentieth centuries, Maryland was a driving force in the nation's memory of the war. The border state's wartime loyalty framed and represented the divisions of the United States that formed during the war and persisted for decades after its conclusion. Maryland was not merely a backdrop for competing memories; it was a central character in the debates over Civil War memory that shaped American society in the wake of the Civil War.

Studying the first century of Maryland's Civil War memory not only sheds light on the importance of loyalty to citizens living in the postwar period but also reveals how varied levels of loyalty played out in commemorations and conversations of the Civil War. Individual veterans strived to maintain their personal loyalties and demonstrated their own devotion through their participation in monument building and fraternal organizations as well as their opposition to reconciliation. Maryland veterans undertook these activities with unmatched earnestness because of the divided loyalty of their state.

Those who lived through the war not only valued and protected their own personal loyalties but also championed the loyalty and devotion of their home states. The loyalty of their state played a significant role in their own identity as Civil War veterans. Marylanders' defense of their state put them on the frontlines for battles over memory because of Maryland's history during the war.

Finally, the concept of border state loyalty and identity held ramifications much larger than personal loyalties or even other state loyalties. The status of Maryland's Civil War loyalty in memory shaped sectional memories of the war. In other words, Maryland's loyalty fueled Unionist and Confederate loyalties well after 1865. The century following the war reveals that Maryland took center stage in America's continued struggle over the Civil War.

The issue of loyalty was also the defining characteristic of Maryland's sesquicentennial commemorations and provides yet another example of how the Old Line State reflects and embodies the nation's memory of the Civil War. In the same fashion as the U.S. government, Maryland did not have a state sesquicentennial commission. This was perhaps a case of both the country and Maryland learning from experiences during the centennial and attempting to avoid controversy. The lack of a national commission and the rarity of state commissions led some historians to question the impact of the sesquicentennial. For instance, in an interview with the Civil War Trust, historian Gary Gallagher characterized the sesquicentennial as "anemic" and stated that "most states have done absolutely nothing." Gallagher noted that part of problem was "that the Civil War still can become very controversial very quickly because you can't talk about it without talking about race." With the lack of national and state commissions, local and county organizations led the commemorative efforts across the country. In this respect, Maryland once again mirrored the nation. The city of Hagerstown, Maryland, noted for its role in the aftermath of the Battle of Antietam, organized a city staff to coordinate sesquicentennial events, including a series of historic markers and a photographic history book of Hagerstown during the Civil War period. Similarly, the Maryland Historical Society published a collection of Maryland Civil War photographs in honor of the sesquicentennial. Local organizations and the National Park Service were active in commemorating the two most important Civil War battles on Maryland soil, the Battles of Antietam and Monocacy. Maryland's collective and vibrant remembrance of the war during the 150th anniversary underscores the centrality of the American Civil War to the memory of Marylanders even in the twenty-first century.[5]

Furthermore, the sesquicentennial is representative of the border state's history in Civil War memory. Throughout the century and a half following the war, Maryland lacked a clear, dominant Civil War identity. Commemorations on the Antietam battlefield mixed reconciliationist sentiment with continued, unmitigated devotion to sectional identity. Plays, novels, historical manuscripts, and a state song promoted specific identities and loyalties for the state, but they were often met with competing memories of the border state's loyalty. Maryland veterans continued their fight on behalf of their state long after the war concluded, and they defended its legacy not only against former foes but also from their comrades who hailed from other states. Finally, during the 1930s and through the Civil War centennial, Maryland's memories of the war fractured along racial lines. The disparate memories of the war that characterized Maryland's memory of the Civil War and the border state's place in American memory persisted and were present in the state's sesquicentennial commemorations.

The sustained controversy over the state song shows how Civil War loyalty continues to influence Maryland society. The debate is exacerbated by the fact that the song is sung annually at the Preakness Stakes. Marylanders continue to put forth numerous petitions and articles calling for the repeal of "Maryland, My Maryland" as the state song, including fourth-grade students at Glen Burnie Park Elementary School of Anne Arundel County in 2009.[6] These petitions, of course, are often met by those promoting the state's Confederate legacy, who claim that removal of the song is distorting the state's history. The *Washington Post* even satirized the song and dispute with its own song titled "O Controversy!" The first few lines were as follows:

> Comes now debate of the state song
> Maryland! My Maryland!
> Seven years since it last came along
> Maryland! My Maryland!
> To some the song is out of date
> It speaks of Lincoln's threat to state
> And so they want to change its fate
> Maryland! My Maryland!
> Since '39, we've sung this ditty
> Maryland! My Maryland![7]

The persistence of Maryland's conflicted Civil War identity not only sheds light on the divisions of the Civil War but also shows how deep those divisions truly are and the hold they have on American society. These divisions have become clearer in the aftermath of the 2015 Charleston church shootings in South Carolina. The convicted shooter, Dylann Roof, authored a racist manifesto, indicating his desire to start a race war. Investigators also discovered photographs of Roof posing with the Confederate flag and firearms.[8]

In the aftermath of the shootings, the debates surrounding the Confederate battle flag and Confederate monuments intensified across the nation as well as within Maryland. The move to curb Maryland's commemorative landscape accelerated after a white supremacist rally was held in Charlottesville, Virginia, in August 2017 to oppose removing a monument of Robert E. Lee. The neo-Nazis inflicted violence on counter-protestors, including a white supremacist who drove a car into the crowd of people protesting racism, injuring many and killing one woman. Calls for removing Confederate monuments reverberated throughout the South in the days that followed the rally. In the early morning hours of August 16, 2017, the city of Baltimore removed its Confederate monuments. Reflecting on the decision to take down the monuments, Baltimore mayor Catherine Pugh said, "It's done. . . . They needed to come down." Maryland's physical manifestations of Confederate memory, much like the nation's, are receding rapidly from public spaces. As the United States's memory of the war evolves, so too does Maryland's.[9]

Marylanders continue to grapple with their Civil War identity more than 150 years removed from the conflict. The conflicted nature of Maryland's Civil War memory explains in part why historians have not thoroughly examined the state's status in collective and popular memory. Maryland does not fit neatly into a larger Unionist or Confederate narrative. Maryland's postbellum history of commemoration and remembrance is messy. In Maryland, we see the most salient legacies of the war: the persistence of the Civil War's divisive memory, its continued impact on society and culture, and the importance of identity and loyalty to American citizens living in the postwar period. The complications and controversies that characterize Maryland in Civil War memory are what make it more interesting and important to our larger understanding of the American Civil War.

NOTES

INTRODUCTION

1. "Proclamation to the People of Maryland," Encyclopedia Virginia, http://www.encyclopediavirginia.org/_Proclamation_to_the_People_of_Maryland_by_Robert_E_Lee_1862.

2. H. L. Mencken, "Maryland: Apex of Normalcy," *The Nation* 114 (1922): 517.

3. In her book *Creating a Confederate Kentucky: The Lost Cause and Civil War Memory in a Border State* (Chapel Hill: University of North Carolina Press, 2010), historian Anne Marshall contends that Kentucky developed an ex post facto Confederate identity in the first century after the Civil War despite the fact that Kentucky never seceded and significantly more Kentuckians fought for the Union than the Confederacy. Marshall persuasively argues that Kentuckians embraced the Lost Cause as well as accepted increased racial violence as a way to attempt to maintain the societal and racial status quo. She argues that this embracing of Confederate memories and ideologies "dominated the historical landscape of postwar Kentucky on the surface" in spite of challenges from former Unionists and African Americans and the "active political and cultural dialogue" that characterized the state. Additionally, she posits that the "efforts of white Kentuckians to celebrate the Confederacy played a major role in cementing and embellishing Kentucky's already-existing southern identity, in effect making it more southern" (p. 4). Historian Aaron Astor presents a similar argument in *Rebels on the Border: Civil War, Emancipation, and the Reconstruction of Kentucky and Missouri* (Baton Rouge: Louisiana State University Press, 2012). He argues, "Although Unionists far outnumbered Confederates in Missouri and Kentucky, the postwar period witnessed dozens of ceremonies, celebrations, and commemorations honoring the Confederate soldiers." This was possible, in part, through the actions of individuals that Astor terms "belated Confederates." They were former Unionists in Kentucky and Missouri "who symbolically

accepted the Confederate cause in the postwar period as the most honorable course" and "helped legitimize the construction of a southern regional identity in the postwar Border States" in response to changes and fear of changes in race relations and citizenship (p. 5). Most recently, Christopher Phillips examines the middle border states during and after the war in *The River Ran Backward: The Civil War and the Remaking of the American Middle Border* (Oxford: Oxford University Press, 2016). Phillips argues that the conflicted nature of the western border states challenges the notion of border states as a boundary between the North-South binary. The divisions within Maryland, in many respects, reflect similar divisions of the middle border states outlined by Phillips in his work.

4. Charles W. Mitchell, *Maryland Voices of the Civil War* (Baltimore: Johns Hopkins University Press, 2007). Mitchell explores the place of Maryland in Civil War memory in his epilogue. Kevin Conley Ruffner, *Maryland's Blue and Gray: A Border State's Union and Confederate Junior Officer Corps* (Baton Rouge: Louisiana State University Press, 1997). A few scholars have offered preliminary investigations into the importance of Maryland to Civil War memory. In her Ph.D. dissertation "Lincoln's Divided Backyard: Maryland in the Civil War era" (Rice University, 2010), Jessica A. Cannon contends that Maryland moved slowly from being a state that possessed a southern identity in 1861 to a state whose "cultural identity resided with the North by April 1865" (p. 237). Although her dissertation focuses primarily on the period from 1861 to 1865, Cannon devotes her conclusion to a discussion of the postwar identity and memory of Maryland. She argues that the promoters of the Lost Cause, such as the United Daughters of the Confederacy and the Ku Klux Klan, "were not the dominant culture." She points to the problem of racism throughout the United States in the postwar period as well as Maryland's industrial and urban development as evidence of the "northernness" of the state. It is important to note that many other southern states also industrialized and urbanized following the Civil War. Her conclusions on the minority opinion of the Lost Cause and Confederate identity also warrant further investigation. Even if those promoting a Confederate, southern identity on behalf of the state of Maryland were in the minority, their impact on the popular and collective Civil War memory of Maryland is still significant and worthy of more in-depth analysis. Cannon characterizes the adoption of "Maryland, My Maryland" as the state song of Maryland in 1939 as representative of the efforts of a "clear minority in a northern society" to challenge "pressure from black Marylanders." She also notes that attendees of the Preakness Stakes still sing the song and this yearly occurrence "baffles the mind" (pp. 237, 239–240). The persistent Confederate legacies of Maryland are easier to discern when the conflicted nature of Maryland Civil War memory is taken into account. By underscoring the multiple voices involved, a more complete picture of Maryland in the Civil War era comes into focus and one in which we see the power of competing memories. Additionally, for the purpose of this book, "memory" refers to different aspects of the war that various groups

promoted with some degree of consensus while the term "legacy" alludes to the broader points these memories attempted to support and promote.

5. This interpretation of Maryland's Civil War memory fits within a growing body of scholarship that examines a national debate defined by the persistence of competing Civil War memories and anti-reconciliation sentiment in the postbellum United States. These scholars put forth an important challenge to the interpretation articulated by David Blight in *Race and Reunion: The Civil War in American Memory* (Cambridge: Harvard University Press, 2001). Blight argues that reconciliation and reunion between white northerners and southerners gained traction during 1880s and 1890s at the expense of African Americans. According to Blight, sectional reunion hinged on the white North capitulating on many social and political issues that surrounded the war, most notably those of race and discrimination. Therefore, reconciliation between white Union and Confederate veterans could take place by focusing on their shared experience in war and the celebration of their heroism on the battlefield. Conversely, historian John Neff proposes in *Honoring the Civil War Dead: Commemoration and the Problem of Reconciliation* (Lawrence: University Press of Kansas, 2005) that there were many Union veterans who resisted reconciliation and expressed this resistance in the rhetoric they employed during commemoration activities and ceremonies honoring their fallen comrades. Additionally, Neff argues that much like in the South, northerners engaged in their own myth-making through the form of the "Cause Victorious," which also inhibited reconciliation. Union soldiers were less willing to forget the cause for which they fought and accept those who fought against it when remembering those who died to preserve the Union. Benjamin Cloyd puts forth a similar argument in *Haunted by Atrocity: Civil War Prisons in American Memory* (Baton Rouge: Louisiana State University Press, 2010). He contends that memories of Civil War prisons in the nineteenth and twentieth centuries kept alive a divisive sentiment among veterans both North and South. Most recently, Caroline Janney offers a definition of reconciliation and its distinction from reunion in her *Remembering the Civil War: Reunion and the Limits of Reconciliation* (Chapel Hill: University of North Carolina Press, 2013). Reunion was the political and literal reunification of the nation that occurred in 1865 and was bolstered by the close of Reconstruction. Reunion did not require reconciliation. Reconciliation was more fluid and the war generation interpreted it in different ways. Veterans North and South, men and women, black and white, all wrestled with reconciliation and its meaning. Reconciliation could be an emotion or feeling; it could also be an act or a political device. The fluidity and complexity surrounding reconciliation compounded by the refusal of the war generation to forget why they fought made widespread, national reconciliation unachievable.

6. William A. Blair, *With Malice toward Some: Treason and Loyalty in the Civil War Era* (Chapel Hill: University of North Carolina Press, 2014).

7. "Augustus W. Bradford (1806–1881)," *Archives of Maryland* (Biographical

Series), http://msa.maryland.gov/megafile/msa/speccol/sc3500/sc3520
/001400/001463/html/1463bi02.html.

CHAPTER 1. MARYLAND ON TRIAL

1. "Virginia Garland Moore Craig letter dated April 19, 1865," Maryland
Digital Cultural Heritage, http://collections.mdch.org/cdm/compoundobject
/collection/mcw/id/58/rec/165.

2. Kevin Conley Ruffner, *Maryland's Blue and Gray: A Border State's Union and
Confederate Junior Officer Corps* (Baton Rouge: Louisiana State University Press,
1997), 20–21.

3. Ibid.

4. Ibid., 17–18.

5. Charles W. Mitchell, ed., *Maryland Voices of the Civil War* (Baltimore: Johns
Hopkins University Press, 2007), 3–4.

6. Ruffner, *Maryland's Blue and Gray*, 23, 26.

7. Ibid., 28, 29.

8. Ibid., 30; Mitchell, *Maryland Voices of the Civil War*, 9.

9. It was later discovered, according to Lucinda Beall, that it was only a
group of students. "Lucinda Rebecca (Lucy) Beall letter dated December 27,
1860," Maryland Digital Cultural Heritage, http://collections.mdch.org/cdm
/compoundobject/collection/mcw/id/549/rec/108.

10. Quoted in Mitchell, *Maryland Voices of the Civil War*, 17–18.

11. "Martin H. Batson letter dated February 5, 1861," Maryland Digital Cultural Heritage, http://collections.mdch.org/cdm/compoundobject/collection
/mcw/id/557/rec/112; Ruffner, *Maryland's Blue and Gray*, 31–32.

12. U.S. War Department, *The War of the Rebellion: A Compilation of the Official
Records of the Union and Confederate Armies*, Series II, Volume I (Washington,
D.C.: Government Printing Office, 1894), 564.

13. Mitchell, *Maryland Voices of the Civil War*, 4, 11; Ruffner, *Maryland's Blue
and Gray*, 34–36.

14. U.S. War Department, *The War of the Rebellion: A Compilation of the Official
Records of the Union and Confederate Armies*, Series I, Volume II (Washington,
D.C.: Government Printing Office, 1880), 7–9.

15. Ibid., 9–11.

16. U.S. War Department, *The War of the Rebellion*, Series II, Volume I,
564–565.

17. Ibid., 565.

18. Ruffner, *Maryland's Blue and Gray*, 39; *Journal of Proceedings of the Senate
of Maryland, April Special Session 1861* (Frederick: Beale H. Richardson, Printer,
1861), 8, 13.

19. Ruffner, *Maryland's Blue and Gray*, 40; Mitchell, *Maryland Voices of the Civil
War*, 5, 149.

20. U.S. War Department, *The War of the Rebellion*, Series II, Volume I, 587–588.

21. "Ex Parte Merryman," Maryland State Archives, 2004, http://teaching .msa.maryland.gov/000001/000000/000107/html/t107.html.

22. Brian McGinty, *The Body of John Merryman: Abraham Lincoln and the Suspension of Habeas Corpus* (Cambridge: Harvard University Press, 2011); Abraham Lincoln Message to Congress, July 4, 1861, transcribed and annotated by the Lincoln Studies Center, Knox College, Galesburg, Illinois, available at *Abraham Lincoln Papers at the Library of Congress*, Manuscript Division (Washington, D.C.: American Memory Project, 2000–2002), http://memory.loc.gov/cgi-bin /ampage?collId=mal&fileName=mal1/105/1050300/malpage.db&recNum=0.

23. U.S. War Department, *The War of the Rebellion*, Series II, Volume I, 678–679.

24. Ibid., 679.

25. John A. Dix to Simon Cameron, Friday, September 13, 1861, transcribed and annotated by the Lincoln Studies Center, Knox College, Galesburg, Illinois, available at *Abraham Lincoln Papers at the Library of Congress*, Manuscript Division (Washington, D.C.: American Memory Project, 2000–2002), http://memory .loc.gov/cgi-bin/query/r?ammem/mal:@field%28DOCID+@lit%28d1163000 %29%29; U.S. War Department, *The War of the Rebellion*, Series II, Volume I, 682–685.

26. U.S. War Department, *The War of the Rebellion*, Series II, Volume I, 595, 684–685.

27. "General Dix's Proclamation," *An American Time Capsule: Three Centuries of Broadsides and Other Printed Ephemera*, Rare Book and Special Collections Division, Library of Congress (Washington, D.C.: American Memory Project, 2000–2002), http://memory.loc.gov/ammem/rbpehtml/.

28. *Savannah Republican*, March 22, 1862.

29. U.S. War Department, *The War of the Rebellion*, Series II, Volume II, 778–790.

30. "Suspension of Civil Liberties in Maryland: The Case of Richard Bennett Carmichael," Maryland State Archives, http://msa.maryland.gov/msa/speccol /sc5500/sc5572/000001/000000/000016/html/t16.html; "Executive Order No. 1—Relating to Political Prisoners," The American Presidency Project, University of California, Santa Barbara, http://www.presidency.ucsb.edu/ws /?pid=69792#axzz2jWcvBQXo.

31. Ruffner, *Maryland's Blue and Gray*, 7–11; Anne E. Marshall, *Creating a Confederate Kentucky: The Lost Cause and Civil War Memory in a Border State* (Chapel Hill: University of North Carolina Press, 2010), 2; Daniel E. Sutherland, *Savage Conflict: The Decisive Role of Guerillas in the American Civil War* (Chapel Hill: University of North Carolina Press, 2009), 166. Maryland's total population in 1860 was 687,049, compared to nearly 1,000,000 each for Kentucky and Missouri (U.S. Census, 1860). Additionally, these troop numbers

do not reflect the different forms of violence, namely, guerilla warfare, which characterized the wartime experiences of Kentucky and Missouri.

32. "Letter Charles H. Russell to Ward Lamon, April 1862," Letters of Charles H. Russell, First Maryland Cavalry, Western Maryland's Historical Library, http://www.whilbr.org/CharlesRussellLetters/index.aspx; "Charles Thornton Moore letter dated August 7, 1863," Maryland Digital Cultural Heritage, http://collections.mdch.org/cdm/compoundobject/collection/mcw/id /83/rec/34.

33. Ted Ballard, *Staff Ride Guide: The Battle of Antietam* (Washington, D.C.: Center of Military History, 2006), 3.

34. Ibid., 4.

35. "Proclamation to the People of Maryland," Encyclopedia Virginia, http://www.encyclopediavirginia.org/_Proclamation_to_the_People_of _Maryland_by_Robert_E_Lee_1862.

36. Joseph Glathaar, *General Lee's Army: From Victory to Collapse* (New York: Simon & Schuster, 2008), 166–167.

37. "Civil War Diary of James Francis Beall," September 1862, Western Maryland's Historical Library, http://www.whilbr.org/JamesFrancisBeall/index .aspx; William Harrison Beach, *The First New York (Lincoln) Cavalry from April 19, 1861, to July 7, 1865* (New York: Lincoln Cavalry Association, 1902), 170.

38. Gary Gallagher, ed., *The Antietam Campaign* (Chapel Hill: University of North Carolina Press, 1999), ix–x; Ballard, *Staff Ride Guide*, 45.

39. *Hagerstown Herald of Freedom and Torch Light*, September 10–24, 1862.

40. Ibid.

41. "Antietam National Battlefield (U.S. National Park Service)," http://www .nps.gov/anti/.

42. Bob Zeller, *The Blue and Gray in Black and White: A History of Civil War Photography* (Westport: Praeger, 2005), 73–75.

43. Earl J. Hess, "A Terrible Fascination: The Portrayal of Combat in the Civil War Media," in *An Uncommon Time: The Civil War and the Northern Home Front*, ed. P. A. Cimbala and R. M. Miller (New York: Fordham University Press, 2002), 20.

44. Zeller, *The Blue and Gray in Black and White*, 65, 80.

45. Earl J. Hess, "Tell Me What the Sensations Are: The Northern Home Front Learns About Combat," in *Union Soldiers and the Northern Home Front*, ed. P. A. Cimbala and R. M. Miller (New York: Fordham University Press, 2002), 123.

46. *New York Times*, October 20, 1862.

47. Zeller, *The Blue and Gray in Black and White*, 77.

48. "Maryland in the Civil War," Enoch Pratt Free Library, http://www .prattlibrary.org/uploadedFiles/www/locations/central/maryland/md_cw _complete.pdf; "Fighting for Freedom: United States Colored Troops from Maryland," Maryland States Archives, http://teaching.msa.maryland.gov

/000001/000000/000118/html/t118.html; Mitchell, *Maryland Voices of the Civil War,* 7. For a thorough discussion of slavery in Maryland during the war, see Barbara Fields, *Slavery and Freedom on the Middle Ground: Maryland During the Nineteenth Century* (New Haven: Yale University Press, 1987).

49. Quoted in Mitchell, *Maryland Voices of the Civil War,* 384–385.

50. Ibid., 185, 187.

51. "Monocacy: The Battle that Saved Washington, D.C.," Maryland State Archives, http://teaching.msa.maryland.gov/000001/000000/000141 /html/t141.html; "Virginia Garland Moore Craig letter dated July 10, 1864," Maryland Digital Cultural Heritage, http://collections.mdch.org/cdm /compoundobject/collection/mcw/id/41/rec/168.

52. *Proceedings and Debates of the 1864 Constitutional Convention,* Maryland State Archives, vol. 102, 723.

53. Abraham Lincoln, 1809–1865, *Collected Works of Abraham Lincoln,* vol. 6 (Ann Arbor: University of Michigan Digital Library Production Services, 2001), 557–558. William Blair includes an in-depth analysis of this exchange and the role military presence at polls had in elections throughout the border states, including Maryland, during the war in *With Malice toward Some: Treason and Loyalty in the Civil War Era* (Chapel Hill: University of North Carolina Press, 2014), 183–184.

54. Quoted in Ruffner, *Maryland's Blue and Gray,* 261.

55. "Virginia Garland Moore Craig letter dated September 13, 1864," Maryland Digital Cultural Heritage, http://collections.mdch.org/cdm /compoundobject/collection/mcw/id/93/rec/170; Mitchell, *Maryland Voices of the Civil War,* 151.

56. Tyler Dennett, ed., *Lincoln and the Civil War in the Diaries and Letters of John Hay* (New York: Dodd, Mead & Company, 1939), 16.

57. Elizabeth D. Leonard, *Lincoln's Avengers: Justice, Revenge, and Reunion after the Civil War* (New York: W. W. Norton, 2004), 4–5.

58. Ibid., 5–7.

59. Ibid., 36–38.

60. Ibid., 36.

61. Michael W. Kauffman, *American Brutus: John Wilkes Booth and the Lincoln Conspiracies* (New York: Random House, 2007), 81; Leonard, *Lincoln's Avengers,* 59, 46, 37, 50, 55, 39.

62. Leonard, *Lincoln's Avengers,* 67, 129–130.

63. Benjamin Perley Poore, *The Conspiracy Trial for the Murder of the President: And the Attempt to Overthrow the Government by the Assassination of Its Principal Officers* (Boston: J. E. Tilton and Company, 1865), vol. 1, 21.

64. Ibid., 59; Edward Steers Jr., ed., *The Trial: The Assassination of President Lincoln and the Trial of the Conspirators* (Lexington: University Press of Kentucky, 2003), xviii.

65. Benjamin Perley Poore, *The Conspiracy Trial for the Murder of the President,*

and the Attempt to Overthrow the Government by the Assassination of Its Principal Officers (Boston: J. E. Tilton and Company, 1865), vol. 2, 494–495.

66. Benn Pitman, *The Assassination of President Lincoln and the Trial of the Conspirators* (New York: Moore, Wilstach and Baldwin, 1865), 127.

67. Ibid., 179–180.

68. Ibid., 142–143.

69. Ibid., 184–185, 191.

70. Poore, *The Conspiracy Trial for the Murder of the President*, vol. 2, 402.

71. Pittman, *The Assassination of President Lincoln*, 128, 130.

72. *Harper's Weekly* 9, no. 440 (1865): 342.

73. George Alfred Townsend, *The Life, Crime, and Capture of John Wilkes Booth* (New York: Dick and Fitzgerald, Publishers, 1865), 42, 50.

CHAPTER 2. "AN UNGENEROUS SNEER"

1. Rev. J. William Jones, *Southern Historical Society Papers, Volume XIV* (Richmond: Southern Historical Society, 1886), 430, 433. Many historians have debated the status of reconciliation during the second half of the nineteenth century and beyond. In *The Romance of Reunion: Northerners and the South, 1865–1900* (Chapel Hill: University of North Carolina Press, 1993), Nina Silber argues that in the growing uncertainty and industrialization of the Gilded Age, "Yankees sought to re-create the Victorian ideal through the reconciliation process." Northerners' image of the South embodied an "idealized feminine sphere" and characterized the South as a region of "domestic comfort" (p. 9). This romanticized notion facilitated reconciliation, according to Silber, and quickened sectional forgetfulness over the issues that brought about the Civil War. Silber helped open the discussion for later historians, including David Blight, who expanded on the notion of forgetfulness. In his seminal work *Race and Reunion: The Civil War in American Memory* (Cambridge: Harvard University Press, 2001), Blight argues that reconciliation gained traction during 1880s and 1890s and occurred at the expense of African Americans. According to Blight, reconciliation could only occur by capitulating on many social and political issues that surrounded the war, most notably those of race, racism, and discrimination. To Silber and Blight, reconciliation was to eclipse Civil War bitterness with the sentimental rejoining of North and South. Paul Buck provided the foundation for analysis on reconciliation in *The Road to Reunion, 1865–1900* (Boston: Little, Brown, 1937). He noted that sectional reconciliation and reunion occurred during the 1880s and 1890s and argued that race played a central role in the process. Blight furthered the reconciliationist thesis with *Race and Reunion*. Edward Blum's *Reforging the White Republic: Race, Religion, and American Nationalism, 1865–1898* (Baton Rouge: Louisiana State University Press, 2005) also falls within this school of interpretation.

2. As noted in the introduction notes, others, including John Neff and Car-

oline Janney, have since challenged the reconciliationist thesis. Janney distinguishes between reunion and reconciliation in *Remembering the Civil War: Reunion and the Limits of Reconciliation* (Chapel Hill: University of North Carolina Press, 2013). Reunion occurred with the conclusion of the war in 1865. Reconciliation was more complex and could be evidenced through something as ambiguous as an emotion or something as visceral as a deliberate act. This complexity, in part, made a large-scale, national reconciliation unattainable. The dynamism and fluidity of reconciliation, as defined by Janney, was evident in multiple historical moments at Antietam and Gettysburg. John Neff's *Honoring the Civil War Dead: Commemoration and the Problem of Reconciliation* (Lawrence: University of Kansas Press, 2005), Barbara Gannon's *The Won Cause: Black and White Comradeship in the Grand Army of the Republic* (Chapel Hill: University of North Carolina Press, 2011), Benjamin Cloyd's *Haunted by Atrocity: Civil War Prisons in American Memory* (Baton Rouge: Louisiana State University Press, 2010), William Blair's *Cities of the Dead: Contesting the Memory of the Civil War in the South, 1865–1914* (Chapel Hill: University of North Carolina Press, 2003), and Caroline Janney's *Remembering the Civil War* counter the reconciliationist thesis put forth by the Blight school.

3. Portions of this section on Antietam National Battlefield and Cemetery appeared originally in my master's thesis: David K. Graham, "To Guard in Peace: The Commemoration History of the Battle of Antietam, 1862–1937" (M.A. thesis, Bowling Green State University, 2011). Charles W. Snell and Sharon A. Brown, *Antietam National Battlefield and National Cemetery: An Administrative History* (Washington, D.C.: U.S. Department of the Interior, 1986), 1; Timothy B. Smith, *A Chickamauga Memorial: The Establishment of America's First Civil War National Military Park* (Knoxville: University of Tennessee Press, 2009), 8; *History of Antietam National Cemetery including A Descriptive List of all the Loyal Soldiers Buried Therein, Together with the Ceremonies and Address on the Occasion of the Dedication of the Grounds, September 17th, 1867* (Baltimore: John W. Woods, Steam Printer, 1869), 7.

4. *History of Antietam National Cemetery*, 7–8.

5. Susan W. Trail, "Remembering Antietam: Commemoration and Preservation of a Civil War Battlefield" (Ph.D. diss., University of Maryland, 2005), 77; *Baltimore American*, reprinted in Hagerstown *Herald and Torch Light*, December 25, 1867, quoted in Trail, "Remembering Antietam," 77.

6. Trail, "Remembering Antietam," 108; Neff, *Honoring the Civil War Dead*, 124.

7. *Lancaster Intelligencer*, May 10, 1865; *New York Times*, July 3, 1866; Trail, "Remembering Antietam," 80–82.

8. *Boonsboro Odd Fellow*, October 11, 1866, quoted in Trail, "Remembering Antietam," 83, 85.

9. Trail, "Remembering Antietam," 91.

10. *History of Antietam National Cemetery*, 36.

11. Ibid., 38.

12. *Daily Evening Bulletin*, September 18, 1867.

13. *History of Antietam National Cemetery*, 22–23.

14. Ibid., 54.

15. Eric Foner, *A Short History of Reconstruction, 1863–1877* (New York: Harper & Row, 1990), 85.

16. *Daily Evening Bulletin*, September 18, 1867; *Boonsboro Odd Fellow*, September 19, 1867, quoted in Trail, "Remembering Antietam," 94.

17. *Village Record*, September 27, 1867.

18. *New York Times*, September 18, 1867; Thomas A. Desjardin, *These Honored Dead: How the Story of Gettysburg Shaped American Memory* (Cambridge: Da Capo Press, 2003), 199.

19. *Daily Evening Bulletin*, September 18, 1867; *Boonsboro Odd Fellow*, September 26, 1867, quoted in Trail, "Remembering Antietam," 95.

20. *Daily Evening Bulletin*, September 18, 1867.

21. *History of Antietam National Cemetery*, 32.

22. *Village Record*, September 27, 1867.

23. Ibid.

24. Ibid.

25. Snell and Brown, *Antietam National Battlefield and National Cemetery*, 23–24.

26. Thomas J. Brown, *The Public Art of Civil War Commemoration: A Brief History with Documents* (Boston: Bedford/St. Martin's, 2004), 24, 26; "Antietam National Cemetery: Private Soldier Monument," U.S. National Park Service, http://www.nps.gov/anti/historyculture/antietam-national -cemetery-part-2.htm.

27. Snell and Brown, *Antietam National Battlefield and National Cemetery*, 24, 26.

28. Trail, "Remembering Antietam," 118–120.

29. *New York Times*, September 18, 1880.

30. For more on the difficulties in creating and transporting the Private Soldier Monument, see Trail, "Remembering Antietam," and Graham, "To Guard in Peace."

31. Timothy B. Smith, *The Golden Age of Battlefield Preservation: The Decade of the 1890s and the Establishment of America's First Five Military Parks* (Knoxville: University of Tennessee Press, 2008), 2; Brown, *The Public Art of Civil War Commemoration*, 6.

32. Jones, *Southern Historical Society Papers, Volume XIV*, 443, 446.

33. *Shenango Valley News*, November 1, 1889.

34. The GBMA was chartered in April 1864 by the Pennsylvania state government. It was originally a small organization led by David McConaughy. By the 1880s, the association had grown through the influx of GAR members who gained controlling membership. See A. J. Meek and Herman Hattaway, *Gettysburg to Vicksburg: The Five Original Civil War Battlefield Parks* (Columbia: University of Missouri Press, 2001), 10.

35. "Minutes of Gettysburg Battlefield Memorial Association Board of

Directors—Maryland Monuments," Gettysburg National Military Park Archives, 1885, 129.

36. Carol Reardon, *Pickett's Charge in History and Memory* (Chapel Hill: University of North Carolina Press, 1997), 69, 92.

37. "Minutes of GBMA," 132–134.

38. Ibid., 133–135; Janney, *Remembering the Civil War*, 356.

39. Janney, *Remembering the Civil War*, 433–434.

40. Ibid., 435–436.

41. David M. Potter, "The Historians' Use of Nationalism and Vice Versa," *The American Historical Review* 67, no. 4 (1962): 924–950.

42. Bettie Alder Calhoun Emerson, *Historic Southern Monuments: Representative Memorials of the Heroic Dead of the Southern Confederacy* (New York: The Neale Publishing Company, 1911), 173.

43. Jones, *Southern Historical Society Papers, Volume XIV*, 436–439.

44. Ibid., 441.

45. Ibid., 443.

46. Ibid., 439.

47. William Blair and William Pencak, eds., *Making and Remaking Pennsylvania's Civil War* (University Park: Pennsylvania State University Press, 2001), 89; David L. Ladd and Audrey J. Ladd, eds., *The Bachelder Papers: Gettysburg in Their Own Words, Volume III, April 12, 1886 to December 22, 1894* (Dayton: Morningside House, 1995), 1461; Caroline Janney discusses Gettysburg as a Union memorial park in her *Remembering the Civil War*.

48. John M. Vanderslice, *Gettysburg: A History of the Gettysburg Battle-field Memorial Association with an Account of the Battle* (Philadelphia: The Memorial Association, 1897), 219; Robert E. Pattison Papers, Pennsylvania State Archives, http://www.phmc.state.pa.us/bah/dam/mg/mg168.htm; James A. Beaver Papers, Pennsylvania State Archives, http://www.phmc.state.pa.us/bah/dam/mg/mg389.htm.

49. *New York Times*, July 3, 1888; Reardon, *Pickett's Charge*, 103–107.

50. *Daily Alta California*, November 4, 1889; *Alexandria Gazette*, October 25, 1889.

51. *Shenango Valley News*, November 1, 1889.

52. *Shenango Valley News*, January 10, 1890; *New York Times*, January 17, 1890.

53. *Anderson Intelligencer*, December 19, 1889.

54. *Winchester Times*, November 6, 1889.

55. Ibid.

56. *Sacramento Daily Union*, November 24, 1889; *Columbus Enquirer*, November 30, 1889; *Evening Gazette*, October 26, 1889; *Shenango Valley News*, November 1, 1889; *Alexandria Gazette*, October 25, 1889.

57. *Columbus Enquirer*, December 22, 1889.

58. *New York Times*, October 26, 1889.

59. Maryland Gettysburg Monument Commission, *Report of the State of Maryland Gettysburg Monument Commission* (Baltimore: William K. Boyle and Son, 1891), 6, 7–8, 16, 98, 109.

60. *New York Times*, September 17, 1896; David Cunningham and Wells W. Miller, *Antietam. Report of the Ohio Antietam Battlefield Commission* (Springfield: Springfield Publishing Company, 1904), 109–112.

61. Trail, "Remembering Antietam," 259–261.

62. Janney, *Remembering the Civil War*, 222–225.

63. Trail, "Remembering Antietam," 259–261.

64. Ibid., 263; *New York Times*, May 31, 1900.

65. Grand Army of the Republic, Department of Maryland, *Proceedings of the Twenty-Fifth Annual Encampment of the Department of Maryland, Grand Army of the Republic, Held at Baltimore Maryland, February 21st and 22nd, 1901* (Baltimore: Shane Printing Company, 1901), 9–10.

66. *Marion Sentinel*, June 14, 1900.

67. *Urbana Daily Courier*, September 18, 1903.

68. *New York Times*, September 18, 1903.

69. Antietam Battlefield Memorial Commission, *Second Brigade of the Pennsylvania Reserves at Antietam, Report of the Antietam Battlefield Memorial Commission of Pennsylvania and Ceremonies at the Dedication of the Monuments Erected by the Commonwealth of Pennsylvania to Mark the Position of Four Regiments of the Pennsylvania Reserves Engaged in the Battle* (Harrisburg: Harrisburg Publishing Company, 1908), 26–29.

CHAPTER 3. THE HEART OF MARYLAND

A large portion of this chapter was originally published in the *Maryland Historical Magazine* 109, no. 1 (Spring 2014): 38–55.

1. John Greenleaf Whittier, "Barbara Frietchie," Poetry Foundation, http:// www.poetryfoundation.org/poem/174751.

2. In 1977, literary scholar Ann Douglas published *The Feminization of American Culture* (New York: Alfred A. Knopf, 1977). In it, she argued that during the second half of the nineteenth century, American society saw a shift in literary production. Works authored by women and works produced for consumption by women started to grow during this time period. The Victorian era's conceptions of women and qualities associated with women (positive and negative) were canonized in mass culture. Douglas attributed this shift in mass culture to the rapid growth of capitalism, urbanization, and industrialization as well as the weakening influence of the church on American society during the nineteenth century. Mass culture represented a respite from an ever-changing world. Although scholars of the past several decades have challenged many aspects of Douglas's assertion, the portrayal of feminine qualities in mass culture offers context to the feminization of Civil War Maryland during the postwar period

(Rose Laub Coser, "Review of The *Feminization of American Culture*," *American Journal of Sociology* 86, no. 2 [September 1980]: 394–396).

More recently than Douglas, Nina Silber and Anne Marshall have made scholarly arguments that are relevant to the postwar southernization and feminization of Maryland. Silber argues that after the Civil War, the South was romanticized in popular culture and also feminized through nostalgic portraits of the South as representative of simpler, purer time in the nation's rapidly changing history. Marshall argues that during the postwar period, Kentucky assumed a Confederate identity. In Maryland, we can see a combination of the processes outlined by Silber and Marshall but there are also aspects of the Old Line State's history that mark it as unique and add another dimension to the historiographical conversations on culture and identity. The feminization of Maryland is distinct from the feminization of the South as a whole because it is based on its experiences during the Civil War. The southernization of Maryland is different when compared to that of Kentucky because with Maryland, postwar writers attempted to create a southern state as opposed to a Confederate one. Nina Silber, *The Romance of Reunion: Northerners and the South, 1865–1900* (Chapel Hill: University of North Carolina Press, 1997); Anne E. Marshall, *Creating a Confederate Kentucky: The Lost Cause and Civil War Memory in a Border State* (Chapel Hill: University of North Carolina Press, 2010).

3. Caroline Janney, "The Lost Cause," Encyclopedia Virginia, Virginia Foundation for the Humanities, 2011.

4. Civil War historians have devoted a substantial amount of research toward investigating the Lost Cause and its significance. For more information, see Charles Reagan Wilson, *Baptized in Blood: The Religion of the Lost Cause, 1865–1920* (Athens: University of Georgia Press, 1980); Gaines M. Foster, *Ghosts of the Confederacy: Defeat, the Lost Cause, and the Emergence of the New South, 1865–1913* (Oxford: Oxford University Press, 1987); Karen Cox, *Dixie's Daughters: The United Daughters of the Confederacy and the Preservation of Confederate Culture* (Gainesville: University Press of Florida, 2003); Gary Gallagher and Alan T. Nolan, eds., *The Myth of the Lost Cause and Civil War History* (Bloomington: Indiana University Press, 2008); Gary Gallagher, *Causes Won, Lost, and Forgotten: How Hollywood and Popular Art Shaped What We Know About the Civil War* (Chapel Hill: University of North Carolina Press, 2008); Caroline E. Janney, *Burying the Dead but Not the Past: Ladies' Memorial Associations and the Lost Cause* (Chapel Hill: University of North Carolina Press, 2007); Marshall, *Creating a Confederate Kentucky*; John M. Coski, *The Confederate Battle Flag: America's Most Embattled Emblem* (Cambridge: Harvard University Press, 2005).

5. James W. Loewen and Edward H. Sebesta, eds., *The Confederate and Neo-Confederate Reader: The "Great Truth" about the "Lost Cause"* (Oxford: University of Mississippi Press, 2010), 249.

6. Edward Alfred Pollard, *The Lost Cause: A New Southern History of the War of the Confederates* (New York: E. B. Treat and Co., 1866), 121–122, 47, 123–124.

7. Robert Lewis Dabney, *Life and Campaigns of Lieut.-Gen. Thomas J. Jackson, (Stonewall Jackson)* (New York: Blelock and Co., 1866), 158.

8. Ibid., 190, 234.

9. Ibid., 546.

10. George Francis Robert Henderson, *Stonewall Jackson and the American Civil War*, vol. 1 (New York: Longmans, Green, and Co., 1898), 146–147.

11. George Francis Robert Henderson, *Stonewall Jackson and the American Civil War*, vol. 2 (New York: Longmans, Green, and Co., 1919), 209.

12. Douglas Southall Freeman, *The South to Posterity: An Introduction to the Writing of Confederate History* (Baton Rouge: Louisiana State University Press, 1998), 56; Frank H. Alfriend, *The Life of Jefferson Davis* (Cincinnati: Caxton Publishing House, 1868), 269.

13. Alfriend, *The Life of Jefferson Davis*, 351.

14. Ibid., 412.

15. Freeman, *The South to Posterity*, 44–45. There were also several memoirs published by Maryland Confederates many years later, including George Booth's *A Maryland Boy in Lee's Army: Personal Reminiscences of a Maryland Soldier in the War between the States 1861–1865* (Baltimore: Privately Published, 1898), W. W. Goldsborough's *The Maryland Line in the Confederate Army, 1861–1865* (Baltimore: Guggenheimer, Weil & Co., 1900), and McHenry Howard's *Recollections of a Maryland Confederate Soldier and Staff Officer under Johnston, Jackson, and Lee* (Baltimore: Williams & Wilkins Company, 1914). List taken from Mitchell's *Maryland Voices of the Civil War*.

16. John Beauchamp Jones, *A Rebel War Clerk's Diary at the Confederate States Capital* (Philadelphia: J. B. Lippincott and Co., 1866), 14.

17. Ibid., 25.

18. Jefferson Davis, *The Rise and Fall of the Confederate Government*, vol. 1 (New York: D. Appleton and Company, 1881), 299.

19. Wilson, *Baptized in Blood*, 139–140.

20. Lamar Hollyday, "Maryland Troops in the Confederate Service," *Southern Historical Society Papers, Volume III* (Richmond: Southern Historical Society, 1877), 130.

21. Bradley T. Johnson, "Memoir of First Maryland Regiment," *Southern Historical Society Papers, Volume IX* (Richmond: Southern Historical Society, 1881), 345.

22. A. M. Keiley, "Our Fallen Heroes," *Southern Historical Society Papers, Volume VII* (Richmond: Southern Historical Society, 1879), 375.

23. Carlton McCarthy, "Camp Fires of the Boys in Gray," *Southern Historical Society Papers, Volume I* (Richmond: Southern Historical Society, 1876), 80.

24. Z. B. Vance, *Southern Historical Society Papers, Volume XIV* (Richmond: Southern Historical Society, 1886), 507.

25. D. H. Hill, *Southern Historical Society Papers, Volume I* (Richmond: Southern Historical Society, 1876), 394.

26. Pollard, *The Lost Cause*, 116–117.

27. Ibid., 125.

28. Davis, *The Rise and Fall of the Confederate Government*, vol. 2 (New York: D. Appleton and Company, 1912), 460; *The Rise and Fall of the Confederate Government*, vol. 1, 337.

29. *Southern Historical Society Papers, Volume I*, 34.

30. Jubal Early, "Relative Strength of the Armies of Generals Lee and Grant," *Southern Historical Society Papers, Volume II* (Richmond: Southern Historical Society, 1876), 14.

31. Glenn Hughes and George Savage, eds., *America's Lost Plays: The Heart of Maryland and Other Plays by David Belasco* (Princeton: Princeton University Press, 1940), 235–236.

32. Marshall, *Creating a Confederate Kentucky*.

33. Hughes and Savage, *America's Lost Plays*, 171–172; *New York Times*, November 19, 1887; *New York Times*, May 23, 1889; Craig Clinton, *Mrs. Leslie Carter: A Biography of the Early Twentieth Century American Stage Star* (Jefferson: McFarland and Co., 2006).

34. Gerald Martin Bordman and Thomas S. Hischak, *The Oxford Companion to American Theatre* (Oxford: Oxford University Press, 2004), 299.

35. Silber, *The Romance of Reunion*, 89.

36. Hughes and Savage, *America's Lost Plays*, 179, 181.

37. Ibid., 183–184.

38. Ibid., 194, 240.

39. Ibid., 176, 193.

40. *New York Tribune* quoted in Hughes and Savage, *America's Lost Plays*, 172; *Macon Telegraph*, December 13, 1898; *New England Magazine* quoted in Silber, *Romance of Reunion*, 111; *New York Times*, April 17, 1898.

41. Hughes and Savage, *America's Lost Plays*, 172.

42. *Courier*, Lincoln, Nebraska, December 29, 1900; *Evening Bulletin*, Philadelphia, Pennsylvania, March, 12, 1900; *Minneapolis Journal*, January 12, 1901; *St. Paul Globe*, December 12, 1897; *New York Times*, April 22, 1896.

43. *New York Times*, October 27, 1895.

44. "Barbara Frietchie," *Atlantic*, http://www.theatlantic.com/magazine/archive/2012/02/barbara-frietchie/8826/.

45. Bordman and Hischak, *Oxford Companion to American Theatre*, 52–53.

46. Clyde Fitch, *Barbara Frietchie: The Frederick Girl* (New York: Life Publishing Company, 1900), 42, 112.

47. *New York Times*, October 3, 1899.

48. *New York Times*, October 5, 1899.

49. *New York Times*, October 10, 1899.

50. *New York Times*, October 13, 1899.

51. *New York Times*, October 14, 15, 29, and November 6, 1899.

52. *Confederate Veteran, Vol. VIII* (Nashville: S. A. Cunningham, 1900), 113.

53. *Confederate Veteran, Vol. XXII* (Nashville: S. A. Cunningham, 1914), 542.

54. Brian C. Pohanka, "For Maryland's Honor: A Story for Southern Independence (review)," *Civil War News,* http://www.civilwarnews.com/reviews/bookreviews.cfm?ID=262.

55. Lloyd T. Everett, *For Maryland's Honor: A Story of the War for Southern Independence* (Boston: Christopher Publishing House, 1922), 11–12, 14.

56. Ibid., 35–36, 54.

57. Ibid., 43, 56, 142.

58. Ibid., 62, 185.

59. *Confederate Veteran, Vol. XXX* (Nashville: S. A. Cunningham, 1922), 78.

60. Ibid.

61. Frank Cirillo, "A Southern Strategy: The *Atlanta Constitution* and the Lincoln Centennial, February 1909" (University of Virginia); Thomas Dixon, *The Southerner: A Romance of the Real Lincoln* (New York: Grosset and Dunlap, 1913), 146–149.

62. Thomas Dixon, *The Victim: A Romance of the Real Jefferson Davis* (Toronto: Copp Clark Co., 1914), 172.

CHAPTER 4. TWO-FRONT WAR

1. *Journal of the Thirty-Eighth National Convention of the Woman's Relief Corps: Auxiliary to the Grand Army of the Republic: Indianapolis, Indiana, September 21, 22, 23, 24, 1920* (Washington, D.C.: National Tribune Company, 1920), 188–189.

2. Ibid., 190. In his work *Imagined Communities: Reflections on the Origin and Spread of Nationalism* (London: Verso, 1983), Benedict Anderson outlines how nationalism develops and evolves. Through his interpretation of nationalism, Anderson suggests that it should be more closely categorized with "kinship" and "religion" (p. 5). Indeed, if we accept the connection between kinship and nationalism it becomes easier to understand how veterans, who created communities based on their shared experiences, would be discerning and defensive of their Civil War community.

3. David M. Potter, "The Historians' Use of Nationalism and Vice Versa," *The American Historical Review* 67, no. 4 (1962): 924–950. As noted in chapter 2, Potter contended that soldiers and citizens possessed both sectional and national loyalties, simultaneously.

4. Stuart McConnell, *Glorious Contentment: The Grand Army of the Republic, 1865–1900* (Chapel Hill: University of North Carolina Press, 1992), 15–16; *Proceedings of the Twenty-Fifth Annual Encampment of the Department of Maryland, Grand Army of the Republic, Held at Baltimore, Maryland, February 21 and 22, 1901* (Baltimore: Shane Printing Company, 1901), 22. In addition to McConnell, for historical analysis of the GAR and its commemorative activities, see Barbara Gannon, *The Won Cause: Black and White Comradeship in the Grand Army of the Republic* (Chapel Hill: University of North Carolina Press, 2011); John R. Neff,

Honoring the Civil War Dead: Commemoration and the Problem of Reconciliation (Lawrence: University Press of Kansas, 2005); Caroline Janney, *Remembering the Civil War: Reunion and the Limits of Reconciliation* (Chapel Hill: University of North Carolina Press, 2013); Gannon, *The Won Cause*, 204.

5. *Register of the Military Order of the Loyal Legion of the United States* (Boston: Commandery of the State of Massachusetts, 1906), 9.

6. *National Roster of the Woman's Relief Corps, Auxiliary to the Grand Army of the Republic, November, 1901* (Bradford, Vt.: Headquarters Grand Army of the Republic), 14; Nina Silber, *Daughters of the Union: Northern Women Fight the Civil War* (Cambridge: Harvard University Press, 2005), 268–274. Historian Caroline Janney also challenges Silber's claim about the WRC in her work *Remembering the Civil War.*

7. *National Tribune,* September 8, 1898.

8. *National Tribune,* September 2, 1909.

9. *Military Essays and Recollections: Papers Read before the Commandery of the State of Illinois, Military Order of the Loyal Legion of the United States, Volume II* (Chicago: A. C. McClurg and Company, 1894), 87; *The National Tribune,* December 20, 1883.

10. *National Tribune,* June 10, 1882; November 10, 1910.

11. Quoted in *National Tribune,* April 5, 1888; *National Tribune,* November 11, 1909.

12. Ziba B. Graham, *On to Gettysburg: Ten Days from My Diary of 1863, a Paper Read before the Commandery of the State of Michigan, Military Order of the Loyal Legion of the U.S.* (Detroit: Winn and Hammond, 1893), 6; *Ceremonies at the Twenty-Fifth Anniversary, American Academy of Music, Philadelphia, April 15, 1890* (Philadelphia, 1890), 17.

13. *National Tribune,* June 3, 1882.

14. *National Tribune,* July 14, 1910.

15. *War Papers Read before the Commandery of the State of Wisconsin, Military Order of the Loyal Legion of the United States* (Milwaukee: Burdick and Allen, 1914), 81; George M. Finch, *In the Beginning: Read before the Ohio Commandery of the Loyal Legion of the United States* (Cincinnati: Peter G. Thomson, 1884), 9.

16. *National Tribune,* April 17, 1890.

17. *The National Memorial Day: A Record of Ceremonies over the Graves of the Union Soldiers, May 29 and 30, 1869* (Washington City: Headquarters Grand Army of the Republic, 1870), 233.

18. *Journal of the Twenty-Fourth Annual Session of the National Encampment, Grand Army of the Republic, Boston, Mass., August 13th and 14th, 1890* (Detroit: The Richmond and Backus Co., 1890), 149.

19. Ibid., 150–151.

20. Ibid., 151–152, 154.

21. *Journal of the Eighth Annual Convention of the Woman's Relief Corps: Auxiliary of the Grand Army of the Republic: Boston, Massachusetts, August 13 and 14,*

1890 (Boston: E. B. Stillings and Company, 1890), 143; *Report of the National Organization Woman's Relief Corps at Denver, Colorado, July 25 and 26, 1883, and Proceedings of the Second National Convention Woman's Relief Corps, Minneapolis, Minnesota, July 23, 24, and 25, 1884* (Boston: Griffith-Stillings Press, 1903), 23–24. Anna Ella Carroll was a trusted advisor to Abraham Lincoln throughout the Civil War; *Journal of the Thirty-Eighth National Convention of the Woman's Relief Corps,* 154.

22. *Journal of the Twenty-Eighth National Convention of the Woman's Relief Corps,* 222; *Journal of the Twenty-First National Convention of the Woman's Relief Corps: Auxiliary to the Grand Army of the Republic: San Francisco, California, August 20, 21, and 22, 1903* (Boston: Griffith-Stillings Press, 1903), 164, 168–169.

23. Janney, *Remembering the Civil War,* 252–253; *Journal of the Fifteenth National Convention of the Woman's Relief Corps: Auxiliary to the Grand Army of the Republic: Buffalo, New York, August 26 and 27, 1897* (Boston: E. B. Stillings, 1897), 148–149, 320.

24. *Journal of the Fifteenth National Convention of the Woman's Relief Corps,* 322–323.

25. Ibid., 323–324.

26. Ibid., 325.

27. Ibid., 327–328.

28. Ibid., 328–329.

29. Ibid., 330.

30. Gannon, *The Won Cause,* 41.

31. *Laws of the State of Maryland, Made and Passed at a Session of the General Assembly Begun and Held at the City of Annapolis on the Second Day of January, 1881, and Ended on the Thirty-First Day of March, 1884, Vol. 424,* Maryland State Archives (Annapolis: James Young, 1884), 365; *Cleveland Gazette,* February 5, 1887.

32. *Journal of the Fifteenth National Convention of the Woman's Relief Corps,* 330.

33. Gannon, *The Won Cause,* 60. The drama that played out across racial lines offers a caveat to the narrative put forth of the WRC in recent literature, namely, the work of Barbara Gannon. In *The Won Cause,* Gannon argues that the GAR was an interracial organization and that, in many ways, it was thoroughly integrated. White Union veterans accepted black Union veterans as their comrades despite the racial climate of the time in which they were living. She writes, "In an era in which race trumped virtually all other social identities, black and white veterans created an interracial organization at both the national and local levels" (p. 6). Gannon's research also touches on the history of the WRC and, specifically, the push of some states to detach their black corps and the policies of the national organization regarding black departments. She notes that African American WRC departments in Louisiana and Mississippi "constituted the official state organization" but received the label of "provisional departments" from the national WRC as a slight to "all-black state

organizations." Gannon suggests that "despite their provisional status, African American women likely welcomed the autonomy they achieved with segregation, particularly when they became the official state WRC" (p. 49).

34. Michael Kammen, *Mystic Chords of Memory: The Transformation of Tradition in American Culture* (New York: Vintage Books, 1993), 381.

35. "History of Battle Abbey," Virginia Historical Society, http://www .vahistorical.org/your-visit/history-battle-abbey; *Confederate Veteran, Volume XXIX* (Nashville: S. A. Cunningham, 1921), 210.

36. *Confederate Veteran, Volume III* (Nashville: S. A. Cunningham, 1895), 213; *Confederate Veteran, Volume VIII* (Nashville: S. A. Cunningham, 1900), 350; *Confederate Veteran, Volume XVI* (Nashville: S. A. Cunningham, 1908), 265.

37. *Confederate Veteran, Volume XVIII* (Nashville: S. A. Cunningham, 1910), 105.

38. For a history of Bradley Johnson's postwar activities, see Thomas E. Will, "Bradley T. Johnson's Lost Cause: Maryland's Confederate Identity in the New South," *Maryland Historical Magazine* 94, no. 1 (Spring 1999); *Confederate Veteran, Volume IX* (Nashville: S. A. Cunningham, 1901), 324.

39. *Confederate Veteran, Volume XVII* (Nashville: S. A. Cunningham, 1909), 458.

40. Ibid., 266.

41. *Confederate Veteran, Volume XIV* (Nashville: S. A. Cunningham, 1906), 65; *Confederate Veteran, Volume XXI* (Nashville: S. A. Cunningham, 1913), 114; *Confederate Veteran, Volume XXX* (Nashville: S. A. Cunningham, 1922), 141; *Confederate Veteran, Volume XXIV* (Nashville: S. A. Cunningham, 1916), 312.

42. *Confederate Veteran, Volume II* (Nashville: S. A. Cunningham, 1894), 260–261.

43. *Confederate Veteran, Volume IV* (Nashville: S. A. Cunningham, 1896), 275.

44. *Confederate Veteran, Volume XX* (Nashville: S. A. Cunningham, 1912), 166; *Confederate Veteran, Volume XXXI* (Nashville: S. A. Cunningham, 1923), 92.

45. *Confederate Veteran, Volume XIII* (Nashville: S. A. Cunningham, 1906), 312.

46. *Confederate Veteran, Volume XXIX* (Nashville: S. A. Cunningham, 1921), 418.

47. *Confederate Veteran, Volume VII* (Nashville: S. A. Cunningham, 1899), 124.

48. *Confederate Veteran, Volume XX*, 562.

49. *Confederate Veteran, Volume I* (Nashville: S. A. Cunningham, 1893), 326.

50. *Confederate Veteran, Volume II*, 366.

51. *Confederate Veteran, Volume XXIX*, 176.

52. For a history of the UDC, see Karen L. Cox, *Dixie's Daughters: The United Daughters of the Confederacy and the Preservation of Confederate Culture* (Gainesville: University Press of Florida, 2003). For analysis of the antecedent of the UDC, see Caroline Janney, *Burying the Dead but Not the Past: Ladies' Memorial Associations and the Lost Cause* (Chapel Hill: University of North Carolina Press, 2008). *Minutes of the Fourteenth Annual Convention of the United Daughters of the Confederacy, Held in Norfolk, Virginia, November 13–16, 1907* (Opelika, Ala.: Post Publishing Company, 1908), Appendix, 40.

53. *Minutes of the Twenty-Third Annual Convention of the United Daughters of the*

Confederacy, Held in Dallas, Texas, November 8 to 11, 1916 (Raleigh: Edwards & Broughton Printing Company, 1917), 362–363; Amanda M. Myers argues in her M.A. thesis "Glory Stands beside Our Grief: The Maryland United Daughters of the Confederacy and the Assertion of Their Identity" that the Maryland UDC fought ardently to secure its place within the national organization and sought recognition from other southern states.

54. *Confederate Veteran, Volume XXVIII* (Nashville: S. A. Cunningham, 1920), 333–336.

55. *Minutes of the Fourth Annual Meeting of the United Daughters of the Confederacy, Held in Baltimore, Maryland, November 10–12, 1897* (Nashville: Foster & Webb, Printers, 1898), 3.

56. *Confederate Veteran, Volume VI* (Nashville: S. A. Cunningham, 1898), 359.

57. *Confederate Veteran, Volume V* (Nashville: S. A. Cunningham, 1897), 499; *Confederate Veteran, Volume X* (Nashville: S. A. Cunningham, 1902), 433; *Confederate Veteran, Volume XVII*, 10; "United Daughters of the Confederacy Monument," National Park Service, http://www.nps.gov/mono/historyculture/confederate-monument.htm; *Confederate Veteran, Volume XXVII* (Nashville: S. A. Cunningham, 1919), 5.

58. *Minutes of the Sixteenth Annual Meeting of the United Daughters of the Confederacy, Held in Houston, Texas, October 19–22, 1909* (Opelika, Ala.: Post Publishing Company, 1909), 314–315.

59. *Minutes of the Twenty-Fourth Annual Meeting of the United Daughters of the Confederacy, Held in Chattanooga, Tennessee, November 14–17, 1917* (Richmond: Richmond Press, Inc., 1918), 374.

60. *Confederate Veteran, Volume XIX* (Nashville: S. A. Cunningham, 1911), 148.

61. Ibid., 148.

62. *Confederate Veteran, Volume XVII*, 106; *Minutes of the Sixteenth Annual Meeting of the United Daughters of the Confederacy, Held in Houston, Texas, October 19–22, 1909*, 314.

63. *A Souvenir Book of the Jefferson Davis Memorial Association and the Unveiling of the Monument, Richmond, Virginia, June 3, 1907* (Richmond: Whittet and Shepperson, 1907).

64. *Confederate Veteran, Volume XI* (Nashville: S. A. Cunningham, 1903), 535.

65. *Confederate Veteran, Volume XII* (Nashville: S. A. Cunningham, 1904), 79–80.

66. Donald E. Collins, *The Death and Resurrection of Jefferson Davis* (Lanham: Rowman and Littlefield, 2005), 147.

CHAPTER 5. MARYLAND, MY MARYLAND

1. *Baltimore Sun*, March 25, 1993; "Maryland! My Maryland!" Maryland State Archives, 2005, http://msa.maryland.gov/msa/speccol/sc5500/sc5572/000001/000000/000010/html/t10.html.

2. Through this process, historian David Blight's thesis on race and Civil War

memory becomes clearer when viewed through the lens of twentieth-century Maryland.

3. *Laws of the State of Maryland, Made and Passed at a Session of the General Assembly Begun and Held at the City of Annapolis on the Second Day of January, 1881, and Ended on the Thirty-First Day of March, 1884* (Annapolis: James Young, State Printer, 1884), 365; Chapter 109, Laws of 1904; Chapter 110, Laws of 1904; Chapter 250, Acts of 1910. Laws accessed courtesy of Teaching American History in Maryland, Maryland State Archives, http://teaching.msa.maryland .gov/000001/000000/000048/html/t48.html.

4. David S. Bogen, "The Forgotten Era," *Maryland Bar Journal* 19, no. 4 (1986): 10–13; *National Tribune*, October 7, 1904.

5. *Baltimore Afro-American*, September 8, 1917, quoted in "Harry S. Cummings (1866–1917), The Road from Frederick to Thurgood: Black Baltimore in Transition, 1870–1920," Maryland State Archives, http://msa.maryland.gov /msa/stagser/s1259/121/6050/html/11427000.html.

6. "George M. Lane (1866–1912), The Road from Frederick to Thurgood: Black Baltimore in Transition, 1870–1920," Maryland State Archives, http:// msa.maryland.gov/msa/stagser/s1259/121/6050/html/12417000.html.

7. "W. Ashbie Hawkins (1861–1941), The Road from Frederick to Thurgood: Black Baltimore in Transition, 1870–1920," Maryland State Archives, http://msa.maryland.gov/msa/stagser/s1259/121/6050/html /12415000.html.

8. *Cleveland Advocate*, May 29, 1920.

9. Barbara A. Gannon, *The Won Cause: Black and White Comradeship in the Grand Army of the Republic* (Chapel Hill: University of North Carolina Press, 2011).

10. "Founder John Henry Murphy Sr.," http://www.pbs.org/blackpress /news_bios/afroamerican.html; "Murphy, John Henry, Sr. (1840–1922)," http://www.blackpast.org/aah/murphy-john-henry-sr-1840-1922; *Afro-American*, October 24, 1987.

11. "Mrs. John L. Woodbury letter (1927) and responses from L. Goldie M. Smith and W. Kennedy Jenkins," United Daughters of the Confederacy Collection, MSA SC 213, Maryland State Archives.

12. "Theophilus Turing (response)," United Daughters of the Confederacy Collection, MSA SC 213, Maryland State Archives. See Grace Hale's *Making Whiteness: The Culture of Segregation in the South, 1890–1940* (New York: Pantheon, 1998).

13. David Blight, *Race and Reunion: The Civil War in American Memory* (Cambridge: Harvard University Press, 2001), 387; Kathleen Ann Clark, *Defining Moments: African American Commemoration and Political Culture in the South, 1863–1913* (Chapel Hill: University of North Carolina Press, 2005).

14. *Baltimore Sun*, April 30, 1939; Caroline E. Janney, *Remembering the Civil War: Reunion and the Limits of Reconciliation* (Chapel Hill: University of North Carolina Press, 2013), 303–304.

15. Suzanne Ellery Greene Chapelle, Jean H. Baker, Dean R. Esslinger, Whitman H. Ridgway, Jean B. Russo, Constance B. Schulz, and Gregory A. Stiverson, *Maryland: A History of its People* (Baltimore: Johns Hopkins University Press, 1986), 244–245; "Race and Mob Violence: The Matthew Williams Case," Teaching American History in Maryland, Maryland State Archives, http://teaching.msa.maryland.gov/000001/000000/000036/html/t36.html; *Philadelphia Record*, December 5, 1931.

16. *Baltimore Post*, December 5, 1931.

17. Grace Elizabeth Hale, *Making Whiteness: The Culture of Segregation in the South, 1890–1940* (New York: Pantheon, 1998), 205–206.

18. *Baltimore Sun*, December 6, 1931.

19. "Race and Mob Violence: The Matthew Williams Case," Teaching American History in Maryland, Maryland State Archives, http://teaching.msa.maryland.gov/000001/000000/000036/html/t36.html; U.S. Census Bureau, "Fifteenth Census of the United States 1930: Baltimore Wards," https://jscholarship.library.jhu.edu/handle/1774.2/35405.

20. *Baltimore Afro-American*, December 5, 1931; February 27, 1932; Sherrilyn A. Ifill, *On the Courthouse Lawn: Confronting the Legacy of Lynching in the Twenty-First Century* (Boston: Beacon Press, 2007), 24–25.

21. *Baltimore American*, December 6, 1931.

22. *Baltimore Post*, March 19, 1932; "Race and Mob Violence: The Matthew Williams Case," Teaching American History in Maryland, Maryland State Archives, http://teaching.msa.maryland.gov/000001/000000/000036/html/t36.html; *Baltimore Sun*, March 20, 1932.

23. "George Armwood (b. 1911–d. 1933)," *Archives of Maryland* (Biographical Series), Maryland State Archives, http://msa.maryland.gov/megafile/msa/speccol/sc3500/sc3520/013700/013750/html/13750bio.html.

24. *Slave Narratives: A Folk History of Slavery in the United States From Interviews with Former Slaves, Maryland Narratives* (Washington, D.C.: Works Progress Administration, 1941), vol. 8, 19–20.

25. Caroline Janney, "War over the Shrine of Peace: The Appomattox Peace Monument and Retreat from Reconciliation," *Journal of Southern History* 77, no. 1 (February 2011): 91–120; W. Fitzhugh Brundage, "White Women and the Politics of Historical Memory in the South, 1880–1920," in *Jumpin' Jim Crow: Southern Politics from Civil War to Civil Rights*, ed. Jane Dailey, Glenda Gilmore, and Bryant Simon (Princeton: Princeton University Press, 2000), 115.

26. *Baltimore Afro-American*, October 17, 1931; Caroline Janney, "Written in Stone: Gender, Race, and the Heyward Shepherd Memorial," *Civil War History* 52, no. 2 (2006): 118.

27. "Current Exhibitions," Maryland Historical Society, http://www.mdhs.org/museum/exhibitions/current; "Civil Rights in Maryland," Maryland State Archives, http://www.msa.md.gov/e cp/45/00028/html/civilrgt.html.

28. "BALTIMORE CITY COURT (Court Papers) including: plaintiff's

exhibit number 2 (R.A. Pearson to Donald G. Murray) 14 December 1934; petitioner's exhibit A (admission application) n.d.; plaintiff's exhibit number 4 (W. M. Hillegeist to Donald G. Murray) 9 February 1935; plaintiff's exhibit number 5 (Donald G. Murray to the Board of Regents) 5 March 1935; plaintiff's exhibit number 6 (R. A. Pearson to Donald G. Murray) 8 March 1935; petitioner's exhibit A (postal money order) 24 January 1935," Maryland State Archives, MSA SC 2221-11-4, http://msa.maryland.gov/megafile/msa/speccol /sc2200/sc2221/000011/000004/html/0000.html.

29. Ibid.

30. Ibid.

31. "BALTIMORE CITY COURT (Court Papers) Stenographer's Record, Donald G. Murray vs. Raymond A. Pearson, et al. 18 June 1935; plaintiff's exhibit number 10; writ of mandamus 25 June 1935," Maryland State Archives, MSA SC 2221-11-6, http://msa.maryland.gov/megafile/msa/speccol/sc2200 /sc2221/000011/000006/html/0000.html.

32. "COURT OF APPEALS (Miscellaneous Papers) including number 53 October Term 1935, petition to advance case for an immediate hearing 6 August 1935; number 53 October Term 1935, answer to petition to advance 31 August 1935. MSA S 397–94. COURT OF APPEALS (Opinions) number 53 October Term 1935 (Pearson, et al. vs. Murray) 15 January 1936," Maryland State Archives, MSA SC 2221-11-8, http://msa.maryland.gov /megafile/msa/speccol/sc2200/sc2221/000011/000008/html/0000.html.

33. Anne E. Marshall, "The 1906 *Uncle Tom's Cabin* Law and the Politics of Race and Memory in Early-Twentieth-Century Kentucky," *The Journal of the Civil War Era* 1, no. 3 (2011): 376.

34. "Maryland State Song—'Maryland, My Maryland,'" Maryland State Archives, http://msa.maryland.gov/msa/mdmanual/01glance/html/symbols /song.html.

35. "Miscellaneous newspaper clippings," Mrs. Ruth A. Krebs Collection, MSA SC 100, Maryland State Archives.

36. "Speech Louis Henry Gosserand at the dedication of James Ryder Randall tablet and Oak Tree, April 26, 1938," Mrs. Ruth A. Krebs Collection, MSA SC 100, Maryland State Archives.

37. Kentucky adopted "My Old Kentucky Home" in 1928, Florida adopted "Old Folks at Home" in 1935, and Virginia adopted "Carry Me Back to Old Virginny" in 1940. "The Old Folks at Home," The Center for American Music at the University of Pittsburgh, http://www.pitt.edu/~amerimus/index.html; James Ramage, *Kentucky Rising: Democracy, Slavery, and Culture from the Early Republic to the Civil War* (Lexington: University Press of Kentucky, 2011), 236; Gary Giddins, *Visions of Jazz: The First Century* (Oxford: Oxford University Press, 1998), 25.

38. *Baltimore Sun*, February 2, 2002; April 30, 1939.

39. "Commencement Address to the Morgan State College Graduating Class

of 1958 delivered by Martin Luther King, Jr., on June 2, 1958, transcribed from the *Baltimore Afro-American*, Late City Edition, June 7, 1958," MSA SC 2221, Maryland State Archives, http://msa.maryland.gov/megafile/msa/speccol/sc2200/sc2221/000012/000039/html/00000001.html.

40. "Civil Rights Movement Veterans," Tougaloo College, http://www.crmvet.org/tim/timhis55.htm.

41. Cindy Kelly, *Outdoor Sculpture in Baltimore: A Historical Guide to Public Art in the Monumental City* (Baltimore: Johns Hopkins University Press, 2011), 198–199.

42. *Free Lance-Star*, April 29, 1948.

43. *Free Lance-Star*, May 1, 1948.

44. *Afro-American*, May 15, 1948.

45. Ibid.

46. Peter Irons, *The Courage of Their Convictions* (New York: The Free Press, 1988), 130; *Baltimore Sun*, June 18, 1960.

47. Irons, *The Courage of Their Convictions*, 136, 140.

48. Robert Cook, *Troubled Commemoration: The American Civil War Centennial, 1961–1965* (Baton Rouge: Louisiana State University Press, 2007); David Blight, *American Oracle: The Civil War in the Civil Rights Era* (Cambridge: Harvard University Press, 2011).

49. "75th Anniversary of the Battle of Antietam," Western Maryland's Historical Library, http://www.whilbr.org/AntietamAnniversary/index.aspx.

50. "Maryland Commemorates the Civil War Centennial: A Manual for the Observation of the Civil War in the Counties and Cities of the State of Maryland," Maryland Civil War Centennial Commission (General File) MSA s131, Maryland State Archives.

51. "Invitation to Sister States," Maryland Civil War Centennial Commission (General File) MSA s131, Maryland State Archives.

52. Maryland Civil War Centennial Commission (General File) MSA s131, Maryland State Archives.

53. "The Maryland Civil War Centennial Commission: A report of its functioning since its inception in 1959 and its Financial Status projected to January 1, 1962," Maryland Civil War Centennial Commission (General File) MSA s131, Maryland State Archives.

54. "Maryland Remembers," Maryland Civil War Centennial Commission (General File) MSA s131, Maryland State Archives. As historian Kevin Conley Ruffner notes in *Maryland's Blue and Gray: A Border State's Union and Confederate Officer Corps* (Baton Rouge: Louisiana State University Press, 1997), 7, "students of the war debate the exact number of Marylanders who served in the Union and Confederate forces" and some "estimates range up to sixty thousand Marylanders in the northern ranks and as many as twenty-five thousand in Confederate service." Ruffner suggests that these "figures . . . must be approached

with caution." The plaque's inscription utilizes the higher estimates while the introduction of this book reflects the more modest estimations.

55. *Baltimore Sun*, October 6, 1964.

56. "Letter Ruby Duval to Park Loy, August 27, 1964," Maryland Civil War Centennial Commission (General File) MSA s131, Maryland State Archives.

57. "Report of President—Ruby Duval (October 1961)," UDC Collection, Maryland Historical Society.

58. "Antietam-South Mountain Centennial Assoc., Minutes of the Board of Directors Meetings, May 22, 1962," Maryland Civil War Centennial Commission (General File) MSA s131, Maryland State Archives.

59. Ibid.

60. David O'Connell, *Furl that Banner: The Life of Abram J. Ryan, Poet-Priest of the South* (Macon: Mercer University Press, 2006), 205.

61. "Letter Park Loy to Francis X. Gallagher, July 28, 1964," Maryland Civil War Centennial Commission (General File) MSA s131, Maryland State Archives.

62. "Letter Edward Egan to Richard Grumbacher, July 17, 1964," Maryland Civil War Centennial Commission (General File) MSA s131, Maryland State Archives.

63. "Letter Park Loy to Francis X. Gallagher, July 28, 1964," Maryland Civil War Centennial Commission (General File) MSA s131, Maryland State Archives.

64. "Letter Edward Egan to Park Loy, August, 1964," Maryland Civil War Centennial Commission (General File) MSA s131, Maryland State Archives.

65. "Civil War Parley Bows on Equality," *New York Times*, [date unknown], Maryland Civil War Centennial Commission (General File) MSA s131, Maryland State Archives.

66. "Letter Park Loy to George L. Radcliffe, October 26, 1961," Maryland Civil War Centennial Commission (General File) MSA s131, Maryland State Archives.

67. *Washington Afro-American*, January 8, 1952; September 24, 1968.

68. *News American*, May 10, 1970.

69. *Washington Post*, September 27, 1979.

70. *Washington Post*, January 30, 1980.

71. *Washington Post*, January 29, 1980; *Evening Capital*, February 16, 1980.

72. Cook, *Troubled Commemoration*; Blight, *American Oracle.*

73. Marshall, "The 1906 *Uncle Tom's Cabin* Law," 371.

EPILOGUE

1. *The Conspirator*, directed by Robert Redford (2010; Santa Monica, Calif.: American Film Company, 2011), script. The film generated interesting and

strong responses from critics and historians. Elizabeth Leonard is right to point out the film's sympathetic portrayal of not only Mary Surratt but also the South as a whole. Elizabeth Leonard, "Elizabeth D. Leonard: A Historian's Review of *The Conspirator*," *UNC Press Civil War 150*, May 11, 2011, http:// uncpresscivilwar150.com/2011/05/elizabeth-d-leonard-a-historians-review-of -the-conspirator/.

2. *Baltimore Sun*, March 26, 1984, Maryland State Archives, Clagett Collection, MSA SC 1718.

3. *Baltimore Sun*, April 1984, Maryland State Archives, Clagett Collection, MSA SC 1718.

4. Jean Baker, e-mail message to author, May 30, 2017.

5. Clayton Butler, "Understanding Our Past: An Interview with Historian Gary Gallagher," http://www.civilwar.org/education/history/civil-war-history -and-scholarship/gary-gallagher-interview.html; "Sesquicentennial of the Civil War," http://www.hagerstownmd.org/index.aspx?NID=426; Ross J. Kelbaugh, *Maryland's Civil War Photographs: The Sesquicentennial Collection* (Baltimore: Maryland Historical Society, 2012); "Civil War Sesquicentennial," http://www .visitfrederick.org/civil-war-150th; "Antietam National Battlefield," National Park Service, http://www.nps.gov/anti/index.htm.

6. "Taking the Northern Scum out of a State Song," NPR, http://www.npr .org/templates/story/story.php?storyId=102218518.

7. *Washington Post*, March 1, 2009.

8. *Washington Post*, August 22, 2016.

9. *Baltimore Sun*, August 16, 2017.

BIBLIOGRAPHY

ARCHIVAL COLLECTIONS

Abraham Lincoln Papers, Library of Congress, Washington, D.C.

The American Presidency Project, University of California, Santa Barbara

An American Time Capsule: Three Centuries of Broadsides and Other Printed Ephemera, Rare Book and Special Collections Division, Library of Congress, Washington, D.C.

Civil War Diary of James Francis Beall, Western Maryland's Historical Library

Clagett Collection, MSA SC 1718, Maryland State Archives

"From Segregation to Integration: The Donald Murray Case, 1935–1937," MSA SC 2221, Maryland State Archives

Letters of Charles H. Russell, First Maryland Cavalry, Western Maryland's Historical Library

Maryland Civil War Centennial Commission (General File), MSA s131, Maryland State Archives

Maryland Digital Cultural Heritage

"Minutes of Gettysburg Battlefield Memorial Association Board of Directors—Maryland Monuments, 1885," Gettysburg National Military Park Archives

Mrs. Ruth A. Krebs Collection, MSA SC 100, Maryland State Archives

Robert E. Pattison Papers, Pennsylvania State Archives

Teaching American History in Maryland, Maryland State Archives

United Daughters of the Confederacy Collection, MSA SC 213, Maryland State Archives

United Daughters of the Confederacy Records, 1936–1984, MS. 2846, Maryland Historical Society

PERIODICALS

Alexandria Gazette
Anderson Intelligencer
Atlantic
Baltimore Afro-American
Baltimore American
Baltimore Post
Baltimore Sun
Boonsboro Odd Fellow
Civil War News
Cleveland Advocate
Columbus Enquirer
Confederate Veteran
Courier (Lincoln, Ne-
braska)

Daily Alta California
Daily Evening Bulletin
Evening Capital
Evening Gazette
Harper's Weekly
Herald and Torch Light
Lancaster Intelligencer
Macon Telegraph
Marion Sentinel
Minneapolis Journal
National Tribune
New York Times
News American

Philadelphia Record
Sacramento Daily Union
Savannah Republican
Shenango Valley News
St. Paul Globe
Urbana Daily Courier
Village Record
Washington Afro-American
Washington Post
Winchester Times

PUBLISHED PRIMARY SOURCES

Alfriend, Frank H. *The Life of Jefferson Davis*. Cincinnati: Caxton Publishing House, 1868.

Antietam Battlefield Memorial Commission. *Second Brigade of the Pennsylvania Reserves at Antietam, Report of the Antietam Battlefield Memorial Commission of Pennsylvania and Ceremonies at the Dedication of the Monuments Erected by the Commonwealth of Pennsylvania to Mark the Position of Four Regiments of the Pennsylvania Reserves Engaged in the Battle.* Harrisburg: Harrisburg Publishing Company, 1908.

Ceremonies at the Twenty-Fifth Anniversary, American Academy of Music, Philadelphia, April 15, 1890. Philadelphia, 1890.

Collected Works of Abraham Lincoln, vol. 6. Ann Arbor: University of Michigan Digital Library Production Services, 2001.

The Conspirator. Directed by Robert Redford. 2010. Santa Monica, Calif.: American Film Company, 2011, script.

Cunningham, David, and Wells W. Miller. *Antietam. Report of the Ohio Antietam Battlefield Commission.* Springfield: Springfield Publishing Company, 1904.

Dabney, Robert Lewis. *Life and Campaigns of Lieut.-Gen. Thomas J. Jackson, (Stonewall Jackson).* New York: Blelock and Co., 1866.

Davis, Jefferson. *The Rise and Fall of the Confederate Government,* vol. 1. New York: D. Appleton and Company, 1881.

———. *The Rise and Fall of the Confederate Government,* vol. 2. New York: D Appleton and Company, 1912.

Dennett, Tyler, ed. *Lincoln and the Civil War in the Diaries and Letters of John Hay.* New York: Dodd, Mead & Company, 1939.

Dixon, Thomas. *The Southerner: A Romance of the Real Lincoln.* New York: Grosset and Dunlap, 1913.

———. *The Victim: A Romance of the Real Jefferson Davis.* Toronto: Copp Clark Co., 1914.

Everett, Lloyd T. *For Maryland's Honor: A Story of the War for Southern Independence.* Boston: Christopher Publishing House, 1922.

Finch, George M. *In the Beginning: Read before the Ohio Commandery of the Loyal Legion of the United States.* Cincinnati: Peter G. Thomson, 1884.

Fitch, Clyde. *Barbara Frietchie: The Frederick Girl.* New York: Life Publishing Company, 1900.

Graham, Ziba B. *On to Gettysburg: Ten Days from My Diary of 1863, a Paper Read before the Commandery of the State of Michigan, Military Order of the Loyal Legion of the U.S.* Detroit: Winn and Hammond, 1893.

Grand Army of the Republic, Department of Maryland. *Proceedings of the Twenty-Fifth Annual Encampment of the Department of Maryland, Grand Army of the Republic, Held at Baltimore, Maryland, February 21st and 22nd, 1901.* Baltimore: Shane Printing Company, 1901.

Henderson, George Francis Robert. *Stonewall Jackson and the American Civil War,* vol. 1. New York: Longmans, Green, and Co., 1898.

———. *Stonewall Jackson and the American Civil War,* vol. 2. New York: Longmans, Green, and Co., 1919.

History of Antietam National Cemetery including A Descriptive List of all the Loyal Soldiers Buried Therein: Together with the Ceremonies and Address on the Occasion of the Dedication of the Grounds, September 17th, 1867. Baltimore: John W. Woods, Steam Printer, 1869.

Jones, John Beauchamp. *A Rebel War Clerk's Diary at the Confederate States Capital.* Philadelphia: J. B. Lippincott and Co., 1866.

Jones, Rev. J. William. *Southern Historical Society Papers, Volume XIV.* Richmond: Southern Historical Society, 1886.

Journal of the Eighth Annual Convention of the Woman's Relief Corps: Auxiliary of the Grand Army of the Republic: Boston, Massachusetts, August 13 and 14, 1890. Boston: E. B. Stillings and Company, 1890.

Journal of the Fifteenth National Convention of the Woman's Relief Corps: Auxiliary to the Grand Army of the Republic: Buffalo, New York, August 26 and 27, 1897. Boston: E. B. Stillings and Company, 1897.

Journal of Proceedings of the Senate of Maryland, April Special Session 1861. Frederick: Beale H. Richardson, Printer, 1861.

Journal of the Thirty-Eighth National Convention of the Woman's Relief Corps: Auxiliary to the Grand Army of the Republic: Indianapolis, Indiana, September 21, 22, 23, 24, 1920. Washington D.C.: National Tribune Company, 1920.

Journal of the Twenty-Eighth National Convention of the Woman's Relief Corps: Auxiliary to the Grand Army of the Republic: Atlantic City, New Jersey, September 21, 22, and 23, 1910. Boston: Griffith-Stillings Press, 1910.

Journal of the Twenty-First National Convention of the Woman's Relief Corps: Auxiliary to the Grand Army of the Republic: San Francisco, California, August 20, 21, and 22, 1903. Boston: Griffith-Stillings Press, 1903.

Journal of the Twenty-Fourth Annual Session of the National Encampment, Grand Army of the Republic, Boston, Mass., August 13th and 14th, 1890. Detroit: The Richmond and Backus Co., 1890.

Laws of the State of Maryland, Made and Passed at a Session of the General Assembly Begun and Held at the City of Annapolis on the Second Day of January, 1881, and Ended on the Thirty-First Day of March, 1884, Vol. 424. Maryland State Archives. Annapolis: James Young, 1884.

Maryland Gettysburg Monument Commission. *Report of the State of Maryland Gettysburg Monument Commission.* Baltimore: William K. Boyle and Son, 1891.

"Maryland State Song—'Maryland, My Maryland.'" Maryland State Archives. http://msa.maryland.gov/msa/mdmanual/01glance/html/symbols/song .html.

Mencken, H. L. "Maryland: Apex of Normalcy." *The Nation* 114 (1922): 517–519.

Military Essays and Recollections: Papers Read before the Commandery of the State of Illinois, Military Order of the Loyal Legion of the United States, Volume II. Chicago: A. C. McClurg and Company, 1894.

Minutes of the Fourteenth Annual Convention of the United Daughters of the Confederacy, Held in Norfolk, Virginia, November 13–16, 1907. Opelika, Ala.: Post Publishing Company, 1908.

Minutes of the Fourth Annual Meeting of the United Daughters of the Confederacy, Held in Baltimore, Maryland, November 10–12, 1897. Nashville: Foster & Webb, Printers, 1898.

Minutes of the Sixteenth Annual Meeting of the United Daughters of the Confederacy, Held in Houston, Texas, October 19–22, 1909. Opelika, Ala.: Post Publishing Company, 1909.

Minutes of the Twenty-Fourth Annual Meeting of the United Daughters of the Confederacy, Held in Chattanooga, Tennessee, November 14–17, 1917. Richmond: Richmond Press, Inc., 1918.

Minutes of the Twenty-Third Annual Convention of the United Daughters of the Confederacy, Held in Dallas, Texas, November 8–11, 1916. Raleigh: Edwards & Broughton Printing Company, 1917.

The National Memorial Day: A Record of Ceremonies over the Graves of the Union Soldiers, May 29 and 30, 1869. Washington City: Headquarters Grand Army of the Republic, 1870.

National Roster of the Woman's Relief Corps, Auxiliary to the Grand Army of the Republic, November, 1901. Bradford, Vt.: Headquarters Grand Army of the Republic, 1901.

Pitman, Benn. *The Assassination of President Lincoln and the Trial of the Conspirators.* New York: Moore, Wilstach and Baldwin, 1865.

Pollard, Edward Alfred. *The Lost Cause: A New Southern History of the War of the Confederates*. New York: E. B. Treat and Co., 1866.

Poore, Benjamin Perley. *The Conspiracy Trial for the Murder of the President: And the Attempt to Overthrow the Government by the Assassination of Its Principal Officers*, vol. 1. Boston: J. E. Tilton and Company, 1865.

———. *The Conspiracy Trial for the Murder of the President: And the Attempt to Overthrow the Government by the Assassination of Its Principal Officers*, vol. 2. Boston: J. E. Tilton and Company, 1865.

Proceedings and Debates of the 1864 Constitutional Convention, Maryland State Archives, vol. 102.

Proceedings of the Twenty-Fifth Annual Encampment of the Department of Maryland, Grand Army of the Republic, Held at Baltimore, Maryland, February 21 and 22, 1901. Baltimore: Shane Printing Company, 1901.

"Proclamation to the People of Maryland." Encyclopedia Virginia. http://www .encyclopediavirginia.org/_Proclamation_to_the_People_of_Maryland_by _Robert_E_Lee_1862.

Register of the Military Order of the Loyal Legion of the United States. Boston: Commandery of the State of Massachusetts, 1906.

Report of the National Organization Woman's Relief Corps at Denver, Colorado, July 25 and 26, 1883, and Proceedings of the Second National Convention Woman's Relief Corps, Minneapolis, Minnesota, July 23, 24, and 25, 1884. Boston: Griffith-Stillings Press, 1903.

Slave Narratives: A Folk History of Slavery in the United States From Interviews with Former Slaves, Maryland Narratives, Volume VIII. Washington, D.C.: Works Progress Administration, 1941.

Southern Historical Society Papers. Richmond: Southern Historical Society. First fourteen volumes edited by J. William Jones, 1876–1886.

A Souvenir Book of the Jefferson Davis Memorial Association and the Unveiling of the Monument, Richmond, Virginia, June 3, 1907. Richmond: Whittet and Shepperson, 1907.

Steers, Edward, Jr., ed. *The Trial: The Assassination of President Lincoln and the Trial of the Conspirators*. Lexington: University Press of Kentucky, 2003.

Townsend, George Alfred. *The Life, Crime, and Capture of John Wilkes Booth*. New York: Dick and Fitzgerald, Publishers, 1865.

U.S. Census Bureau. "Fifteenth Census of the United States 1930: Baltimore Wards."

———. "Population of the United States in 1860." Washington, D.C.: Government Printing Office, 1864.

U.S. War Department. *The War of the Rebellion: A Compilation of the Official Records of the Union and Confederate Armies*, Series I, Volume II. Washington, D.C.: Government Printing Office, 1880.

Vanderslice, John M. *Gettysburg: A History of the Gettysburg Battle-field Memorial Association with an Account of the Battle*. Philadelphia: The Memorial Association, 1897.

War Papers Read before the Commandery of the State of Wisconsin, Military Order of the Loyal Legion of the United States. Milwaukee: Burdick and Allen, 1914.

Whittier, John Greenleaf. "Barbara Frietchie." Poetry Foundation. http://www.poetryfoundation.org/poem/174751.

SECONDARY SOURCES

"75th Anniversary of the Battle of Antietam." Western Maryland's Historical Library. http://www.whilbr.org/AntietamAnniversary/index.aspx.

Anderson, Benedict. *Imagined Communities: Reflections on the Origin and Spread of Nationalism.* London: Verso, 1983.

"Antietam National Battlefield (U.S. National Park Service)." http://www.nps.gov/anti/.

"Antietam National Cemetery: Private Soldier Monument." U.S. National Park Service. http://www.nps.gov/anti/historyculture/antietam-national-cemetery-part-2.htm.

Astor, Aaron. *Rebels on the Border: Civil War, Emancipation, and the Reconstruction of Kentucky and Missouri.* Baton Rouge: Louisiana State University Press, 2012.

"Augustus W. Bradford (1806–1881)." *Archives of Maryland* (Biographical Series). http://msa.maryland.gov/megafile/msa/speccol/sc3500/sc3520/001400/001463/html/1463bio2.html.

Ballard, Ted. *Staff Ride Guide: The Battle of Antietam.* Washington, D.C.: Center of Military History, 2006.

Beach, William Harrison. *The First New York (Lincoln) Cavalry from April 19, 1861, to July 7, 1865.* New York: Lincoln Cavalry Association, 1902.

Blair, William. *Cities of the Dead: Contesting the Memory of the Civil War in the South, 1865–1914.* Chapel Hill: University of North Carolina Press, 2003.

———. *With Malice toward Some: Treason and Loyalty in the Civil War Era.* Chapel Hill: University of North Carolina Press, 2014.

———, and William Pencak, eds. *Making and Remaking Pennsylvania's Civil War.* University Park: Pennsylvania State University Press, 2001.

Blight, David W. *American Oracle: The Civil War in the Civil Rights Era.* Cambridge: Harvard University Press, 2011.

———. *Race and Reunion: The Civil War in American Memory.* Cambridge: Harvard University Press, 2001.

Blum, Edward J. *Reforging the White Republic: Race, Religion, and American Nationalism, 1865–1898.* Baton Rouge: Louisiana State University, 2005.

Bogen, David S. "The Forgotten Era." *Maryland Bar Journal* 19, no. 4 (1986): 10–13.

Bordman, Gerald Martin, and Thomas S. Hischak. *The Oxford Companion to American Theatre.* Oxford: Oxford University Press, 2004.

Brown, Thomas J. *The Public Art of Civil War Commemoration: A Brief History with Documents.* Boston: Bedford/St. Martin's, 2004.

Buck, Paul H. *The Rod to Reunion, 1865–1900*. Boston: Little, Brown, 1937.

Butler, Clayton. "Understanding Our Past: An Interview with Historian Gary Gallagher." http://www.civilwar.org/education/history/civil-war-history-and-scholarship/gary-gallagher-interview.html.

Cannon, Jessica A. "Lincoln's Divided Backyard: Maryland in the Civil War Era." Ph.D. diss., Rice University, 2010.

Chapelle, Suzanne Ellery Greene, Jean H. Baker, Dean R. Esslinger, Whitman H. Ridgway, Jean B. Russo, Constance B. Schulz, and Gregory A. Stiverson. *Maryland: A History of Its People*. Baltimore: Johns Hopkins University Press, 1986.

Cimbala, Paul A., and Randall M. Miller, eds. *An Uncommon Time: The Civil War and the Northern Home Front*. New York: Fordham University Press, 2002.

———, eds. *Union Soldiers and the Northern Home Front*. New York: Fordham University Press, 2002.

Cirillo, Frank. "A Southern Strategy: The Atlanta Constitution and the Lincoln Centennial, February 1909." University of Virginia.

"Civil Rights in Maryland." Maryland State Archives. http://www.msa.md.gov/e cp/45/00028/html/civilrgt.html.

"Civil Rights Movement Veterans." Tougaloo College. http://www.crmvet.org/tim/timhis55.htm.

"Civil War Sesquicentennial." http://www.visitfrederick.org/civil-war-150th.

Clark, Kathleen Ann. *Defining Moments: African American Commemoration and Political Culture in the South, 1863–1913*. Chapel Hill: University of North Carolina Press, 2005.

Clinton, Craig. *Mrs. Leslie Carter: A Biography of the Early Twentieth Century American Stage Star*. Jefferson: McFarland and Co., 2006.

Cloyd, Benjamin G. *Haunted by Atrocity: Civil War Prisons in American Memory*. Baton Rouge: Louisiana State University Press, 2010.

Collins, Donald E. *The Death and Resurrection of Jefferson Davis*. Lanham: Rowman and Littlefield, 2005.

Cook, Robert. *Troubled Commemoration: The American Civil War Centennial, 1961–1965*. Baton Rouge: Louisiana State University Press, 2007.

Coser, Rose Laub. "Review of *The Feminization of American Culture*." *American Journal of Sociology* 86, no. 2 (September 1980): 394–396.

Coski, John M. *The Confederate Battle Flag: America's Most Embattled Emblem*. Cambridge: Harvard University Press, 2005.

Cox, Karen L. *Dixie's Daughters: The United Daughters of the Confederacy and the Preservation of Confederate Culture*. Gainesville: University Press of Florida, 2003.

"Current Exhibitions." Maryland Historical Society. http://www.mdhs.org/museum/exhibitions/current.

Dailey, Jane, Glenda Gilmore, and Bryant Simon, eds. *Jumpin' Jim Crow: Southern Politics from Civil War to Civil Rights*. Princeton: Princeton University Press, 2000.

Desjardin, Thomas A. *These Honored Dead: How the Story of Gettysburg Shaped American Memory.* Cambridge: Da Capo Press, 2003.

Douglas, Ann. *The Feminization of American Culture.* New York: Alfred A. Knopf, 1977.

Emerson, Bettie Alder Calhoun. *Historic Southern Monuments: Representative Memorials of the Heroic Dead of the Southern Confederacy.* New York: Neale Publishing Company, 1911.

"Ex Parte Merryman." Maryland State Archives, 2004. http://teaching.msa .maryland.gov/000001/000000/000107/html/t107.html.

Fields, Barbara. *Slavery and Freedom on the Middle Ground: Maryland During the Nineteenth Century.* New Haven: Yale University Press, 1987.

"Fighting for Freedom: United States Colored Troops from Maryland." Maryland State Archives, http://teaching.msa.maryland.gov/000001/000000 /000118/html/t118.html.

Foner, Eric. *A Short History of Reconstruction, 1863–1877.* New York: Harper & Row, 1990.

Foster, Gaines M. *Ghosts of the Confederacy: Defeat, the Lost Cause, and the Emergence of the New South, 1865–1913.* Oxford: Oxford University Press, 1987.

"Founder John Henry Murphy Sr." http://www.pbs.org/blackpress/news_bios /afroamerican.html.

Freeman, Douglas Southall. *The South to Posterity: An Introduction to the Writing of Confederate History.* Baton Rouge: Louisiana State University Press, 1998.

Gallagher, Gary, ed. *The Antietam Campaign.* Chapel Hill: University of North Carolina Press, 1999.

———. *Causes Won, Lost, and Forgotten: How Hollywood and Popular Art Shaped What We Know About the Civil War.* Chapel Hill: University of North Carolina Press, 2008.

———, and Alan T. Nolan, eds. *The Myth of the Lost Cause and Civil War History.* Bloomington: Indiana University Press, 2000.

Gannon, Barbara A. *The Won Cause: Black and White Comradeship in the Grand Army of the Republic.* Chapel Hill: University of North Carolina Press, 2011.

"George Armwood (b. 1911–d. 1933)." *Archives of Maryland* (Biographical Series). Maryland State Archives.

Giddins, Gary. *Visions of Jazz: The First Century.* Oxford: Oxford University Press, 1998.

Glathaar, Joseph. *General Lee's Army: From Victory to Collapse.* New York: Simon & Schuster, 2008.

Graham, David K. "To Guard in Peace: The Commemoration History of the Battle of Antietam, 1862–1937." M.A. thesis, Bowling Green State University, 2011.

Hale, Grace. *Making Whiteness: The Culture of Segregation in the South, 1890–1940.* New York: Pantheon, 1998.

"History of Battle Abbey." Virginia Historical Society. http://www.vahistorical
.org/your-visit/history-battle-abbey.

Hughes, Glenn, and George Savage, eds. *America's Lost Plays: The Heart of Mary-land and Other Plays by David Belasco.* Princeton: Princeton University Press, 1940.

Ifill, Sherrilyn A. *On the Courthouse Lawn: Confronting the Legacy of Lynching in the Twenty-First Century.* Boston: Beacon Press, 2007.

Irons, Peter. *The Courage of Their Convictions.* New York: The Free Press, 1988.

Janney, Caroline E. *Burying the Dead but Not the Past: Ladies' Memorial Associations and the Lost Cause.* Chapel Hill: University of North Carolina Press, 2007.

———. "The Lost Cause." Encyclopedia Virginia. Virginia Foundation for the Humanities, 2011.

———. *Remembering the Civil War: Reunion and the Limits of Reconciliation.* Chapel Hill: University of North Carolina Press, 2013.

———. "War over the Shrine of Peace: The Appomattox Peace Monument and Retreat from Reconciliation." *Journal of Southern History* 77, no. 1 (February 2011): 91–120.

———. "Written in Stone: Gender, Race, and the Heyward Shepherd Memorial." *Civil War History* 52, no. 2 (2006): 117–141.

Kammen, Michael. *Mystic Chords of Memory: The Transformation of Tradition in American Culture.* New York: Vintage Books, 1993.

Kauffman, Michael W. *American Brutus: John Wilkes Booth and the Lincoln Conspiracies.* New York: Random House, 2007.

Kelbaugh, Ross J. *Maryland's Civil War Photographs: The Sesquicentennial Collection.* Baltimore: Maryland Historical Society, 2012.

Ladd, David, and Audrey J. Ladd, eds. *The Bachelder Papers: Gettysburg in Their Own Words, Volume III, April 12, 1886 to December 22, 1894.* Dayton: Morningside House, 1995.

Leonard, Elizabeth. "Elizabeth D. Leonard: A Historian's Review of *The Conspirator.*" *UNC Press Civil War 150.* May 11, 2011. http://uncpresscivilwar150
.com/2011/05/elizabeth-d-leonard-a-historians-review-of-the-conspirator/.

———. *Lincoln's Avengers: Justice, Revenge, and Reunion After the Civil War.* New York: W. W. Norton, 2004.

Loewen, James W., and Edward H. Sebesta, eds. *The Confederate and Neo-Confederate Reader: The "Great Truth" about the "Lost Cause."* Oxford: University of Mississippi Press, 2010.

Marshall, Anne E. "The 1906 *Uncle Tom's Cabin* Law and the Politics of Race and Memory in Early-Twentieth-Century Kentucky." *The Journal of the Civil War Era* 1, no. 3 (2011): 368–393.

———. *Creating a Confederate Kentucky: The Lost Cause and Civil War Memory in a Border State.* Chapel Hill: University of North Carolina Press, 2010.

"Maryland in the Civil War." Enoch Pratt Free Library. http://www.prattlibrary

.org/uploadedFiles/www/locations/central/maryland/md_cw
_complete.pdf.

McConnell, Stuart. *Glorious Contentment: The Grand Army of the Republic, 1865–1900.* Chapel Hill: University of North Carolina Press, 1992.

McGinty, Brian. *The Body of John Merryman: Abraham Lincoln and the Suspension of Habeas Corpus.* Cambridge: Harvard University Press, 2011.

Meek, A. J., and Herman Hattaway. *Gettysburg to Vicksburg: The Five Original Civil War Battlefield Parks.* Columbia: University of Missouri Press, 2001.

Mitchell, Charles W., ed. *Maryland Voices of the Civil War.* Baltimore: Johns Hopkins University Press, 2007.

"Monocacy: The Battle that Saved Washington, D.C." Maryland State Archives. http://teaching.msa.maryland.gov/000001/000000/000141/html/t141.html.

"Murphy, John Henry, Sr. (1840–1922)." http://www.blackpast.org/aah/murphy-john-henry-sr-1840-1922.

Myers, Amanda M. "Glory Stands Beside Our Grief: The Maryland United Daughters of the Confederacy and the Assertion of Their Identity." M.A. thesis, University of Mississippi, 2010.

Neff, John R. *Honoring the Civil War Dead: Commemoration and the Problem of Reconciliation.* Lawrence: University Press of Kansas, 2005.

O'Connell, David. *Furl that Banner: The Life of Abram J. Ryan, Poet-Priest of the South.* Macon: Mercer University Press, 2006.

"The Old Folks at Home." The Center for American Music at the University of Pittsburgh. http://www.pitt.edu/~amerimus/index.html.

Phillips, Christopher. *The River Ran Backward: The Civil War and the Remaking of the American Middle Border.* Oxford: Oxford University Press, 2016.

Potter, David M. "The Historians' Use of Nationalism and Vice Versa." *The American Historical Review* 67, no. 4 (1962): 924–950.

Ramage, James. *Kentucky Rising: Democracy, Slavery, and Culture from the Early Republic to the Civil War.* Lexington: University Press of Kentucky, 2011.

Reardon, Carol. *Pickett's Charge in History and Memory.* Chapel Hill: University of North Carolina Press, 1997.

"The Road from Frederick to Thurgood: Black Baltimore in Transition, 1870–1920." Maryland State Archives.

Ruffner, Kevin Conley. *Maryland's Blue and Gray: A Border State's Union and Confederate Junior Officer Corps.* Baton Rouge: Louisiana State University Press, 1997.

"Sesquicentennial of the Civil War." http://www.hagerstownmd.org/index.aspx?NID=426.

Silber, Nina. *Daughters of the Union: Northern Women Fight the Civil War.* Cambridge: Harvard University Press, 2005.

———. *The Romance of Reunion: Northerners and the South, 1865–1900.* Chapel Hill: University of North Carolina Press, 1993.

Smith, Timothy B. *A Chickamauga Memorial: The Establishment of America's First Civil War National Military Park.* Knoxville: University of Tennessee Press, 2009.

————. *The Golden Age of Battlefield Preservation: The Decade of the 1890s and the Establishment of America's First Five Military Parks.* Knoxville: University of Tennessee Press, 2008.

Snell, Charles W., and Sharon A. Brown. *Antietam National Battlefield and National Cemetery: An Administrative History.* Washington, D.C.: U.S. Department of the Interior, 1986.

Sutherland, Daniel E. *Savage Conflict: The Decisive Role of Guerillas in the American Civil War.* Chapel Hill: University of North Carolina Press, 2009.

"Taking the Northern Scum out of a State Song." NPR. http://www.npr.org /templates/story/story.php?storyId=102218518.

Trail, Susan W. "Remembering Antietam: Commemoration and Preservation of a Civil War Battlefield." Ph.D. diss., University of Maryland, 2005.

"United Daughters of the Confederacy Monument." National Park Service. http://www.nps.gov/mono/historyculture/confederate-monument.htm.

Will, Thomas E. "Bradley T. Johnson's Lost Cause: Maryland's Confederate Identity in the New South." *Maryland Historical Magazine* 94, no. 1 (Spring 1999).

Wilson, Charles Reagan. *Baptized in Blood: Religion of the Lost Cause, 1865–1920.* Athens: University of Georgia Press, 1980.

Zeller, Bob. *The Blue and Gray in Black and White: A History of Civil War Photography.* Westport: Praeger, 2005.

INDEX

Abell, Arunah Shepherdson, 81
abolitionists, 12, 21, 31, 90, 105, 149. *See also* slaves and slavery
African Americans: in centennial celebrations, 167; Civil War memory of, 148–49; disenfranchisement of, 138–40; dual-identity of, 116; free black populations, 10, 11; GAR membership of, 104–5, 116; Lost Cause ideology on, 77; in political office, 139; reconciliation at expense of, 179n5, 184n1; as soldiers, 31, 116, 117; WRC membership of, 114–18, 194–95n33. *See also* civil rights activism; Jim Crow era; slaves and slavery
Aiken, Frederick, 39
Alfriend, Frank H., 80–81
Ambler, James Murray, 140
"The American Conflict" (Greeley), 105–6
amnesty policies, 47
Anderson, Benedict, 192n2
Anderson, James S., 109
Antietam, Battle of (1862), 26–30, 50–52, 72–74, 160, 174
Antietam National Battlefield, 69–74
Antietam National Cemetery, 42–55; Confederate burial controversy at, 43–44; dedication ceremony for, 5, 43, 45–52; Lee's Rock at, 44–45; ownership of, 53; Private Soldier Monument at, 45, 52–55; proposition for, 42–43

Argabright, Charles F., 156
Armwood, George, 148, 150
Army of Northern Virginia, 1, 24–25, 41, 82
Army of the Potomac, 31–32
Arnold, Samuel, 35, 36
Arp, Bill, 66
Astor, Aaron, 177–78n3
Atzerodt, George, 35, 36

Bachelder, John B., 57, 58, 63, 67, 74
Baer, John W., 169
Baker, Jean, 172
Ball, Isabel Worrell, 103
Baltimore (Md.): African Americans in, 139, 146; civil rights activism in, 146, 150–51, 157, 159; commemorations in, 107, 129, 130, 157–59, 175; desegregation in, 116–17, 150–51; divisions within, 1, 11; federal occupation of, 17, 18, 25; population demographics, 11, 146; riot of 1861, 10, 13–18, 27, 78, 82, 101; secessionist sentiment in, 79, 106, 109
Banks, Nathaniel P., 20, 21
Barbara Frietchie (Fitch), 7, 87, 93–98
Barger, W. D., 125
Barker, Florence, 113
Batterson, James C., 52
battlefield preservation efforts, 42, 55

CPSIA information can be obtained
at www.ICGtesting.com
Printed in the USA
LVHW040427070423
743674LV00003B/368

9 780820 364889